CAREER DEVELOPMENT
in RECREATION, PARKS, *and* TOURISM

A Positioning Approach

CAREER DEVELOPMENT in RECREATION, PARKS, and TOURISM

A Positioning Approach

Robert B. Kauffman, PhD

Frostburg State University

Human Kinetics

Library of Congress Cataloging-in-Publication Data

Kauffman, Robert B.
  Career development in recreation, parks, and tourism : a positioning approach / Robert B. Kauffman.
    p. cm.
  Includes bibliographical references and index.
  ISBN-13: 978-0-7360-7633-3 (soft cover)
  ISBN-10: 0-7360-7633-6 (soft cover)
  1. Recreation--Vocational guidance. 2. Parks--Vocational guidance. 3. Tourism--Vocational guidance. I. Title.
  GV160.K38 2010
  790.07--dc22

                                        2009019518

ISBN-10: 0-7360-7633-6 (print)   ISBN-10: 0-7360-8747-8 (Adobe PDF)
ISBN-13: 978-0-7360-7633-3 (print)   ISBN-13: 978-0-7360-8747-6 (Adobe PDF)

The Web addresses cited in this text were current as of July 2009, unless otherwise noted.

Acquisitions Editor: Gayle Kassing, PhD; **Developmental Editor:** Jacqueline Eaton Blakley; **Assistant Editors:** Lauren B. Morenz, Elizabeth Evans, and Anne Rumery; **Copyeditor:** Patsy Fortney; **Indexer:** Bobbi Swanson; **Permission Manager:** Dalene Reeder; **Graphic Designer:** Joe Buck; **Graphic Artist:** Yvonne Griffith; **Cover Designer:** Bob Reuther; **Photo Asset Manager:** Laura Fitch; **Visual Production Assistant:** Joyce Brumfield; **Photo Production Manager:** Jason Allen; **Art Manager:** Kelly Hendren; **Associate Art Manager:** Alan L. Wilborn; **Illustrators:** Joe Jaharus (cartoons) and Tammy Page; **Printer:** Versa Press

Printed in the United States of America   10 9 8 7 6 5 4 3 2 1

The paper in this book is certified under a sustainable forestry program.

Human Kinetics
Web site: www.HumanKinetics.com

United States: Human Kinetics
P.O. Box 5076
Champaign, IL 61825-5076
800-747-4457
e-mail: humank@hkusa.com

Canada: Human Kinetics
475 Devonshire Road Unit 100
Windsor, ON N8Y 2L5
800-465-7301 (in Canada only)
e-mail: info@hkcanada.com

Europe: Human Kinetics
107 Bradford Road
Stanningley
Leeds LS28 6AT, United Kingdom
+44 (0) 113 255 5665
e-mail: hk@hkeurope.com

Australia: Human Kinetics
57A Price Avenue
Lower Mitcham, South Australia 5062
08 8372 0999
e-mail: info@hkaustralia.com

New Zealand: Human Kinetics
Division of Sports Distributors NZ Ltd.
P.O. Box 300 226 Albany
North Shore City
Auckland
0064 9 448 1207
e-mail: info@humankinetics.co.nz

E4626

To my parents, Frank and Maribelle Kauffman.

CONTENTS

Chapter 8   The One-on-One Interview
Who within the organization can hire me?   **127**

Chapter 9   The Formal Interview
How should I prepare for a traditional interview?   **147**

Chapter 10   You and Your Resume
Does my resume reflect who I am?   **173**

PREFACE

This book fills a need in the recreation, parks, and tourism field regarding career development. Most people don't find a job through the traditional job search process in which many people apply for the same job and the employer narrows the field of applicants to a finalist. Rather, most people determine where they want to work and then actively seek a job there. This book systematizes a process that over half of job seekers have been using for many years. The process is called *positioning*.

Positioning is the technique of placing yourself in close proximity to the person for whom you want to work, the organization in which you want to work, and/or the position that fulfills your career goal. This book will change how you approach your job search. If you can answer the question of where you want to work for your next job, you can use the positioning model.

This book starts by addressing the question of where you want to work next, or your career goal. It explains the need to be proactive in your job search and then focuses on specific job search techniques. What knowledge, skills, abilities, and experience (KSAEs) do you need for this position? How can you build a bridge to your next job by acquiring these KSAEs? Who can help you obtain this job? What else do you need to know about the place where you want to work? And finally, how do you contact the person who can hire you and obtain an interview with that person?

In addition to using the positioning job search model, you may also encounter the traditional model, in which you apply for a job along with many others. This book explains techniques for this process also, addressing resumes, cover letters, e-mails, portfolios, and business cards. Each chapter includes activities to help you apply the concepts of the positioning process to your own job search.

The positioning model provides the skills and tools you will need in order to find your next job. Positioning is a new way to look at an old process. This book will change how you approach your job search.

ACKNOWLEDGMENTS

Like most new things, positioning has been an evolving concept. As presented in this book, the concept is quite different from its original incarnation. It has matured considerably. This is due partly to the actual process of organizing, developing, and writing this book and partly to the help of people along the way. These people include our graduate assistants, Jessica Leer, Amber Cox, and Josh Hierstetter. If I needed an article along the way, Jessica or Amber helped to track it down. In the library, Mary Jo Price provided invaluable assistance in finding that elusive reference. And, there was the assistance of our administrative assistant, Karen Frink, who reviewed the manuscript.

I would like to extend special thanks to Marcy Childs. Marcy was involved in the project during its early phases. She saw the value of the concept and was extremely supportive regarding the need for the book. In addition, her comments were helpful in developing the proposal and in writing the book. She played an important role in the development of this book.

I would also like to thank the many other people, too numerous to name, who assisted in the project. In addition, I want to acknowledge the support of our faculty. Although they didn't contribute directly to the content, they provided the continued support I needed in order to complete the project. They are Diane Blankenship, Veronica Hill, Maureen Dougherty, Susan Gray, and Ken Witmer, our dean. Last, I would like to thank my wife, Sally. Without her support, the creation of this book could not have occurred.

chapter 1

The New Paradigm

Remember when you were in high school and you wanted to get close to a special person? Did you sit next to that person at lunch, or did you sit three tables away? For most people, the answer is obvious: You need to sit next to the person at lunch.

This question reveals the essence of the concept of positioning. It is really this simple. People use the concept of positioning throughout their lives, from sitting next to that special person at lunch to obtaining their next job. In career development, positioning is the technique of placing yourself in close proximity to the person for whom you want to work, the organization in which you want to work, or the position that fulfills your career goal. This book addresses the principles and techniques of positioning.

Consider the experience of Marty, a junior in the recreation and parks management program who was looking for summer employment. Like many students, he hoped to gain experience in the field he was preparing to work in. Marty made a list of job criteria for his summer employment. His list was typical. He wanted a job in his major where he could gain professional experience. He wanted to work with youth. He wanted to be active. He wanted to work close to home. At this point in his career development, he was not giving serious consideration to obtaining a full-time job after graduation. He simply wanted a summer job close to home that would give him experience in his major.

Marty's search for summer employment led him to a Boys and Girls Club in northern Virginia and to Connie, the director of the center. He had a good summer working at the club.

A little less than a year later, it was time for him to complete his internship. We shouldn't be surprised that he chose to do his internship at the Boys and Girls Club: he had positioned himself to do his internship there. For him, it was as if he was sitting next to that very special person in high school. He liked the job. He knew something about the organization, its mission, and the clientele it served. He had a realistic idea of what the work entailed. He knew the director, and she knew him. Since he had already worked there, she knew his capabilities and work performance. Stated another way, she wasn't taking much of a chance with Marty. From her perspective, he was a known commodity. Marty consulted about the potential internship with his faculty supervisor, who affirmed that the Boys and Girls Club would be a logical choice for his internship.

Marty's experience is anecdotal, but variations of his experience are played out daily within the workplace. And similar scenarios are described in the job search literature. Several sources suggest that between 50 and 80 percent of job vacancies in the U.S. are filled before the position is advertised outside of the organization (Ganske, 2005; Kopiske, 2003; O'Donnell, 2004). Kopiske noted that "it's estimated that between 70 and 80 percent of all the jobs that get filled

A TALE OF TWO MODELS

Chapters 1 through 12 of this book include a section called A Tale of Two Models. This section compares the traditional and positioning job search models. Juxtaposing the two models helps explain the positioning model and when you should use each of the models.

In the traditional job search model, the organization identifies a position that it needs, or one that is unfilled and needs to be filled. Next, it advertises the position in newspapers, in trade journals, on the Internet, and through other standard media. You see the advertisement for the position and, along with many others, apply for the position. You send the firm your cover letter, resume, references, and anything else required. Those in charge of hiring for the firm sort through the applications and invite you for an interview. Finally, if you are the last person standing, the firm offers you the position.

In contrast to the traditional model is the positioning model. This model begins with your deciding on your career goal or at least where you want to work. Next, you identify positions in organizations that will potentially advance your career goal. You then research the organizations in terms of their viability in advancing your career, asking yourself several basic questions: *Is this an organization where I would like to work? Will this organization advance my career? If I take a position with this organization, how quickly will it advance my career?* The next step is to identify and approach a person in the organization and explore ways you can become involved. Depending on the situation, your involvement could be volunteer, part-time, or even full-time employment. Finally, your involvement with the organization leads to full-time employment or to a promotion depending on whether you were previously employed full- or part-time. Often, a new position appears, and you are the only one interviewed. Or, if the position is opened up to the public, it is merely a formality to satisfy the human resources department because the managers have already decided to hire you. As noted, the positioning model is most likely the norm regarding how most people obtain their next job.

In some cases, the two models work in concert with each other. Although the organization may need to use the traditional model to officially search for the candidate, the positioning model may have already been working to select the candidate who will eventually be chosen. For example, the candidate may already be working at the agency, and the formal search process is merely a formality that must be completed to satisfy human resources. Or, the organization is in the process of a traditional job search, and one of the applicants is someone who worked there previously or someone who is known through their professional contacts. These candidates have enhanced the likelihood of being selected because they have positioned themselves.

Most people are familiar with the traditional job search model. Most career advice books are written from the perspective of this model. Although the positioning model is theoretically new, most people have already used aspects of it throughout their lives without realizing it. And, because a significant number of positions are awarded to people within the organization, it is the new paradigm that represents the norm in the job search process.

The positioning model is the primary model delineated in the job search process described in this book. The process requires that you proactively seek the position you want. You decide where and for whom you want to be employed. You case the joint to make sure it is the place for you. By working there, you place yourself in close proximity to the position that will advance you and your career. Or, by developing the skill set necessary for the position that you seek, you are able to build a bridge to the new position.

are by people who first heard about the position through word-of-mouth" (2003, p. 53). Marty could relate to this statistic since neither the summer job nor the internship was advertised. He found his jobs through word-of-mouth and simple investigation on his part.

Many vacant positions are referred to as hidden because they are not yet known to the public. O'Donnell (2004) suggested that 30 to 35 percent of these positions are posted only in the hiring manager's thoughts and are the most hidden. Another 30 to 50 percent of positions are partially hidden in that they are advertised only within the organization (e.g., to key employees, on the cafeteria wall, on the company's intranet, or through internal announcements). Only 20 to 30 percent of positions are public, or not hidden. These positions reach the public as advertisements in newspapers, on online job sites, and through recruiters.

DISCOVERING THE POSITIONING MODEL

Like many other people, I practiced positioning with only a partial understanding of the concept. I was interested in a position at a university in western Maryland. The current professor in the program had a long-term illness that, unfortunately, was rendering him ineffective in the program and was threatening to result in the elimination of the program. At the time, I was living off a modestly thriving consulting business and two grants. Rather than wait for the position to formally open up, I approached the chair of the department and the dean with a proposal to fund a part-time position for myself. Essentially, my objective was to position myself within the university.

By being proactive, I offered the chair and the dean a potential solution to their problem. (Because their faculty member was chronically ill, enrollment in the program had dropped off, and the program was in danger of elimination.) In addition, my proposal made a valuable statement about my work ethic and demonstrated that I was proactive and not reactive. They saw a potential faculty member who identified an opportunity and pursued it rather than waited to be told what to do. My behavior demonstrated that I would potentially be a proactive faculty member.

The ill faculty member took a leave of absence and subsequently retired on disability. Initially, I was hired in a full-time contractual position. A year later the position was converted back to a full-time tenure-track position. As part of the process, the department was required to complete a search for the position. However, it was more of a formality than an active search. Because I was already doing the job, I was the logical choice for the position. In essence, I had positioned myself quite well for the very position that I sought in the first place.

The concept of positioning crystallized for me when I was working with student interns. Had it not been for them, I would have most likely considered my experience a lucky aberration and never developed it into the positioning model. I found myself constantly articulating its basic techniques to my students. First, I would ask them what they wanted to do or where they wanted to work once they graduated. It was a simplistic way of asking them their career goals. Then I would explain that they needed to make the transition from school to their career. With one hand, I would signal that they were "here," and with the other hand, I would signal that they needed to be "over there." I began to use the word *positioning* to describe the process. The next step was to codify what I was describing.

POSITIONING AND THE SEVEN-STEP SALES MODEL

The seven-step sales model has been modified and adapted for use in many settings, from retail sales to consulting. The positioning model incorporates the seven-step sales model. Although I describe the model in several chapters, chapter 8, The One-on-One Interview, focuses on fully incorporating the model.

The steps in the model are as follows:

1. Identify your prospect.
2. Engage the decision maker.
3. Survey.
4. Design.
5. Propose.
6. Close the deal.
7. Follow up.

Using my own experience as an example, I engaged the chair of the department and then the dean. They were the decision makers. I had already surveyed their needs and decided how I could fit into their organization. For the design phase, I suggested a part-time position that was essentially self-funded. They countered a few days after our meeting and suggested their standard off-the-shelf full-time contractual position. Their offer was far superior to mine. We closed the deal, and I was hired. The follow-up involved acclimatizing me to the job. This involved meeting the faculty, showing me the classrooms, and filling out the paperwork for human resources.

The seven-step sales model assumes you know what business you are in. Because many students are still determining what business they are in, I devote several chapters in the beginning of this book to helping you determine the knowledge, skills, abilities, and experiences (KSAEs) you will need in order to sell yourself using the positioning model.

POSITIONING IN RECREATION, PARKS, AND TOURISM

The traditional model has become institutionalized as *the* career development model. It is the model generally used by business schools. However, there are systemic differences between the industries associated with business schools and those associated with recreation, parks, and tourism programs. Generally, the business community consists of a large number of huge companies with large personnel departments that draw from a continual supply of workers. It makes sense for

them to participate in career fairs in which they can sift through large numbers of applicants and select their workers. For them, it is a situation of the cream rising to the top; the large companies simply skim off the best students, hire them, and retrain them for their corporate systems. The traditional model works well in the business world (although this does not preclude the use of the positioning model).

For students majoring in recreation, parks, and tourism, as in many other majors, there are often no job fairs or large interview sessions in which organizations visit the campus and interview prospective employees. Most recreation, parks, and tourism majors have spent a substantial portion of their college careers developing their professional networks to position themselves for their formal entry into the field. In other words, many students in this field use the positioning model. Although it has gained a lot of use, it is generally not recognized as the primary method of making the transition from college to career. Regardless, the positioning model has become the preferred model for many disciplines.

Within the recreation, parks, and tourism field, students need to use both curricular and non-curricular activities to position themselves for their careers. Often, the curriculum offers several ways to make use of the positioning model. For example, students may attend professional conferences to expand their professional networks. Some programs require that students attend such conferences; others have a culture of encouraging students to do so. Many students use professional conferences to position themselves and to line up senior internships or summer jobs.

Many programs require students to complete an internship during their senior year. For many students, the internship provides the transition phase into their first full-time career position. It is an important transition. They have already begun to build their professional networks through a series of summer jobs, field experiences, class activities, and other experiences.

Positioning is as simple as putting yourself where you want to be.

Their professional network is complemented or augmented by the professional network already developed by the instructors in the program. It is important for recreation, parks, and tourism students to begin building their network infrastructure by the time they complete their internship and before graduation.

Many students complete their internships and return to school having been offered a position. Sometimes these positions are created specifically to hire the intern as a full-time employee. If this scenario occurred only rarely, it would be considered a coincidence. However, it is close to the norm, which suggests that the positioning model is active in the field of recreation, parks, and tourism.

Sometimes, students return from internships without having been offered a job. Perhaps there were simply no positions available, or the organization engaged several interns with the intention of hiring only one at the end of the experience. Some organizations have a permanent internship position so they can use interns as inexpensive labor and have little or no intention of offering continued employment after the internship.

Regardless of the circumstances, you can still position yourself for the transition into your career, particularly if you have cased the joint well and know the potential problems prior to the experience. Internship programs often provide excellent training for jobs with similar organizations. Even if you aren't hired at the end of your internship, you are well trained for entry into the field. It can help to network with other professionals in other organizations during your internship so that you have people to contact later when you are searching for a position.

The positioning model represents a paradigm shift from the traditional job search model, and I believe it should be a formal part of the curriculum in recreation, parks, and tourism departments. It is a life skill that will serve students throughout their employment careers. Until recently, students didn't receive a formal course on the topic. There wasn't a book that put it together under one cover. Instead, students learned the lessons of positioning informally through a series of life experiences that taught them many of the processes described in this book. These positioning skills include being proactive, bridging, thinking evaluation, professional networking, casing the joint, and succeeding in the one-on-one interview. These positioning steps and skills are briefly discussed in the next section, which also serves as an overview of this book.

NINE STEPS TO POSITIONING YOURSELF

The steps of the positioning process form the structure of this book. Each step includes a question that summarizes the goal of that step; these are the questions you will be trying to answer as you go about the positioning process. Some of the questions are very similar to the questions that are traditionally asked of applicants during interviews. However, they take on a different meaning when applied to the concept of positioning because you are asking them of yourself.

Proximity Is Everything . . . Well, Almost Everything

Where do I want to work?

Positioning starts with determining where you want to work, or your career goal, if you know what it is. Because most people have trouble delineating their career goal, the emphasis at this point is on the immediate goal of determining your next job. Then it is a question of positioning yourself close to the people, job, and organization that will advance you in fulfilling your career goal. When you ask yourself, Where do I want to work? you are already in the process of moving toward the position you seek. Chapter 2 walks you through the process of answering this question and provides examples of people who have successfully positioned themselves.

Being Proactive, not Reactive

Do I actively seek the job I want, or do I wait for it to come to me?

Attitude is a vital component of positioning. A proactive person has a curious attitude and finds out what needs to be done and then does it rather than waiting to be told what to do. When I sought a position in western Maryland, my actions suggested to others that I had a proactive attitude. In turn, when you seek a field experience or internship, you are demonstrating a proactive attitude. For the most part, the job search process associated with the traditional model is reactive, whereas the job search process associated with the positioning model is very proactive. As the question suggests, in the traditional model, you wait for the job to come to you. You wait for the organization to advertise the job, and then you apply for it. Chapter 3 applies the principles of being proactive to your career development. Don't get upset if you don't view yourself as a proactive person. By following the positioning model and the techniques described in this book, you will become more proactive in your job search. An added bonus is that people who are proactive get better positions, promotions, and advancements.

Think Evaluation

Why should they hire me?

How do you prepare yourself for your next job? Whether you use the traditional or positioning model, you will find chapter 4 unlike any other

in most career development books because it approaches the job search process by starting at the end of the process, evaluation. This chapter provides an insight into the link between the evaluation instrument (the documents and rubrics hiring organizations use to evaluate candidates for employment) and the *job description*. You will also learn how your application will be evaluated in the traditional model. With this insight comes key knowledge of how to prepare for eventual employment. The chapter also shows how to use job announcements to determine the knowledge, skills, abilities, and experiences (KSAEs) you will need in order to prepare yourself for your next job. By starting your career development at the end, with evaluation, you are actually starting at the beginning.

Bridging

Am I prepared for the job I seek?

If you are on one side of a river and want to get to the other side, you build a bridge. You don't sit there and watch the water flow by. In chapter 4,

you first determine the knowledge, skills, abilities, and experiences you need for the job you seek. Then you develop a plan to obtain them. Bridging is the process of obtaining the appropriate skills for your desired job, whether it is a new job (horizontal bridging) or a promotion (vertical bridging). Chapter 5 describes several bridging techniques and offers advice on developing the KSAEs you need for your next job. It starts with the selection of your major and includes obtaining field experiences, internships, and even summer jobs. Professional development is also discussed.

Professional Networking

How do I meet the person who will hire me?

Although the concept of networking has been around for a while, it needs reexamination, particularly in terms of professional positioning. Chapter 6 introduces the concept of professional networking. It is more than just making

By starting at the end of the process, you are actually starting at the beginning.

contacts; it is making quality contacts, or the right contacts, and it includes addressing technical and content competency. Professional development is one of the key avenues for developing professional contacts in any field, and it is an important aspect of networking. Think of it this way: If you position yourself, you will know who will hire you. In fact, you have probably already met this person. And, because you have already met and talked with this person, in all probability you have already networked with him. In other words, you have assessed what he can do for you in terms of your career, and conversely, he has assessed what you can do for him in terms of his needs.

Casing the Joint

Do I know everything about the organization and the job I seek?

Now that you know where you want to work and have prepared yourself for the job, you need to investigate the organization. *Casing the joint* is another way of saying *researching the organization*. In the seven-step sales model, this is the survey phase. It doesn't matter whether you are reactively responding to a position announcement you saw on the Internet or using the positioning model to proactively seek an organization where you can potentially work. The more you know about where and for whom you want to work, the better able you are to position yourself for the job. Chapter 7 reviews some of the traditional research techniques from the perspective of the positioning model. It describes a methodology for researching the field, organization, and position to determine whether this is where you want to work.

The One-on-One Interview

Who within the organization can hire me?

As part of your job search process, you identify the person within the organization whom you need to contact regarding a job. Your next step is to contact that person or someone who can introduce you to that person. This initial contact is what we call the one-on-one interview, in which you explore job opportunities and how the organization can use your skills. This interview incorporates most of the steps in the seven-step sales model. The one-on-one interview is unlike the traditional interview in that it occurs at the beginning rather than at the end of the process, and you are not in competition with anyone else for the position at that time.

The Formal Interview

How should I prepare for a traditional interview?

Depending on your circumstances, even within the positioning model it's entirely possible that you will take part in a formal interview as part of the job search process. In the formal interview process, the organization announces the job and people apply and compete for the position. In some cases, it is a formal process. If you have positioned yourself well for the job, it may be more of a formality. Chapter 9 helps you prepare for the traditional interview.

Developing Your Communication Tools

Do I have the communication tools I need to obtain my job?

Three chapters focus on the communication tools that you will need to obtain your job. In the positioning model, you might never be asked for a copy of your resume. However, you should certainly be prepared in case you are, or in case you are applying for a position through the traditional model. Chapter 10 addresses the nuts and bolts of preparing an effective resume. There are other ways, though, to communicate your skills to a prospective employer besides a resume. Chapter 11 discusses the value of preparing a portfolio and business cards. Finally, because you may need to send a letter or e-mail to the person who will employ you, it is helpful to know the proper format and etiquette for writing cover letters and e-mails. These are addressed in chapter 12. All of these communication tools are sales instruments that sell you and what you are capable of doing. They are you.

CASE STUDY: SALLY HERR

To illustrate the steps of the positioning model, this book features the ongoing case study of Sally Herr, a fictitious student who is finishing her last semester at State College University and seeks to become an aquatics director at the fictitious Anytown Association of Family Centers (AFC). Like many students, Sally has done some things that will help to prepare her to make the transition in the workplace (some summer jobs and some other experiences, including her internship), but she hasn't done everything that she could have done to prepare herself to become an aquatics director. In exercise 1.1 at the end of this chapter, you can compare Sally's resume to your own to begin to get an idea of how prepared you are for the kind of job you are interested in.

PARADIGM SHIFT

Every book on the job search process or career development claims to be unique. It may be hyperbole to suggest that the positioning model represents a paradigm shift in the approach to the job search process. However, it is clear that this book documents a process that has been occurring under the noses of all of the other job search publications. In addition, it formalizes the process and provides step-by-step instructions that will help you in 50 to 80 percent of hiring situations. Does this constitute a paradigm shift? Perhaps. You can decide for yourself as you read the book.

Many of my students get that "ah-ha" feeling when the concept of positioning becomes clear. It makes perfect sense. It is like a reordering of a deck of cards to create a new and very different hand of cards to play. This realization often occurs when they complete their internship and a position suddenly appears where there wasn't one before. (If you want to know if Marty gets the job after his internship, read chapter 13.) It occurs when the employer asks for the resume only as an afterthought in the application process. Or, it occurs when a student attends a professional conference and ends up interviewing for a job that may or may not have been advertised to the public. If you obtain the same ah-ha feeling as you read this book, then positioning is a paradigm shift for you regarding how you approach your job search.

PUTTING IT ALL TOGETHER

In high school, if you wanted to meet a special person, you positioned yourself close to her by sitting next to her at lunch. You joined the drama club if she was in the school play. And, if you were lucky, you also increased your skill as an actor. Perhaps you became a cheerleader if he was on the football team. Or, maybe you joined the yearbook committee if he was on that committee. And again, you probably found yourself improving your writing skills too. Maybe you had a mutual friend introduce you to the person you wanted to meet.

Intuitively, you placed yourself in close proximity to this special person. You also learned new skills. In a sense, you created a bridge to the person you wanted to meet. You were proactive. You didn't wait for the person to come to you; you sought her out. You were already practicing many of the techniques of positioning. These same techniques will help you find a satisfying and meaningful career.

REFERENCES

Ganske, N. (2005). Networking for students. *Intercom, 52* (3), 10-13.

Kopiske, W. (2003). Networking etiquette: Respecting your professional contacts. *Government Finance Review, 19* (5), 53-54.

O'Donnell, P. (2004). Selling to the hidden job market. *Intercom, 51* (6), 26-29.

Comparing Your Resume With Sally Herr's

The purpose of this exercise is to compare your resume with Sally Herr's (see below). Although the content will be different, in terms of experiences, do you view her as better prepared for her job than you are for yours, about the same, or less prepared? If you view yourself as less prepared, then you might want to consider what you need to do to prepare yourself better for your next job.

____ Sally is better prepared than I.

__X__ We are both about the same in preparation.

____ I am better prepared than Sally.

Note: Remember that we noted that Sally's resume is probably typical of a lot of students'. She has gained experience during the summer and some part-time work. However, her resume is not exceptional.

Sally K. Herr
8310 Oakford Drive
Springfield, Virginia 56001
Home: 507-555-2223
e-mail: skherr@statecollege.edu

OBJECTIVE

Seek an aquatics director position in a community or nonprofit setting

HONORS

All-American—Earned All-American honors in swimming
President—Student Recreation and Parks Club

EDUCATION

State College University
BS degree in Recreation and Parks
Option: Therapeutic Recreation
Expected graduation: May 2008

CAREER EXPERIENCES

Summer 2007   **Rolling Hills AFC**, Rolling Hills, MD
ASSISTANT AQUATICS DIRECTOR and INTERNSHIP
- Administered the pool, including five lifeguards
- Worked with the director and CEO in administering the pool
- Choreographed the women's aquatic exercise program

Summer 2006   **Rolling Hills AFC**, Rolling Hills, MD
HEAD SWIM COACH
- Coached a swim team of over 100 children
- Conducted swimming meets and organized field trips
- Team won first place in regional tournaments

Fall 2005   **American Red Cross**, Harrisburg, PA
ADAPTED AQUATICS INSTRUCTOR
- Taught disabled students to swim as part of an American Red Cross Adapted Aquatics program

Summer 2003   **Browne Summer Camp**, Alexandria, VA
HEAD CAMP COUNSELOR
- Planned special projects and participated in camp productions for children aged three and four

EMPLOYMENT

Spring 2006   **State College University**, University Park, MD, to present
RESIDENT ASSISTANT
- Counseled students and worked with seven other resident assistants

Spring 2005   **Springfield High School**, Springfield, VA
SUBSTITUTE TEACHER
- Instructed high school classes in physical education, science, business, mathematics, and art

Exercise 1.2

Surveying Your Hidden Jobs

The purpose of this exercise is to review jobs you have had (including significant promotions) to determine how many of them you obtained through the traditional job search process and how many were hidden. Using the table below, list your most recent jobs (including full-time jobs, part-time jobs, summer jobs, significant promotions, internships, and field experiences) and then indicate whether you obtained the job using the traditional job search model or whether you got it without formally applying for it. If any part of the formal job process was not performed, check the second box.

Were most of your positions obtained using the traditional job search process? Did you obtain any of your jobs or significant promotions through a nontraditional job search? If you are completing this exercise as a class, discuss your findings in terms of the traditional and positioning models. Did your percentage coincide with the national percentage (i.e., between 50 and 80 percent of positions are hidden)? Did you use a hybrid, or variation, of one model or the other in the process of obtaining any of your jobs?

	Job	I got the job using the traditional job search method.	I got the job without formally applying for it.
1.		[ ]	[ ]
2.		[ ]	[ ]
3.		[ ]	[ ]
4.		[ ]	[ ]
5.		[ ]	[ ]
6.		[ ]	[ ]
7.		[ ]	[ ]
8.		[ ]	[ ]
9.		[ ]	[ ]
	Total each column; divide the number of checks in each column by the total number of jobs. Multiply by 100, or move the decimal point two points to the right to convert your score into a percentage.		

Exercise 1.3

Determining Your Hidden Jobs

The purpose of this exercise is to examine a hidden job you have had and analyze it.

Think back over the jobs you have had. Use the list from the previous exercise, if appropriate. List the jobs or significant promotions you have had that weren't advertised or, if they were advertised, were really yours.

1. _____

2. _____

3. _____

4. _____

5. _____

6. _____

Why did you want to work there? Was it for the money, the experience, convenience, or for all of these reasons?

_____

_____

_____

_____

_____

Did you actively seek the position, or did you wait for it to come to you? Briefly describe what you did and how you actively sought the job.

_____

_____

_____

_____

_____

What knowledge, skills, abilities, and experiences did you need for the job? List these here.

_____

_____

_____

_____

_____

How did you obtain the knowledge, skills, abilities, and experiences that you needed for the job? Did you have all the skills you needed? Did your employer provide you with the training that you needed? Were there any knowledge, skills, abilities, or experiences that you learned while on the job that you wish you had had before you took the job?

_____

_____

_____

_____

_____

How much did you know about the organization and the job before you obtained the job? If you knew nothing or only a little, was there anything you wish you would have known before taking the job? If so, explain. Why did you wish you had known it?

_____

_____

_____

_____

_____

Who hired you, and how did you meet this person? Did you already know this person? If you did, was it in a personal or professional capacity? If it was professional, note how you initially made contact.

_____

_____

_____

_____

_____

Did the person who hired you help you to advance your career? If so, describe how.

_____

_____

_____

_____

_____

Did this job lead to additional jobs or promotions? List those jobs or promotions here. Were they hidden or advertised publicly?

_____

_____

_____

_____

_____

2

Proximity Is Everything . . . Well, Almost Everything

Where do I want to work?

Where do I want to work? Would you rather hire someone you don't know, or someone you know who is already doing the job? The answer is obvious: You would hire the person you know.

Proximity is everything, or almost everything. Actors in search of work in the movies move to Hollywood. A person who wants to work as a programmer in a YMCA works in a YMCA. Those who want to run their own businesses start businesses. *If you want to be close to something, position or move yourself closer to it.* This is intuitive. Chapter 1 defined positioning as the technique of placing yourself in proximity to the person for whom you want to work, the organization in which you want to work, or the position that fulfills your career goal. This chapter describes how you can begin to do just that.

As suggested by the question at the beginning of this chapter, to position yourself close to the job you seek, you need to know where you want to work, why you want to work there, and which job you seek. In this chapter you will consider

your career goals, but it's not necessary at this point to know what you want to do for the rest of your life. For now, it's enough to simply determine where you want to work for your next job. Most people can answer this question or at least have a pretty good idea of what they would like to do next. If you can answer this question, you know where you are going; once you know where you are going, positioning becomes doable.

SEEKING PROXIMITY IN YOUR JOB SEARCH

In terms of jobs, the ways people seek proximity may be analyzed in terms of the following:

- People
- Places
- Organizations
- Networking events
- Knowledge, skills, abilities, and experiences (KSAEs)

A TALE OF TWO MODELS

Whether you are using the traditional model or the positioning model, you are trying to move yourself closer to where you want to work. In the traditional model, when you apply for a job, you are attempting to place yourself close to where you want to work and whom you want to work for. In contrast, in the positioning model, you seek the position you want and in doing so seek to place yourself close to the person who can help you get it or the organization where you want to work. Differences between the two models are not readily evident in terms of proximity. Other differences will become more evident in the later chapters. This chapter discusses the importance of proximity to positioning.

Most people seek proximity in their job searches to more than one of the preceding factors.

Proximity to People

There are two ways to position yourself close to other people for the purpose of finding a job. First, you can seek a prominent person in the field who can act as your mentor and help you to advance your career. Very often instructors play this role for students. In graduate school, I studied under Dr. Betty van der Smissen, a significant leader in the field. Studying under her helped my career in many ways. She helped me obtain a position in the field upon graduation, for one thing. Also, I became a member of a special group of people who had the common experience of having studied under her, which further benefited my career.

To consider another example, Joe was a student who wasn't sure where he wanted to work. A faculty member had connections with MWR (Morale, Welfare and Recreation), the service branch that provides recreational services to military personnel and their families. In discussions with the faculty member, Joe decided that he wanted to work in MWR. The faculty member assisted Joe in the application process and making the necessary connections to obtain an internship at the Kodiak Coast Guard station in Alaska. After completing his internship, Joe applied for MWR's training program. He was accepted, and he is now on a direct career path in MWR management. Initially, the faculty member mentored Joe and helped him obtain the internship. From there he was able to position himself for the next step in his career.

Like Joe, you can use a third party to act as a catalyst and link you with an employer. Like mentors, faculty members often help students obtain jobs. (This benefit is discussed further in chapter 6 in the section Developing Your Professional Family.) I recall helping Virgil, the executive director of a national nonprofit organization that promotes boating safety, to hire Amanda, a former student of mine. Virgil's organization needed someone with strong organizational and writing skills. Although the job announcement had been distributed nationally, the pool of applicants had been exhausted, so he was looking at alternative ways to fill the position.

After her internship Amanda had obtained a contractual position with an outdoor education center near St. Louis. She had gone to St. Louis, in part, because of a personal relationship that had later evaporated, so she was willing to move.

Virgil and I discussed Amanda's qualifications and potential to do the job. I called Amanda, and we chatted about the job and its opportunities for her. I e-mailed her a copy of the job description, and she e-mailed Virgil a copy of her resume. Virgil invited her in for an interview and subsequently hired her for the position. (As a footnote, Amanda's meeting with Virgil was a variation of the one-on-one interview, which is discussed in detail in chapter 8.) My acting as a catalyst was a vital factor in Amanda's securing a job that worked out well for her and her employer.

Proximity to Place

Location usually plays an important role in selecting jobs. It is probably more important than most people would like to admit. If you want a particular job, sometimes you need to move closer to where the job is located. Place can also play a big part in your job search if you are bound to a particular location—for example, if your spouse or significant other is working or studying there.

Consider Helen, a college student from the eastern United States who wanted to move west—ideally, to Montana or Wyoming. In addition, she wanted to work on a dude ranch because she loved horses. She knew what she wanted, and she began her planning in ample time. She researched dude ranches and narrowed the search to the one that most appealed to her.

Helen's plan was to obtain an internship with the dude ranch she had selected and then to use the internship as a vehicle to position herself for a full-time job with that ranch or one nearby. The strategy was not without risks. There was no guarantee that once she completed her internship she would obtain a full-time job. Also, there was an inherent bias. She was competing against people who had done this sort of thing all their lives. And because she was from the East, it was simply assumed that she didn't have the necessary skills and abilities to do the job. She had to prove herself.

Helen obtained the internship. She had fortitude and perseverance, she applied herself, and she worked hard during her internship. She proved herself, and she obtained the job she sought with the dude ranch after graduation. She had boarded her own horses during her internship. She put them in her horse trailer and moved to Montana and her new job on the ranch. She chose where she wanted to work, and her efforts to position herself on a dude ranch in Montana were successful.

Helen's case is interesting and somewhat typical in that she worked for two years in Montana and then moved back to a similar job in the East that was closer to family and friends. Helen made this move early in her career. Many people consider family ties later in their careers when parents and relatives become older and more in need of assistance. Helen was again able to position herself where she wanted to be, this time closer to family and friends.

Proximity to an Organization

Before universities turned out journalism majors, if you wanted to become a news reporter, you started by working in a newsroom. Usually, your career started not with reporting the news, but with sweeping the floors. Over time, you worked your way into a reporter's position. As your career advanced, you became an associate editor, and if you were really good or ambitious, you became an editor. If you wanted to be a newspaper person, you worked in a newsroom, even if it meant sweeping the floors. The adage was: *If you want to work there, work there.* This point is fundamental to positioning.

If you want a job with the park and planning commission, you might not think to look there for a summer job. You might, for example, work construction instead, figuring it's a way to earn a good amount of money. Granted, sometimes people have to make the hard choice between earning money during the summer and preparing themselves for their careers. Nevertheless, as you choose your experiences in your academic career, it's worth remembering that they are all preparing you for something.

Don't leave your career choice to chance.

Again, it is as simple as remembering that if you want to work there, work there. Many executives at park and planning started their careers by figuratively sweeping the floors; they then advanced up the chain of command to directorships. Sometimes you may need to take a lesser position than you want. The lesser position may be necessary for getting you into the organization, giving you the credentials to stay with the organization, or keeping you employed in the organization until the desired position becomes open.

Raymond grew up in Washington, D.C. For him, it was an obvious choice to want to do his internship with the D.C. Parks and Recreation Department. He secured an internship in the department's outdoor program as part of the summer camp program. Unfortunately, he had little experience in this area. He had to learn the program, hone his skills, and apply them at the summer camp. He did.

When Raymond's camp supervisor decided to leave her position to start a bed and breakfast, she recommended him for her position. Not only had he positioned himself well for the job, but he had also demonstrated an ability to learn, adapt, and apply himself. He accepted the job and is working full-time for the department. He wanted to work close to home (place), and he wanted to work for the D.C. Parks and Recreation Department (organization). He positioned himself well for the camp director's position and was pleased when he obtained the position.

Ellen sought a career in the front office of the Altoona Curves, a minor league baseball team. In addition to her major degree, she had a minor in business administration. She engineered an internship with the team in sales. An internship in sales was the typical avenue for anyone who wanted to get a foot in the door with the organization. Sales was where you started; it was the ground floor that led to other positions in the organization. Also, sales was fundamental to understanding the organization because everything else depended on it.

Note that many organizations use their internship programs to procure inexpensive labor; they hire interns with no intention of offering them full-time positions after the internship. Or, they may hire three or four interns with the intention of hiring only one of them after the internship. Often, hiring is based on the normal turnover of employees (i.e., someone has to leave for a position to open). Raymond's situation was an example of a position opening up when someone left. In contrast, Ellen faced a situation in which there were several interns and probably only one would be hired after the internship.

Although obtaining the internship was competitive, Ellen was accepted. She completed her internship with no guarantee of full-time employment. Full-time jobs with the organization were also competitive because, generally, the number of people seeking entry-level positions was greater than the number of positions available. After doing a good job on her internship, Ellen obtained a full-time job with the Altoona Curves. Currently, she is the Curves' director of community relations and is responsible for all of the club's community programs and special events. Also, she serves as an on-field host during games.

Ellen positioned herself well with her internship and eventually was offered employment. For Ellen, proximity was everything—well, almost everything. She also had to perform well in her job. And she did.

Chip wanted to be a climbing guide at Seneca Rocks in West Virginia. This is often a hard market to penetrate. First, there is always a supply of young climbers who are willing to do what you want to do for free or for very little money. This is the nature of the market. Unless you start your own business, it is often difficult to make the appropriate contacts with climbing employers. Although there is always someone ready to take your place, however, not everyone makes a suitable employee. This is because there is a profound difference between climbing as an individual activity and leading or guiding others in a climb. However, finding an opportunity to demonstrate that you will subjugate your personal climbing needs for the good of the company can be difficult.

Chip knew what he wanted to accomplish, and he knew the difficulty of breaking into the field as a professional. He also knew that he needed to serve an apprenticeship if he were to have even a hope of making it into the field as a professional. He needed to use his internship to strategically position himself as a professional guide.

Chip interned with one of the premier climbing schools at Seneca Rocks in West Virginia, during which he proved himself as having the potential as a guide and instructor. Furthermore, during his internship, he networked on a professional level with the people who could hire him after his internship, or who could provide him with the references and referrals to obtain a job with another reputable guide service.

In a highly competitive market that is hard to break into, Chip developed a viable strategy to obtain his objective. Currently, he is actively employed as a climbing guide.

Do I take a job just to take a job, or do I take a job that positions me for where I want to go?

Katie did her internship with the park and planning commission. She did an outstanding job, and they wanted to keep her. As part of her responsibilities, she helped plan a new community center. Her supervisors within the commission suggested that she take a lesser position in the commission until a position at the new center became available. She did so, strategically positioning herself for the job in the new center when it becomes available.

You should keep in mind that taking a lesser position can raise serious questions regarding your employability and career path. The most obvious question is, Why are you taking a lesser position when you are obviously more qualified for something better? This is less of a problem for students who are entering the workforce than for people who already have well-developed career paths. Katie can easily answer this question. She has the support of key people within the organization who will help facilitate her movement within the organization when the time is right.

Proximity Through Networking Events

Networking events such as professional conferences and professional development activities can be important vehicles to obtaining the job you want. As previously noted, sometimes the people or organizations you come across through networking can serve as facilitators, or midwives, in the positioning process. Professional and community involvement can bring the same kinds of career-changing results.

Take Bud, who had worked summer camps most of his life and dreamed of becoming a camp director. But becoming a camp director can be tricky. Some organizations treat the camp director position as a part-time job within the parent organization, requiring the director to hold another position in the organization also. Private camps present a different problem. Unless you have the capital resources to purchase a private camp, you need to find a camp whose owner is looking for someone to manage it. Often, this is because the owner is no longer interested in operating the camp but is not yet ready to sell it. Given Bud's situation, this was the most attractive alternative for him.

The issue for Bud was how to make a link with the appropriate camp. He reviewed advertisements for open positions in the American Camp Association (ACA) magazine and made preliminary contact with several camps regarding their need for a camp director. Then Bud made arrangements to interview several camps at the annual conference of the ACA. He attended the conference during the fall, interviewed several owners, and eventually secured a position as the director of a camp in Maine.

A key component in Bud's obtaining this job was his professional involvement, which included his attendance at the professional conference. The professional organization linked the job hunter with the camp owner. Without it, Bud would never have found his job.

Proximity by KSAEs

By developing the appropriate knowledge, skills, abilities, and experiences (KSAEs), you can position yourself for a job even if you may not have been actively seeking it. Kathy was a student with considerable event management skills; however, she had no skill as a canoeist or kayaker. She had never even been in a canoe. For her, it was a question of identifying an area in which to apply her talents. The executive director of the American Canoe Association hired her for her skills and then provided the necessary competencies in canoeing and kayaking as part of her training.

Many students participated in the Whitewater Parks and Courses Conference as part of the service learning experiences associated with one of their classes. Kathy demonstrated her organizational abilities in events management and her work ethic at the conference. Matt, who was one of the co-organizers of the conference, said of Kathy's contribution: "Kathy was the unsung hero. She worked hard, took little credit, and made the registration process easy on the attendees. My understanding is she's in the hospitality track in the department. It seems to be working! She'll go far."

Kathy went far. Pam, the executive director of the American Canoe Association, who was in attendance at the conference and who had close connections with Matt, offered Kathy a job as the special events coordinator for their Subaru Rendezvous. Now, Kathy travels around the country coordinating grassroots special events in paddlesports for the public.

Because of her knowledge, skills, abilities, and experiences in event management, Kathy had positioned herself for this job. Actually, through a series of events, she backed into this job because of the KSAEs she possessed. Although she didn't

know the first thing about canoeing or paddlesports, she had the organizational and event management skills necessary for the job. She got the job as a result of serendipitous circumstances, faculty connections, and the KSAEs she possessed. Kathy's KSAEs were not in the content area of canoeing and kayaking. In retrospect, she found a home in event management and planning. She would never have guessed that it was in the area of paddlesports.

DETERMINING YOUR CAREER GOAL OR WHERE YOU WANT TO WORK

In most of the examples we have reviewed so far, the people made conscious decisions that they wanted to work for specific people, for specific organizations, in specific locations, or at specific jobs because they possessed the KSAEs needed for performing those jobs. Occasionally, people back into their jobs or take advantage of opportunities as they became available. Kathy, for example, wanted to be an event planner. She hadn't identified the content area in which she wanted to work, but circumstances put her in contact with the American Canoe Association.

This returns us to the question at the beginning of the chapter: Where do you want to work? Until you are able to answer this question or the broader question of what your career goal is, it will be difficult to develop a plan and position yourself for your next job. The problem is that most people have a hard time identifying their career goals. You can test this for yourself. If you have a hard time writing your career goal, try exercise 2.4. It asks you who, what, where, when, and why, or the five Ws, regarding the job you seek. Answering these questions will help you articulate a career goal that is typical of what most publications recommend—that is, a description of the job you want.

Sally Herr completed the five Ws exercise (exercise 2.4); her completed form is shown in figure 2.1. She synthesized her career goal as follows: *My career goal is to obtain an aquatics position and, if possible, an assistant aquatics director position at the Anytown AFC upon my gradua-*

The Five Ws and Developing Your Career Goal

In this exercise you will determine the five Ws (who, what, where, when, and why) regarding where you want to work. In some cases, this may be all you really know about what you want to do. Completing this exercise will give you the minimal information you need in order to position yourself.

1. For whom (what organization) do you want to work?

   I would like to work for the AFC.

2. What position do you want (job title, job description, or both)?

   I would like an aquatics position and, if possible, an assistant aquatics director position.

3. Where (location) do you want to work?

   Anytown, MD

4. When do you want to begin working there?

   May 2xxx

5. Why do you want this job? (e.g., you respect the product or service the organization delivers, it will advance your career, or the person who would supervise you is someone you want to learn from)

   I have worked for two summers with the AFC. I like the organization and, if possible, I would like to make a career with the AFC in aquatics.

6. Using your answers thus far, write a working career goal.

   My career goal is to obtain an aquatics position and, if possible, an assistant aquatics director position at the Anytown AFC upon my graduation in May. I would eventually like to become the aquatics director.

Figure 2.1   Sally Herr's completed five Ws exercise.

Finding a Job Announcement on the Internet

In this exercise you will find an online announcement for a job that appeals to you and then analyze what you like and dislike about the job. Try several search engines to find one that lists several potential jobs. Don't find one job quickly just to complete this exercise. Rather, review lots of job announcements and let one or two of them rise to the surface. Go with your feeling as much as with logic.

1. In exercise 2.4, you created a working career goal for yourself.

My career goal is to obtain an aquatics position and, if possible, an assistant aquatics director position at the Anytown AFC upon my graduation in May. I would eventually like to become the aquatics director.

2. Search the Internet and find at least one announcement for a job that most closely approximates the job you seek in terms of the title, duties, organization, location, and simply how it feels. For example, you may find a job that appeals to you, but the organization may seem too large for you, too rural, or too urban. If you have a hard time finding a job announcement that matches the job you want, and you are familiar with a job that is what you want, write a brief description of the job and use that in this exercise.

3. Briefly analyze the job announcement to determine what you like and dislike about the job. Do you like the service or product that you would be delivering? Do you believe you could make a difference in this job? List what you like about this job here:

   a. *It is an aquatics position.*
   b. *It involves teaching and instruction.*
   c. *It involves deck time.*
   d. _____
   e. _____
   f. _____

   List what you don't like about this job here:

   a. *It does not have administrative responsibilities.*
   b. *I might like to do the swim team coaching.*
   c. _____
   d. _____
   e. _____
   f. _____

4. Is the job you are searching for realistic in terms of the job announcements you are reviewing? Compare what you like and dislike about the job with what is your job description in step 2. Does what you like about the job seem to satisfy what is requested in the job description? If not, you may need to search for some more for positions or change what you want to do.

I like the position, although I would like more administrative responsiblities. The position is realistic in terms of its responsibilities and what is available at AFCs. I may not get both administrative and coaching responsibilities together.

Figure 2.2 Sally Herr's completed job announcement exercise.

tion in May. I would eventually like to become the aquatics director. This is a good working career goal that she can alter as needed for different positions for which she might be applying. For example, she could tailor or change the sentence about wanting to become an aquatics director to meet the specific needs of the job for which she is applying. Sally's career goal articulates what she wants to do and where she wants to go with her career.

Several other exercises can also help you focus on what you want to do. In exercise 2.5 you search the Internet for job announcements to find a job that suits you. Exercises 2.6 and 2.7 help you examine your past to determine what you may want to do for your career. Exercises 2.6 and 2.7 complement each other by leading you through an analysis of your favorite and least favorite jobs.

Sally completed several of the exercises. She did the Internet search in exercise 2.5 (see figure 2.2, page 20) and found a job announcement in St. Louis that was close to the type of job she was seeking (figure 2.3). In chapter 5 she will learn how an Internet search can help her determine the KSAEs she will need for the position she is currently seeking. At this point, her Internet search allows her to determine how well job descriptions match her career goal. She concluded that although there are some differences, what she is seeking is not too far off from what others are offering.

As long as you know where you want to go, the positioning model will help you get there. If you are like most people, you have an idea of what you want to do for your next job. Perhaps you have even determined the job you want after the next one also. Generally, the further out you can determine what you want to do, the better it is for your career development. Try completing a career goal for yourself even if it is as specific as Sally Herr's. For Sally, her career goal was a more generalized version of the next job she seeks.

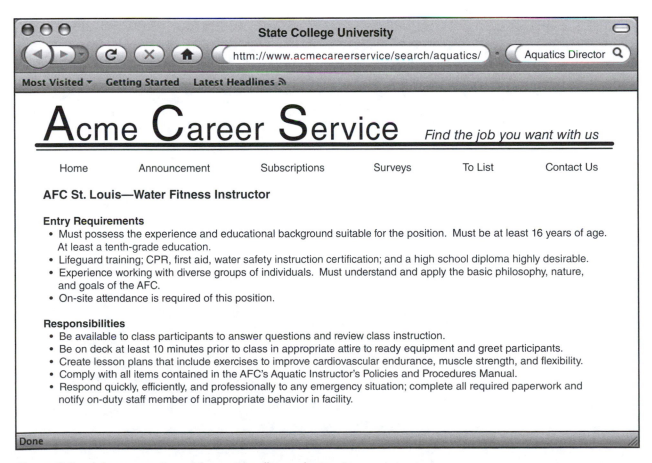

Figure 2.3 Job announcement for a water fitness instructor.

PUTTING IT ALL TOGETHER

To position yourself well for the job you want, you need to move closer to the people, places, organizations, and positions that are in proximity to that job. You have answered the question at the beginning of the chapter regarding where you want to work. Keep in mind that the best way to get a job is to already be working in that job. Find jobs and experiences that will move you closer to where you eventually want to work.

In addition to finding the job you want, you need to know your career goal or at least where you want to work next. As long as you know where you are headed in your career, you can apply the positioning model delineated in this book.

As the title of this chapter says, proximity isn't everything. In every one of the examples used in this chapter, the people who eventually obtained the jobs they wanted displayed other important characteristics. They demonstrated perseverance, enthusiasm, desire, and a good work ethic. In addition, they had the basic KSAEs that prepared them for their jobs. Don't discount the importance of these other attributes. Proximity will put you in the vicinity of the job you seek, but then you have to show them what you're made of.

Analyzing Sally Herr's Career Path

Examine Sally Herr's resume on page 9. Forget for the moment that she wants to become an aquatics director. Put yourself in the role of a guidance counselor who is looking at her resume to assess what she might want to do careerwise. What careers might you suggest based on her experiences? Is her desire to become an aquatics director a logical extension of the experiences listed on her resume? With this in mind, complete the next exercise, the blank resume.

The Blank Resume

This fairly simple exercise will help you begin preparing for your next job. Take a blank sheet of paper and create a heading at the top of the page. Type your name, address, phone number, and e-mail address. Underneath it type the following major headings: Education, Professional Experiences, Certifications. Next, fill in the blanks with the education, experiences, and certifications that you want to obtain before you graduate or in the next three years.

If you are already working, complete this exercise shortly after obtaining your job. This will keep you focused on where you are going. Because most people stay in their jobs for five to seven years before moving on to their next jobs, it is good to focus on your next job while you still have ample time to prepare yourself.

Be realistic in filling in your blank resume. If this is the resume you would like to have in three years, then the question is, How will you obtain the KSAEs listed on your resume in the next several years? Discuss how you might acquire the experiences you have listed.

Exercise 2.3

Which Student Example Is Closest to Your Story?

The stories in this chapter show people who have positioned themselves well to advance their careers. Comparing your story to theirs will help you position yourself for your next job.

1. Which story is closest to yours? Which story do you identify with the most? Why?

_____

_____

_____

_____

_____

2. Write a vignette on how you have positioned yourself for a past job.

_____

_____

_____

_____

_____

3. Write a vignette on how you will position yourself for your next position.

_____

_____

_____

_____

_____

4. If this is a class activity, discuss your vignettes. Are there any similarities in how people plan to position themselves?

_____

_____

_____

_____

_____

_____

The Five Ws and Developing Your Career Goal

In this exercise you will determine the five Ws (who, what, where, when, and why) regarding where you want to work. In some cases, this may be all you really know about what you want to do. Completing this exercise will give you the minimal information you need in order to position yourself.

1. For whom (what organization) do you want to work?

_____

_____

_____

2. What position do you want (job title, job description, or both)?

_____

_____

_____

3. Where (location) do you want to work?

_____

_____

_____

4. When do you want to begin working there?

_____

_____

_____

5. Why do you want this job? (e.g., you respect the product or service the organization delivers, it will advance your career, or the person who would supervise you is someone you want to learn from)

_____

_____

_____

6. Using your answers thus far, write a working career goal. (For an example, see the Sally Herr example in figure 2.1.)

_____

_____

_____

_____

Exercise 2.5

Finding a Job Announcement on the Internet

In this exercise you will find an online announcement for a job that appeals to you and then analyze what you like and dislike about the job. Try several search engines to find one that lists several potential jobs. Don't find one job quickly just to complete this exercise. Rather, review lots of job announcements and let one or two of them rise to the surface. Go with your feeling as much as with logic.

1. In exercise 2.4, you created a working career goal for yourself. For example, Sally Herr wants to become an aquatics director. List the job that you seek here.

   _____

   _____

   _____

2. Search the Internet and find at least one announcement for a job that most closely approximates the job you seek in terms of the title, duties, organization, location, and simply how it feels. For example, you may find a job that appeals to you, but the organization may seem too large for you, too rural, or too urban. If you have a hard time finding a job announcement that matches the job you want, and you are familiar with a job that is what you want, write a brief description of the job and use that in this exercise.

   _____

   _____

   _____

   _____

   _____

3. Briefly analyze the job announcement to determine what you like and dislike about the job. Do you like the service or product that you would be delivering? Do you believe you could make a difference in this job? List what you like about this job here:

   a. _____

   _____

   b. _____

   _____

   c. _____

   _____

   d. _____

   _____

   e. _____

   _____

   f. _____

   _____

List what you don't like about this job here:

a. _____

_____

b. _____

_____

c. _____

_____

d. _____

_____

e. _____

_____

f. _____

_____

4. Is the job you are searching for realistic in terms of the job announcements you are reviewing? Compare what you like and dislike about the job with what is your job description in step 2. Does what you like about the job seem to satisfy what is requested in the job description? If not, you may need to search for some more for positions or change what you want to do.

_____

_____

_____

_____

_____

_____

Exercise 2.6

My Favorite Job

In this exercise you will analyze your favorite job to determine what you really liked about it, and then to determine whether any of these reasons relate to your career goal.

1. Think about your favorite job. It could have been a full-time, summer, or part-time job. Write the job title and the basic job description here:

    _____

    _____

    _____

    _____

    _____

2. Think about the job, what you did, and the person you worked for. Also, think about your life circumstances. Did you have this job when you were freer and had fewer responsibilities or less pressure? List several reasons why this was your favorite job:

    a. _____

    _____

    b. _____

    _____

    c. _____

    _____

    d. _____

    _____

    e. _____

    _____

    f. _____

    _____

3. (Optional) Can you make a living at this job if you wanted? Why or why not? What would it take for you to make a living at this job?

    _____

    _____

    _____

    _____

My Least Favorite Job

This exercise is similar to the previous one except that you are analyzing your least favorite job. In this exercise you will analyze your least favorite job to determine what you really didn't like about the job and then to determine whether any of these reasons relate to your career goal.

1. Think about your least favorite job. It could have been a full-time, summer, or part-time job. Write the job title and the basic job description here:

    _____

    _____

    _____

    _____

    _____

    _____

2. Think about the job, what you did, and the person you worked for. Also, think about your life circumstances. List several reasons why this was your least favorite job:

    a. _____

    _____

    b. _____

    _____

    c. _____

    _____

    d. _____

    _____

    e. _____

    _____

    f. _____

    _____

3. Divide the items in step 2 into two groups. The first group includes circumstantial reasons for not liking your job, such as the fact that you did not like your boss, one of your coworkers made working there miserable, or you were ill and didn't perform as well as you could have. These reasons are specific to the circumstances of this job and won't transfer to another one. List the circumstantial reasons you didn't like your job here:

    a. _____

    _____

b. _____

_____

c. _____

_____

d. _____

_____

e. _____

_____

f. _____

_____

The reasons in the second group are more general, or transferable. For example, you didn't like sales, you didn't like the product or service you were delivering, or you wanted a more flexible work schedule. List these general, or transferable, items here:

a. _____

_____

b. _____

_____

c. _____

_____

d. _____

_____

e. _____

_____

f. _____

_____

4. Compare your findings here with those in exercise 2.6 to determine whether the things you didn't like about your least favorite job are the opposite of the things you liked about your favorite job.

_____

_____

_____

_____

_____

_____

The Blank Resume—Part II

Now that you have completed the other exercises and in particular a review of job announcements from the Internet, go back to exercise 2.2 and revise your resume with the information you now have. Is it the same resume? How did it change?

chapter 3

Being Proactive, not Reactive

Do I actively seek the job I want, or do I wait for it to come to me?

Being proactive—or reactive—is a question of attitude. In her book *How to Work a Room: The Ultimate Guide to Savvy Socializing in Person and Online,* Susan RoAne noted that 80 percent of people view themselves as shy. Often, this shyness is reflected in reactive job searches. People wait for job announcements, submit their resumes, and wait hopefully for interviews. They wait for positions to come to them rather than go after them before they are advertised. They believe that the traditional model best describes the job search process. They are reactive, not proactive.

Being proactive is a cornerstone of the positioning model. It is exemplified in the following chapters. Think evaluation and bridging are about actively taking control of your career development. Casing the joint involves researching the organization you want to work for, and the one-on-one interview usually requires that

you initiate contact with someone in the organization. In general, each of these steps requires you to be proactive in your job search and career development.

This chapter is not meant to make you proactive in everything you do; rather, it should help you become more proactive in your job search and in your approach toward your career development, an important factor in positioning yourself in today's employment environment. In addition, it also shows the employer that you have initiative and self-determination.

BENEFITS OF A PROACTIVE ATTITUDE

The first and perhaps most significant benefit of having a proactive attitude is that you can often obtain the job you seek. In most of the examples used in chapter 2, students were able to obtain the

A TALE OF TWO MODELS

There is a profound difference between the positioning and traditional models in terms of being proactive. The positioning model tends to be more proactive, whereas the traditional model tends to be more reactive.

In the traditional model, you wait for the job to come to you. The employer determined the job she needs filled. She develops a job description and advertises the job. You react to her job announcements and apply for the job. You wait for an invitation for an interview. You interview and react to the questions the employer asks. If you are lucky, you obtain the job.

In contrast, in the positioning model you decide where and for whom you would like to work. This requires you to be proactive. You analyze job announcements to determine the knowledge, skills, abilities, and experiences you will need in the job you want. You develop a plan to acquire those KSAEs. You seek ways to increase your professional network. You investigate potential employers and approach them to seek a position. If you have done your groundwork well and if you have positioned yourself, you have a good chance at getting the job.

In the positioning model the roles of the employer and job seeker are somewhat reversed. The employer tends to be reactive, at least initially. You have done all the work to position yourself, and it is usually not until the end of the process that the employer becomes involved in the process. By being proactive, you can often create a job where there might not have been one otherwise.

jobs they wanted because they were acting proactively. Helen obtained the job she sought on the dude ranch. Ellen positioned herself in sales with the Altoona Curves, and Chip positioned himself as a climbing guide in Seneca, West Virginia. Joe obtained a position as a recreation programmer at the U.S. Coast Guard station in Kodiak, Alaska, and Bud obtained a position as camp director. In these examples, the students decided where they wanted to work and then developed plans to obtain the job. In each case, the proactive approach bore fruit.

The second benefit of a proactive approach is that it reveals positive attributes to a potential employer. Most recreation positions require people who can act somewhat independently within an organization to deliver programs and services that meet the goals of the organization. In many cases, people are assigned a task and then they are expected to complete it with little direct supervision. Many people choose this field because of the freedom it offers.

When Chip is climbing at Seneca Rocks and when Helen is conducting a trail ride on the dude ranch, they are acting somewhat independently within the organization. As a camp director, Bud acts with little direct supervision from the owners. As a recreation programmer, Joe determines the

recreation programs for those stationed at the Coast Guard station and then conducts them. The same proactive and take-charge attitude toward programming that is often found in the typical job in recreation, parks, and tourism is demonstrated by the positioning process.

The benefits of being proactive are not unique to this field and to positioning. Considerable research has been conducted on the proactive personality as it relates to the job search and career development. Studies suggest that people with proactive personalities do better in their job searches (Brown, Kane, Cober, Levy, & Shalhoop, 2006; Mueller & Wanberg, 2003). People with proactive personalities are better at determining where they want to work, and they are better at matching their skill sets to the advertised positions. They are better at making the transition into the workplace because they have researched the organization, or cased the joint. Once in the job, they advance more quickly in their career paths, again, because of their proactive personalities. The findings of this research consistently support the basic hypothesis set forth in this book.

Even if you don't have a proactive personality, just using the positioning model delineated in this book suggests a proactive attitude on your part. And, employers seek this attitude in their employees. The better able you are to incorporated proactive attributes into your job search, the more successful you will be in obtaining the job you seek, and once employed, the more successful you will be in advancing yourself with the organization.

As you follow the Sally Herr example used throughout this book, you will see that she is proactive in her job search. Remember, she is not an exceptional student, but a typical student. In chapter 2, she decided where she wanted to work. In chapter 4 you will see how she assessed the position she sought and developed a plan to acquire the knowledge, skills, abilities, and experiences (KSAEs) she needed for the position. She did considerable research before finally approaching Mr. Muncheck in the AFC organization in the one-on-one interview (discussed in chapter 8). By using the positioning job search model, she demonstrated a proactive attitude.

ASSESSING HOW PROACTIVE YOU ARE

Bateman and Crant (1993) developed a 12-question instrument to measure a person's proactive personality. We have adapted this instrument to help you determine how proactive you are regarding your career development. Figure 3.1 lists the 12 adapted questions.

Most of the statements in figure 3.1 address a proactive attitude. Are you on the lookout for new ways to advance your career? Are you proactive when you seek out new career positions, or do you wait for them to come to you? This attitude is foundational to the concept of positioning. Do you see what you need to do to develop your career and then pursue it, even if others oppose it? The statements are discussed in detail in the following section.

Exercise 3.1 gives you the opportunity to assess how proactive you are in your career development. The higher your score, the more proactive you are. There is a minimum score of 12 and a maximum score of 48. A score above 30 indicates that you tend to be proactive in your career development. If you score between 12 and 30, you tend to be less proactive in your career development.

Exercises 3.2 and 3.3 build on the proactive career development instrument and help you apply its findings to help you position yourself. Exercise 3.2 asks you to apply the proactive questions to the next job you seek. In contrast, exercise 3.3 helps you examine more closely your attitude toward both your career development and your job search in terms of the instrument's questions.

---

1. I am constantly on the lookout for new ways to advance my career.
2. I feel driven to make a difference with my career.
3. I seek out new career positions rather than wait for them to come to me.
4. Wherever I have been, I have been a powerful force in my career development.
5. Nothing is more exciting than eventually obtaining the position that I seek.
6. If I see something in my career development that I don't like, I fix it.
7. I will do what is necessary to develop my career, even if others oppose it.
8. I excel at identifying my career opportunities.
9. Regarding my career development, I am always looking for better ways to do things.
10. If I need a new skill to advance my career, I will develop it even if I have to pay for it myself.
11. I have recently had a new job or a major promotion.
12. I can spot a good career opportunity long before others can.

Figure 3.1 Twelve statements used to measure how proactive you are in terms of your career development and job searches.

Adapted, by permission, from T.S. Bateman and J.M. Crant, 1993, "The proactive component of organizational behavior: A measure and correlates," *Journal of Organizational Behavior* 14: 103-118.

PROACTIVE CAREER DEVELOPMENT TRAITS

This section describes each of the statements in figure 3.1 and discusses how they differ from the original statements used in Bateman and Crant's (1993) study.

I am constantly on the lookout for new ways to advance my career.

For a proactive job seeker, seeking to advance your career goes without saying. Proactive job seekers are constantly looking for ways to improve and advance their careers. Chapter 5, Bridging, helps to formalize this process and describes specific ways you can acquire the knowledge, skills, abilities, and experiences you need in order to develop your career. Sally Herr will identify the knowledge, skills, abilities, and experiences she needs to become an aquatics director, and then she will develop a simple plan to acquire them.

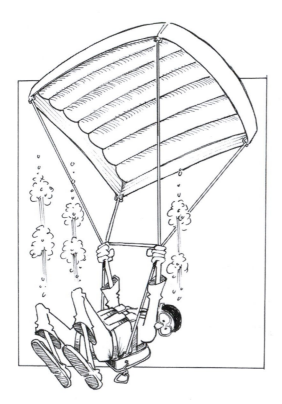

Strap on your parachute now while you still have time to prepare yourself for your next job. Be proactive and plan ahead.

I feel driven to make a difference with my career.

Do you feel driven to make a difference with your career? Sally Herr may not be driven in the traditional sense, but she would like a job as the aquatics director at the AFC. In this sense, she is proactive and driven to make a difference in her career.

I seek out new career positions rather than wait for them to come to me.

Do you take the initiative, or do you follow after others have taken the initiative? This statement reflects the question at the beginning of this chapter. The proactive job seeker takes the initiative and goes after the job. By following the positioning model and seeking the job at the AFC, Sally Herr went after the job she desired.

Wherever I have been, I have been a powerful force in my career development.

Do you take charge of your job search and career development? If so, you are a powerful force in your career development. By using the positioning model, you demonstrate that you have taken charge of your job search and career development. Sally Herr did. This question illustrates a subtle but important paradigm shift in the job search process. When people become proactive in their job search, the locus of control shifts away from the employer and toward the job seeker. Often, the employer does not become actively involved in the employment process until the one-on-one interview described in chapter 8.

Nothing is more exciting than eventually obtaining the position that I seek.

Exciting may be a slight overstatement; perhaps *satisfying* better describes the feeling you get from obtaining the position you seek. What could be more satisfying than identifying the position that you want, seeking it out, and then obtaining it? When Sally Herr finally obtained her job with the AFC, though, she was excited.

If I see something in my career develoment that I don't like, I fix it.

This statement is about showing initiative and having a take-charge attitude. Sally Herr determined that she needed to gain programming experience in water aerobics, and so she completed a water aerobics certification program at her local community college (see chapter 4). In terms of her career development, she fixed a hole in her career development.

I will do what is necessary to develop my career, even if others oppose it.

In a very real sense, this statement measures the intensity of your commitment to and your perseverance regarding your career development. The statement does this in two ways. First, it states it as a positive—that you will do what is necessary to develop your career. Second, it suggests that there might be a cost to your commitment. In the face of the opposition of others, will you still do what is necessary to attain your career goal? It is easy to say that you will do what is necessary to develop your career. Who wouldn't? However, the statement suggests that there might be a price to pay. Are you willing to pay it?

It is important to note that others will often oppose your career development. Change is often upsetting not only to the person making the change but also to those surrounding the person. Your spouse may look at change as a potential loss of income. Some people will react out of jealousy because you are seeking change while they are trapped in their current circumstances. Others will view you as seeking change to get ahead of them in the fictitious race of life. Many people judge their career progression according to those around them.

The first position I obtained after college was in a bank. After working there for a year, I decided to go back to the university to study recreation and parks. My immediate career goal at the time was to become a camp director. My mother was very unhappy about my decision. The simplest way to put it is to say that it was outside of her comfort zone. Although she didn't overtly oppose my decision, she made her opposition known.

I excel at identifying my career opportunities.

In the positioning model, the first step is to decide where you want to work. You may be able to articulate this in terms of your career goal. Chapters 4 and 5, on think evaluation and bridging, will help you identify your career opportunities. Sally

Herr identified her career opportunities and then pursued them.

Regarding my career development, I am always looking for better ways to do things.

Better ways to do things can include identifying and acquiring the necessary KSAEs, casing the joint, or seeking a one-on-one interview. They may also involve more traditional actions such as developing your resume and cover letter.

If I need a new skill to advance my career, I will develop it even if I have to pay for it myself.

In a sense, this is a variation of statement 7. It has two parts, challenging you first to develop a new skill to advance your career, and second, to pay for it yourself. The cost of obtaining the new skill includes not only money, but time. This statement reflects perseverance and dedication.

Sally Herr determined that she needed a four-year degree and to increase her programming diversity. She planned to strengthen her credentials by obtaining a water aerobics certification at the local community college. Although her parents were contributing to her tuition, she was willing to pay for the certification, if necessary.

I have recently had a new job or a major promotion.

Are you complacent and satisfied with your career, and with what you are currently doing? If so, are you proactive in terms of your career development? Probably not. The inference of this statement is that if you have recently had a new job or a major promotion, your career is active and you are moving along on your career path. Because Sally Herr is a graduating senior entering the field for the first time, this statement has less relevance for her.

I can spot a good career opportunity long before others can.

This statement embodies the main principles of this book. Proactive job seekers have a good idea of the job they are seeking. Once they know this, they actively seek this position. They network. They case the joint. These are all signs of spotting a good career opportunity long before others can.

The principles of positioning described in this book will help you spot good career opportunities before others do and will help you to become more proactive in your job search.

The positioning model gives you the opportunity to see potential career opportunities that others have not seen. It can also help you create a job where one didn't exist previously. Sally Herr spotted a potential career opportunity at the Anytown AFC and then pursued it using the positioning model. It doesn't really matter whether she created a new position where one didn't previously exist, or whether she simply uncovered a job that others didn't see.

Many people who are positioning themselves become fearful that someone else will recognize the career opportunity that they see and steal it from underneath them. This is a natural fear. In most cases, however, you can lay this fear to rest because everyone else is generally oblivious to the career opportunity you see. This is because they haven't put in the time and energy that you have to research the position. In most cases, when you are positioning yourself, you are the only one competing for the position.

PUTTING IT ALL TOGETHER

The positioning model requires some degree of proactive behavior on your part. This chapter will help you become more proactive in your job search. Proactive people tend to obtain better jobs, receive higher salaries, and obtain more promotions. If you are not a proactive person, then adapt as many of the proactive traits that you are comfortable with as part of your job search. Remember that 50 to 80 percent of positions in this country are never advertised. Therefore, the norm for seeking a job is really the nontraditional model of positioning.

The positioning model is itself proactive. By simply following this model as described in the following chapters on think evaluation, bridging, professional networking, casing the joint, and the one-on-one interview, you will become more proactive. Your first decision is whether you want the job. Once you decide that you do, follow the steps in chapters 4 through 8. By using the positioning model, you will become more proactive in your job search.

REFERENCES

Bateman, T.S., & Crant, J.M. (1993). The proactive component of organizational behavior: A measure and correlates. *Journal of Organizational Behavior, 14,* 103-118.

Brown, D.J., Kane, K., Cober, R.T., Levy, P.E., & Shalhoop, J. (2006). Proactive personality and the successful job search: A field investigation with college graduates. *Journal of Applied Psychology, 91* (3), 717-726.

Mueller, J.D., & Wanberg, C.R. (2003). Unwrapping the organizational entry process: Disentangling multiple antecedents and their pathways to adjustment. *Journal of Applied Psychology, 88* (5), 779-794.

RoAne, S. (2000). *How to Work a Room: The Ultimate Guide to Savvy Socializing in Person and Online.* New York: HarperCollins, 5.

Seibert, S., Crant, J., & Kraimer, M. (1999). Proactive personality and career success. *The American Psychological Association, Inc.* 0021-9010/99.

Proactive Career Development Instrument

Complete the career development assessment in table 3.1 to gauge how proactive you are in your career development. Respond to each of the statements, indicating how strongly you agree or disagree with each.

Total your points in the far right column of the instrument. The higher your score, the more proactive you are in terms of your job search. There is a minimum score of 12 and a maximum score of 48. A score above 30 indicates that you tend to be proactive in your career development.

After completing the instrument, do you feel that it accurately reflects how proactive you are in terms of your job search? Think about and discuss your findings with friends. Do you need to become more proactive? If you are already proactive in your career development, is there is anything else you could do to improve?

Table 3.1   Proactive Career Development

	Strongly agree	Agree	Disagree	Strongly disagree	Score
1. I am constantly on the lookout for new ways to advance my career.	4	3	2	1	
2. I feel driven to make a difference with my career.	4	3	2	1	4
3. I seek out new career positions rather than wait for them to come to me.	4	3	2	1	
4. Wherever I have been, I have been a powerful force in my career development.	4	3	2	1	
5. Nothing is more exciting than eventually obtaining the position that I seek.	4	3	2	1	
6. If I see something in my career development that I don't like, I fix it.	4	3	2	1	3
7. I will do what is necessary to develop my career, even if others oppose it.	4	3	2	1	
8. I excel at identifying my career opportunities.	4	3	2	1	
9. Regarding my career development, I am always looking for better ways to do things.	4	3	2	1	
10. If I need a new skill to advance my career, I will develop it even if I have to pay for it myself.	4	3	2	1	3
11. I have recently had a new job or a major promotion.	4	3	2	1	
12. I can spot a good career opportunity long before others can.	4	3	2	1	
Total score					

Adapted, by permission, from T.S. Bateman and J.M. Crant, 1993, "The proactive component of organizational behavior: A measure and corrrelates," *Journal of Organizational Behavior* 14: 103-118.

Exercise 3.2

Proactive Job Search

In this exercise, you will apply the factors in the Proactive Career Development instrument (in exercise 3.1) to your job search.

Identify the next job you seek.

_____

_____

_____

_____

_____

Review the 12 statements in table 3.1. Which of these statements, if any, can you apply to your job search?

_____

_____

_____

_____

_____

_____

_____

What can you do or do you need to do to apply this statement to your job search?

_____

_____

_____

_____

_____

_____

_____

Proactive Job Search Skills

Review your answers to each of the statements in table 3.1. Pick your four lowest scores and write those statements here:

1. _____
   _____
2. _____
   _____
3. _____
   _____
4. _____
   _____

Briefly review the focus of these four statements and what they were attempting to measure on pages 36 to 38 of this chapter. Why do you think you rated yourself low on each of the statements? Did you have four statements with which you disagreed (*Strongly disagree* and *disagree*)? How many of the statements did you strongly disagree with versus just disagree?

Select your three lowest scored items in terms of strongly disagree and disagree. Examine these questions and list three things you might do to improve yourself regarding these statements in terms of your career development.

1. _____
   _____
2. _____
   _____
3. _____
   _____

Now pick your three highest scores (*Strongly agree* and *agree*) and write them here:

1. _____
   _____
2. _____
   _____
3. _____
   _____

Briefly review the focus of these statements and what they were attempting to measure on pages 36 to 38 of this chapter. Why do you think you rated yourself high on each of the statements? How many of these statements did you strongly agree with versus just agreeing with? What do these four statements tell you about yourself, if anything?

_____

_____

_____

_____

_____

_____

_____

_____

chapter 4

Think Evaluation

Why should they hire me?

This chapter gives you the power to prepare yourself for your next job. Once you know which knowledge, skills, abilities, and experiences (KSAEs) are required for the job you seek, it then becomes a simple matter of developing a plan to acquire those KSAEs. These are the same KSAEs your potential employer will use to evaluate you if you apply for a job. If you need a bachelor's degree in recreation, parks, and tourism or a related field, or a certification, then you need to obtain it.

This chapter shows you how to use the evaluation process to determine the KSAEs you need for the job you want. In doing so, you will be able to answer the question at the beginning of this chapter, Why should they hire me? They should hire you because you have the appropriate knowledge, skills, abilities, and experiences. This is what we mean when we say that we start at the end of the process, with evaluation. Actually, though, it is the beginning.

In the traditional model, you analyze the job announcement to determine the KSAEs you need to focus on in your cover letter and your interview. Because you are already involved in the application process, there is little or no time to acquire new KSAEs. However, by identifying the KSAEs needed for the job, you can focus your thoughts and tailor your application to the needs identified in the job announcement. In addition, you can use the KSAEs you identify as talking points during the interview.

Think evaluation is fundamental to the positioning model. As soon as you know the job you

want to pursue, you can seek out similar job announcements that will provide you with a list of the KSAEs that you will need to acquire to prepare yourself for the job. Chapter 5 addresses how you can acquire these KSAEs, or build a bridge to your next job, through academic training, professional development, and volunteer service. This will help you create your professional network in chapter 6 because you can seek out people who will help you acquire your KSAEs and prepare you for your next job.

Once you know the KSAEs that you need, you can develop a hypothetical job description as part of casing the joint, chapter 7. This should be fairly close to the job description and individualized job announcement that you and your employer develop during the one-on-one interview described in chapter 8. Even employers who use a standard off-the-shelf description of the position are often willing to tweak it to address your talents. Either way, you have prepared yourself for your next position. The skills learned in this chapter form a foundation for the remaining chapters.

STARTING WITH THE EVALUATION INSTRUMENT

In class, when students ask what will be on the test, they really want to know how they will be evaluated. They simply want to know how to prepare. Likewise, in the traditional job search

A TALE OF TWO MODELS

Think evaluation is important in both job search models—traditional and positioning. The major difference is time. In the traditional model you don't have time to acquire new KSAEs because you are most likely in the application and interview process.

model, you want to know how your application packet will most likely be evaluated, and in the positioning model, you want to know what KSAEs you will need for the job. In both cases, evaluation plays an important role in your preparation. By knowing how you will be evaluated, you know how to prepare. Conceptually, think evaluation is no different from preparing for an examination for which you already know the questions.

In the traditional job search model, a large number of applicants must be narrowed until a final candidate emerges. To help accomplish this task, most search committees develop an *evaluation instrument* based on the KSAEs listed in the job announcement to sort, rank, and select candidates. An example of an evaluation instrument is shown in figure 4.1. Of secondary importance is the fact that you may soon be in the position of an employer developing the job announcement and evaluation instrument. For this reason, you should understand the close connection between the job description and the evaluation instrument used to evaluate the application packets. So close is this relationship that many employers develop their evaluation instruments concurrently with the job descriptions on the job announcements.

From the employer's perspective, the purpose of the evaluation instrument is threefold. First, it enables the employer to sort applicants to select the best candidates to move on to the next round. The requirements for the job listed in the job description must be convertible into an evaluation instrument. The following example is illustrative of how easily this can become problematic. If the job description states that a BS degree is required, then a highly qualified applicant with only an AA degree would not be eligible for the position and would be disqualified for not meeting minimum require-

ments. In contrast, if the job description states that a BS degree is preferred, then the same applicant can be kept in the applicant pool. A simple wording change from *required* to *preferred* can have significant implications in the evaluation process.

Review the evaluation instrument in figure 4.1. It was constructed to evaluate applicants for the Chicago aquatics director announcement in figure 4.2. It is illustrative of transforming the requirements in the job description into quantifiable scales. Although there are many ways to construct an instrument, does the one in figure 4.1 accurately reflect the criteria listed in the job description? Do the scales accurately define their items? In your opinion, are there items missing that should have been included on the instrument?

The second purpose of the evaluation instrument is to sort and rank the candidates. It needs to separate the most qualified from those who are less qualified. If everyone ranks high or has the same score after the evaluation, the evaluation instrument has not done its job. A good evaluation instrument incorporates the major job requirements listed in the announcement and generates a wide range of applicant scores.

Again, review the evaluation instrument in figure 4.1. Do the individual scales provide sufficient separation among candidates? For example, the supervision scale is not a proportional scale. By design, it amplifies certain tendencies. An applicant with one year or less of experience would score low. Someone with two or more years would rate higher. However, five or more years are only marginally valued over two to four years.

The evaluation instrument should not underrepresent or overrepresent criteria listed in the job description. The scales should be weighted to

Applicant: _____

Evaluator: _____

Applicant number: _____   Score from evaluation: _____

Overall comments: _____

_____

_____

Application items: The following items are needed in order to complete the application package. A *No* indicates an incomplete application.

Cover letter	[ ] Yes	[ ] No
Resume	[ ] Yes	[ ] No
Three references	[ ] Yes	[ ] No

The following items are required for continued evaluation. A *No* disqualifies the applicant.

18 years of age	[ ] Yes	[ ] No
Lifeguard, first aid, CPR/AED certifications	[ ] Yes	[ ] No

Evaluation

					Score
Experience—Previous AFC experience	0 years 0	1-2 years 1	3-5 years 3	5+ years 4	
Multicultural—Experience in a multicultural work environment	No experience 0	Some experience 1	A lot of experience 2		
Philosophy—Understanding and application of the philosophy and goals of AFC	None 0	A little 1	Some 3	A lot 4	
Supervision—Ability to work with staff and volunteers including hiring, training, supervising, and evaluating department employees	0 years 0	1 year 1	2-4 years 3	5+ years 4	
Programs—Evidence of having designed and implemented new aquatics programs	No evidence of implementing new programs 0	1-2 new programs 2	3+ new programs 4		
Programs—Actively participate in aquatics activities. Evidence of (1) swim instruction, (2) swim team, (3) water aerobics, (4) other activities, (5) senior as well as youth activities	No evidence 0	1-2 items 2	3-5 items 4	6-7 items 6	
Membership—Ability to recruit and retain new members	No experience 0	Some experience 1	A lot of experience 2		
Between the cracks—Maturity, sound judgment, ability to perform the job not directly measured, etc.	Not good 0	Good 2	Very good 4	Excellent 6	
Total					

Figure 4.1 An example of a well-done evaluation instrument.

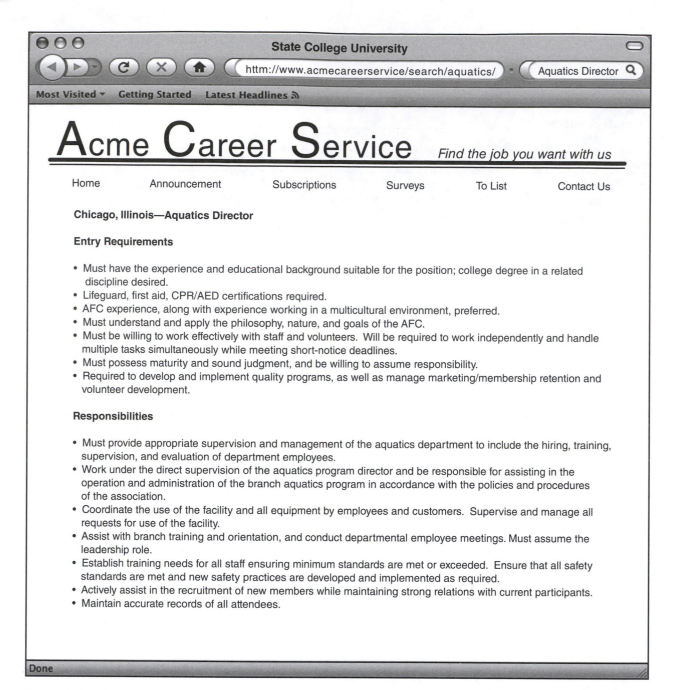

State College University

httm://www.acmecareerservice/search/aquatics/   •   Aquatics Director 🔍

Most Visited ▾   Getting Started   Latest Headlines ⟋

Acme Career Service *Find the job you want with us*

Home   Announcement   Subscriptions   Surveys   To List   Contact Us

Chicago, Illinois—Aquatics Director

Entry Requirements

• Must have the experience and educational background suitable for the position; college degree in a related discipline desired.
• Lifeguard, first aid, CPR/AED certifications required.
• AFC experience, along with experience working in a multicultural environment, preferred.
• Must understand and apply the philosophy, nature, and goals of the AFC.
• Must be willing to work effectively with staff and volunteers. Will be required to work independently and handle multiple tasks simultaneously while meeting short-notice deadlines.
• Must possess maturity and sound judgment, and be willing to assume responsibility.
• Required to develop and implement quality programs, as well as manage marketing/membership retention and volunteer development.

Responsibilities

• Must provide appropriate supervision and management of the aquatics department to include the hiring, training, supervision, and evaluation of department employees.
• Work under the direct supervision of the aquatics program director and be responsible for assisting in the operation and administration of the branch aquatics program in accordance with the policies and procedures of the association.
• Coordinate the use of the facility and all equipment by employees and customers. Supervise and manage all requests for use of the facility.
• Assist with branch training and orientation, and conduct departmental employee meetings. Must assume the leadership role.
• Establish training needs for all staff ensuring minimum standards are met or exceeded. Ensure that all safety standards are met and new safety practices are developed and implemented as required.
• Actively assist in the recruitment of new members while maintaining strong relations with current participants.
• Maintain accurate records of all attendees.

Done

Figure 4.2   The evaluation instrument in figure 4.1 was written to select applicants for this job description.

accurately reflect the intent of the job announcement. For example, the not-so-good evaluation instrument in figure 4.3 was developed for the Chicago aquatics director job announcement in figure 4.2. A quick review of the instrument reveals that the aesthetics of the cover letter and resume represent 6 points on an evaluation instrument of 24 points. Is it appropriate to base 25 percent of the evaluation instrument on the aesthetics of the resume and cover letter?

Applicant: _____

Evaluator: _____

Score from evaluation: _____

Overall comments: _____

_____

_____

Application items (must be met for continued evaluation):

  18 years of age   [   ] Yes   [   ] No

Evaluation

					Score
Certifications—Lifeguard, first aid, CPR/AED	None 0	Few 1	Some 2	A lot 3	
Cover letter—Quality, neatness, content	Poor 0	Okay 1	Good 2	Excellent 3	
Resume—Attractiveness, format	Poor 0	Okay 1	Good 2	Excellent 3	
Philosophy—Understanding and application of the philosophy and goals of AFC	None 0	A little 1	Some 2	A lot 3	
Administration—Administrative skills including budgeting and hiring, training, evaluating, and supervising staff and volunteers	Poor 0	Okay 1	Good 2	Excellent 3	
Program—Evidence of having designed and implemented new aquatics programs	None 0	Few 1	Some 2	A lot 3	
Between the cracks—Maturity, sound judgment, ability to perform the job not directly measured, etc.	Not good 0	Good 2	Very good 4	Excellent 6	
Total					

Figure 4.3   An example of a not-so-well-done evaluation instrument.

DETERMINING YOUR KSAES FROM JOB ANNOUNCEMENTS

If you climb to the summit of a hill, you get a broad view of your surroundings—the valleys, streams, and ridges. You see the lay of the land. Likewise, when you identify the KSAEs needed for the job you want, you see the lay of the land in terms of what you need to do to become employable. The activities in this section are designed to help you determine the KSAEs you need for your next job. Once you know what they are, you can begin to acquire them.

You will review several job announcements to synthesize the KSAEs you need for the job you seek. With Sally Herr as the example, you will use a nine-step process to identify the KSAEs you need.

Step 1: Obtain Similar Job Announcements

The first step is to obtain several similar job announcements for the job you seek. You can think of this step as a sampling process. If you have the job description of the exact job you want, this is ideal. However, it is a good idea to seek other job descriptions even if you are targeting one position to get the lay of the land in terms of the position.

The easiest way to find online job announcements is to use one of the many search engines such as Google. However, don't overlook the direct approach of asking your potential employer for the description of the job you want. In her Internet search, Sally Herr noted in the announcement of the Chicago job that there might be written documentation regarding the position she was interested in. Because Sally worked in an AFC, she had contacts there. She could ask the people she knows if there is a manual that contains the requirements for the job she is looking for. If so, her task of acquiring the necessary KSAEs is simplified. Regardless, using the job announcements she found on the Internet, she knows the KSAEs for the position she seeks because they will parallel fairly closely those recommended by the parent association.

Most likely, Sally will obtain several job announcements as part of her Internet search. Figures 4.2 and 4.4 show two of these—one for a job in Chicago and the other for a position in Smallville, Minnesota. In the next step, you can complete this process with only one job announcement, but we recommend that you analyze two or three that are most representative of the position you seek. After you have completed your analysis, you can go back and compare other job announcements to determine if there is general agreement between them and the two or three you used.

Step 2: Select Two or Three Job Announcements

Sift through the job announcements you have found and select two or three for jobs that are most similar to the one you seek in terms of the position itself, the location, and the size of the organization. Narrowing your selection to two or three announcements makes the analysis process easier in the synthesis steps described in step 6 when you add the next job announcement to the process.

Step 3: Create a Working Table

Create a working table similar to the one in figure 4.5. Along the top of the table list the two or three organizations you selected in step 2. Write *KSAEs* at the top of the last column. This is for the KSAEs that you will synthesize from your analysis of the job announcements.

Along the side of the table, list the KSAE categories. As a starting point, list those used in figure 4.5: age, education, certifications, administration, personal traits, philosophy, membership, and programming. As you synthesize the KSAE categories in the next step, you will add some categories and delete some. For example, because the AFC is a membership organization, the membership category is appropriate. Professionals in other disciplines may find that membership is of little importance and drop it as a category.

Step 4: Group Similar Types of KSAEs on the Job Descriptions

In this step you group similar types of KSAEs required on the job description. For example, in the Chicago job announcement (figure 4.2), several items could be grouped together under the administration category. The first bullet indicates supervision and management including "the hiring,

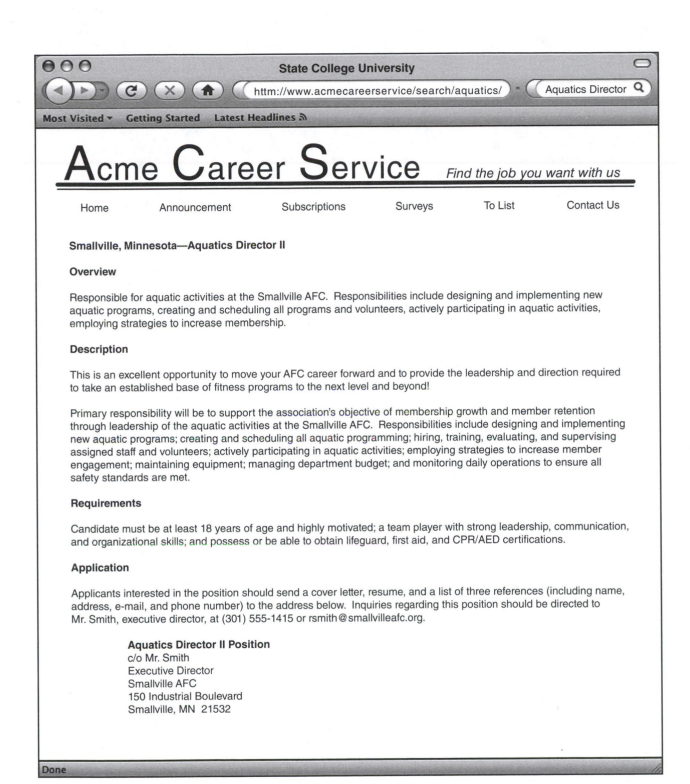

Figure 4.4 A job description for an aquatics director position in Smallville, Minnesota.

	Chicago, IL (figure 4.2)	Smallville, MN (figure 4.4)	KSAEs
Age	Not specified.	Must be at least 18 years of age.	Minimum age already met.
Education	College degree in a related discipline desired.	Not specified.	KSAE 1: Education—College degree in related field needed.
Certifications	Lifeguard, first aid, CPR/AED certifications required.	Possess or be able to obtain lifeguard, first aid, CPR/AED certifications.	KSAE 2: Certifications—Lifeguard, first aid, CPR/AED certifications required.
Administration	Able to work effectively with staff and volunteers; work independently and handle multiple tasks simultaneously while meeting short-notice deadlines.	Able to manage department budget; ensure that all safety standards are met; create and schedule all aquatics programming; hire, train, evaluate, and supervise assigned staff and volunteers.	KSAE 4: Administration—Strong leadership and organizational skills: Able to work effectively with staff and volunteers including hiring, training, supervising, and evaluating employees.
Personal traits	Maturity, sound judgment, and a willingness to assume responsibility.	Highly motivated team player with strong leadership, communication, and organizational skills.	Difficult to quantify; combined with philosophy.
Philosophy	Must understand and apply the philosophy and goals of the AFC.	Not specified.	KSAE 3: Philosophy—AFC experience along with experience working in a multicultural environment preferred.
Membership	Able to develop and implement quality programs, including marketing, membership retention, and volunteer development programs.	Able to employ strategies to increase member engagement and maintain equipment.	KSAE 5: Membership—Can actively assist in the recruitment of new members, while maintaining strong relations with current members.
Programming	Not specified.	Able to design and implement new aquatics programs; actively participate in aquatics activities.	KSAE 6: Programming—Able to design and implement a variety of aquatics programs (e.g., swim team, water aerobics, water therapy).

Figure 4.5   This working table compares the job descriptions in figures 4.2 and 4.4.

training, supervision, and evaluation of department employees." Scheduling under the third bullet might be considered administration, as might the leadership role described under the fourth bullet. These were combined into one item in figure 4.5.

Step 5: Tailor the KSAE Categories to Your Needs

In a continuation of the process described in step 4, add or delete categories as appropriate. Sally Herr grouped these administrative experiences under the rubric of administration. If she

were seeking a truly administrative position, she might break the KSAEs she grouped together under administration into separate categories. For example, she might have developed new categories titled staff supervision, facility scheduling, and training programs.

Because Sally is seeking more of a programming position, she categorized all of these functions under *administration*. However, she also made a mental note that some positions involve considerable administrative responsibilities. This is valuable information for her in her job search process.

Step 6: Add the Next Job Announcement and Repeat Steps 4 and 5

Sally repeated the grouping process for the Smallville AFC. In addition, she tried to see how the two job positions compare. For example, Sally noted that both positions have fairly similar requirements on membership.

Step 7: Keep or Split Categories

Where there is a lack of agreement, decide whether the item is sufficiently important to keep as a separate category. For example, the Chicago position requires an understanding of the AFC philosophy; the Smallville position doesn't. At this point in the process Sally kept the category representing AFC philosophy as its own category. If appropriate, she can merge this category with another later in the process. The same situation occurred for age and programming abilities. Smallville had a minimum age and required programming competencies; Chicago didn't.

Step 8: Synthesize the KSAEs

In the last column, Sally Herr synthesized the KSAEs. In this step, you merge categories such as personal traits and philosophy when appropriate. Number the KSAEs, and give them abbreviated titles that are the same as or similar to the titles used in columns on the left side of the table. Using titles provides a convenient way to identify the KSAEs.

Step 9: List the KSAEs Determined

List the KSAEs you determined on a separate sheet of paper (figure 4.6). You now have a working list of the KSAEs you need for your next job. In chapter 5, Bridging, you will develop ways to acquire these KSAEs to prepare for your next job including a promotion or the next step on your career ladder. These KSAEs will reemerge when you case the joint in chapter 7, where they will assist you in developing a description of the job you seek, and then again in chapter 8, when you develop your individual job announcement. Determining the KSAEs you need is fundamental to your future career development.

THINK EVALUATION AS PART OF THE TRADITIONAL JOB SEARCH PROCESS

The process described in the previous section can also be used with the traditional job search model. The difference is that you use one job announcement rather than two or three. If the job

---

Sally Herr

Analysis of KSAEs

Aquatics Director Position

KSAE 1: Education—College degree in related field needed.
KSAE 2: Certifications—Lifeguard, first aid, CPR/AED certifications required.
KSAE 3: Philosophy—AFC experience along with experience working in a multicultural environment preferred.
KSAE 4: Administration—Strong leadership and organizational skills: Able to work effectively with staff and volunteers including hiring, training, supervising, and evaluating employees.
KSAE 5: Membership—Can actively assist in the recruitment of new members, while maintaining strong relations with current members.
KSAE 6: Programming—Able to design and implement a variety of aquatics programs (e.g., swim team, water aerobics, water therapy).

Figure 4.6   Sally Herr has decided that she needs these KSAEs to position herself for the job she wants.

announcement is well laid out, the KSAEs will be fairly easy to identify. Most federal job announcements, for instance, list the KSAEs required for the position.

There is considerable value to understanding the lay of the land in terms of the position you seek, even in the traditional model. This is of particular value to you if you sense that the employer advertising the position has not articulated it well. This may be because he does job searches infrequently, he is struggling with internal politics, he recycled the last job announcement but the job has morphed into something slightly different, or he really wants something other than what he is advertising for. In this case you may have a better understanding of what he needs than he does.

Identifying the KSAEs required helps you to significantly strengthen your cover letter. If Sally Herr were applying for an aquatics director position, think how beneficial it would be to mention in her cover letter the following passages that relate directly to the KSAEs she identified in figure 4.6. She might begin like this: *As part of my internship, I worked at the Rolling Hills AFC, where I gained an excellent understanding of the philosophy, administration, and programs of the AFC including the importance of membership to the organization.* With this passage she indicates that she understands the philosophy (KSAE 3) and the importance of membership to the organization (KSAE 5). The following passage addresses KSAE 2 directly: *I have my lifeguard, first aid, and CPR certifications.* In the last passage, she addresses both administration (KSAE 4) and programming skills (KSAE 6): *In addition, I have hired, trained, and supervised lifeguards in my summer jobs. Also, I have skills in aquatics, slimnastics, aerobics, and other AFC programs.*

Knowing the KSAEs required for the position will also help you prepare for the formal interview. Not only do they help focus your thoughts and comments, but they also help you develop your talking points. Sally, for example, when asked a question in the interview, can use any one of the preceding passages. This process is covered in more depth in chapter 9.

PUTTING IT ALL TOGETHER

Sometimes how you think about a topic becomes instrumental to your success. Putting yourself in the employer's shoes is useful because it gives you an understanding of how that person approaches the job search process. This understanding enables you to better prepare your application packet.

In addition, evaluating job announcements helps you identify the KSAEs you will need to prepare and position yourself for the job you seek. The working table in figure 4.5, in which you identified the KSAEs you need from the job announcements, is the heart of this process, which is equally valuable in the traditional job search process.

For Sally Herr, the KSAEs she identified in this chapter that are necessary for an aquatics director position will reemerge throughout the positioning process and again in the later chapters. The KSAEs she identified are the building blocks for bridging in chapter 5, professional networking, casing the joint, and the one-on-one interview in the following chapters. By starting at the end of the process, evaluation, Sally was actually starting at the beginning. Also, through proper planning, she answered the question *Why should they hire me?* It is no different for you.

Evaluating Sally Herr's Resume

Assume that Sally Herr has applied for an aquatics director position at the Chicago AFC (figure 4.2). Use the evaluation instrument in figure 4.1 to evaluate her for this position. Use the cover letter in figure 12.3 (page 214) and either resume 10.1 or 10.2 (page 186 or 187). Analyze your results. Do you believe that the instrument accurately evaluated and reflected her KSAEs?

_____

_____

_____

_____

_____

_____

Exercise 4.2

The Hiring Unit

This exercise is a group or class exercise. The exercise is in two parts. The first part focuses on what the typical job hunter encounters in the resume and application process. The second part focuses on the evaluation process; the group becomes the search committee in this hypothetical search for the organization. Tailor this activity to meet the specific needs of your institution and class.

Part 1

Prepare your application for the job described below. Your application will be evaluated in terms of your adherence to procedures and the quality of your application packet (cover letter, resume, references, etc.).

Job Description

The university student union is creating a new position for a recreation programmer to develop recreation programs for students. The position requires 20 hours per week and pays $10 per hour.

Applicants should discuss in their cover letter their area of programming interest and the types of programs that they might like to provide. Submit the following materials:

- Cover letter
- Resume
- Career goal
- Five references (name, position title, address, daytime phone numbers, nighttime phone number, e-mail)

Responsibilities: The recreation programmer will develop and conduct recreation programming for students who patronize the student union, including planning concerts, organizing outings, working with clubs, and other responsibilities found in a student union. The union will tailor the position to emphasize the applicant's speciality area (e.g., adventuresports, special events, etc.).

Part 2

As if you were the search committee reviewing all of the applications, use the table on the next page to evaluate all of the applications. Your evaluations will be judged on the quality of the following:

- Memo from the search committee to the administration indicating its recommendations (e.g., structure, purpose, procedures, selection, etc.)
- Table listing the applications reviewed, their ranking, and scores
- Individual review sheets attached to the memo

Applicant: _____

Evaluator: _____

Score from evaluation: _____

Overall comments: _____

_____

_____

Application items: Applicants are required to submit the following items. A *No* response disqualifies the applicant; enter DNQ (does not qualify) as the evaluation score above, but continue with the full evaluation.

Cover letter	[ ] Yes	[ ] No
Resume	[ ] Yes	[ ] No
Career goal (in cover letter, separate document, or resume)	[ ] Yes	[ ] No
Names of five references	[ ] Yes	[ ] No
Addresses of five references	[ ] Yes	[ ] No
Phone numbers of five references	[ ] Yes	[ ] No

Evaluation

						Weight factor	Score
Appearance of cover letter, resume, etc.	Very poor 1	Poor 2	Good 3	Very good 4	Excellent 5	× 2	
Length of programming experience	Less than 6 months 1	6-9 months 2	9-12 months 3	1-2 years 4	More than 2 years 5	× 1	
Variety of programming experience	No areas 1	1-2 areas 2	3-4 areas 4	More than 5 areas 5		× 1	
Evidence of having developed new programs	Developed no new programs 1	Assisted in developing 1 new program 2	Assisted in developing 2 or more new programs 3	Developed 1 new program alone 4	Developed 2 or more new programs alone 5	× 1	
Total							

Exercise 4.3

Determining Your KSAEs

Follow the steps outlined in the section on determining your KSAEs from job announcements. Obtain several announcements from the Internet for jobs that are similar to the next job you would like to have. Narrow the announcements down to the two or three announcements for jobs that are closest to the job you would like to have in terms of responsibilities, location, and so on. Develop a working table similar to the one in figure 4.5 to determine the KSAEs you will need to acquire to prepare yourself for your next job.

chapter 5

Bridging
Am I prepared for the job I seek?

If you want to cross a river, you need a bridge to get to the other side; if you want a career change or promotion, you need a bridge to the next position. How do you build that bridge? By obtaining the knowledge, skills, abilities, and experiences (KSAEs) necessary for the next job.

Bridging is a fundamental component of career development and of positioning. In the previous chapter on think evaluation, you identified the KSAEs you will need for the job you seek. This chapter focuses on how to acquire these KSAEs so that you will be qualified for the next job. In the following chapters you will use these KSAEs to develop a job description for the position you seek and to merge your needs with the needs of the organization, which you identified from casing the joint and from actually discussing potential job opportunities with the employer in the one-on-one interview.

Unfortunately, many people don't practice bridging. They sit and watch the water flow by rather than build a bridge to the other side of the river. Many people believe that the best way to prepare for their next position is to do well in their current position. This belief betrays an attitude of entitlement; they believe they are owed the next position because they have done well in their current position. In contrast, the person who is

proactively developing his career is determining the KSAEs needed for the next position he wants and creating a plan of action for acquiring them.

This chapter will help you develop a plan of action for acquiring the KSAEs you need. You can add and subtract elements to the plan to tailor it to meet your needs. Using this process, you build a bridge to your future.

Again, the element of time is critical in the process. Sally Herr is completing her last semester of school; she is two months from graduation. As this chapter unfolds, it will become obvious that she could have done more to prepare herself to obtain an aquatics director position. At this point, she is limited in what she can do to prepare herself. However, she has done more than many students to prepare for the transition. Her summer jobs and other experiences will help her make the transition from school to her first job.

UNDERSTANDING BRIDGING

Bridging is defined as the process of preparing yourself for your next position by developing the skill set (KSAEs) necessary for that position. Bridging is one of the simplest and most direct routes to positioning yourself. To enter the nursing

A TALE OF TWO MODELS

In the traditional model, bridging comes under the rubric of career development. As noted in chapter 4, once you are in the traditional job search process of responding to a job announcement, there is little you can do to prepare yourself for the job.

In contrast, using the positioning model, you are developing a bridge from where you are now to where you want to be in terms of your KSAEs. This is career development. However, it is career development with the specific purpose of preparing you for the next job, the job you are currently seeking. Bridging is career development with a specific focus.

Whether you apply for an advertised job or develop a new position through the one-on-one interview process, you need to prepare for your next job. In contrast to most traditional career development, bridging involves acquiring KSAEs based on the specific requirements of the next job. There is a direct link between the KSAEs you identified in chapter 4, your plan of action in this chapter, and the requirements of the job you want.

field, you need to obtain an academic degree in nursing from an accredited nursing program to build a bridge to your future career. If you need to demonstrate written communications, writing a newsletter for a professional organization will help you become known among your peers. If you need to demonstrate your presentation and communication skills to groups, don't overlook the Sunday school classes that you teach each week as an example of formal teaching experience.

In addition, bridging often positions you in close proximity to the person who can hire you or the organization where you will obtain your next job. Sally Herr worked a summer job as an assistant director of Rolling Hills AFC. She gained administrative experience that related directly to the KSAEs she needed, as well as general experience regarding the operation of the pool.

There are two types of bridging, vertical and horizontal. Vertical bridging involves obtaining the KSAEs needed for a promotion within the organization or for your next career position. Generally, vertical bridging moves you up the chain of command. For example, most students who attend college do so to create a vertical bridge into the career of their choice. Most of the examples in chapter 2 of students who obtained jobs are examples of vertical bridging. Future doctors attend medical school to do the same. Also, future lawyers attend law school, and future managers seek out MBA programs. The easiest way to think about vertical bridging is to equate it with the concept of promotions.

Horizontal bridging involves obtaining the KSAEs necessary for making a lateral move into a new discipline or career. When most students change their major, they do so to create a horizontal bridge to a new discipline. For example, if you are an accountant who wants to become a high school teacher, you will need to develop the skill set for teaching in a high school. In addition, you will need to obtain the appropriate credentials, including certifications and licensing. Although the techniques used for vertical and horizontal bridging are the

If you want to cross the river, build a bridge to the other side.

same, horizontal bridging usually requires more extensive effort since you are developing yourself for a new job.

Judy's example is illustrative of horizontal bridging. Judy had a bachelor's degree in history. She had some experience in the park and recreation field, primarily summer experiences. She wanted to switch career paths and enter the park and recreation field. As part of her effort, she enrolled in a master's program to gain the necessary academic credentials. Judy quickly realized that the master's degree was only one component in developing a bridge to her new career. Although it provided her with credentials, it didn't give her practical experience in the field. To make the transition into the field, she also needed practical work experience.

Although it was not officially required as part of her master's program, Judy completed an internship and mentorship program. The internship gave her work experience in park and planning. In the mentorship program she studied directly under a key administrator in the park and planning commission. The internship and mentorship programs gave her experience in the field and also the opportunity to network with key people in the field. Her plan worked, and she made the transition into the field. She was hired by the commission as the director of a community center. Her mentor was instrumental in her hiring.

Bridging is important because the skill set required for your next position is often different from the skill set necessary for your current job. The skill set required of an activity leader is quite different from that of an administrator. An activity leader needs good face-to-face leadership skills and certifications in her content area. In contrast, an administrator needs good administrative skills including an understanding of budget and personnel. Simply doing a good job as an activity leader is no guarantee that you will do a good job as an administrator. This is why it is important to identify the KSAEs you need for your next job.

Jill was a programmer at the local YMCA. She wanted to enter administration and eventually become a CEO of a YMCA. She examined several job announcements and discussed her plans with two YMCA CEOs whom she had befriended through her professional involvement. She concluded that she needed a master's degree, one

or more of the YMCA's leadership/management certifications, and professional experience as an assistant director of a small to medium-sized YMCA.

Jill enrolled in a master's program and obtained the necessary academic credentials. She completed the YMCA's executive training school. Although it cost her several thousand dollars, she believed that the executive training school was money well spent. Along with the knowledge she gained, she now understood the management culture of the YMCA. In addition, she made contact with people at the national office who might be able to help her become an assistant director. They regularly survey participants in the school for new talent and rising stars. She applied for and was hired as the assistant director of a medium-sized YMCA in the Midwest. She had the blessing of a national YMCA administrator who helps local YMCAs hire their administrators; she had met Jill during the executive training program.

Jill developed a bridge to her new position. It involved academic credentials, management training, and an understanding of the YMCA culture. She was able to use the assistant director position as a stepping-stone to becoming a CEO. She correctly recognized that she needed to develop a new skill set if she wanted to become a CEO and that her current skill set was not adequate. Her example illustrates the principle that simply doing a good job in your current position is no guarantee that you will be able to move to the position you want. You need to develop the skill set required for the next position. Jill did this, and after several years as an assistant director, she became a YMCA CEO.

Generally, bridging involves academic preparation, professional development, and volunteer activities.

ACADEMIC PREPARATION

Academic preparation is one of the easiest and most familiar ways to develop your skill set. For most people, the most common method of academic preparation is to take courses or complete a course of study at a community college or university. One of the reasons most students go to college is to study a subject that will help them gain entry into the field of their choice. People who are interested in changing careers (i.e., building a horizontal bridge) often enroll in a college degree program that will give them the credentials or certifications they need for their new career. Others enroll in specific courses to obtain specialized skills needed for furthering their careers.

Many national and nonprofit organizations provide standardized courses of instruction, including the Red Cross, YMCA, and Boy Scouts. In addition, as the following example suggests, local organizations also provide valuable academic programs. As a graduate student interested in entering the interpretive services field, I took a blacksmithing course offered at the nearby national park because I wanted to have firsthand knowledge of historic interpretation. Although the course was geared for artisans interested in starting their own businesses, it provided me with valuable insights into the blacksmithing process. Also, I learned basic blacksmithing skills.

Selecting Your Course of Study or Major

Whether you are choosing a new major or are already progressing toward graduation in your major, you might want to consider the following

Academic preparation is an important strategy in bridging.

three components in selecting your major or in approaching your education within your major. These three components are the academic content of the program, the networking capabilities of the faculty, and the service learning activities provided. Many people focus only on the academic content of the program. However, the other two components should be equally important in the selection process.

Academic Content of the Program

Your major or course of study needs to provide the knowledge necessary for entering the field or advancing to the next level in your career. The question to ask is fairly straightforward: Do the courses both individually and collectively prepare you for entry into the field or for advancement?

An important factor to consider is whether the program is accredited. Accredited programs incorporate the KSAEs necessary for becoming a professional in the field into the course work of the program. The NRPA Council on Accreditation program examines academic programs in the recreation, parks, and tourism area in terms of the minimum requirements for students to become professionals in the field. A benefit of graduating from an NRPA-accredited program is that you have met the minimum standards necessary for becoming a professional in your field. Because of your specialized preparation, you are permitted to sit for the Certified Park and Recreation Professional (CPRP) examination directly after graduation and obtain your certification without additional experience or study. Also, some programs in the outdoor area have used the Association of Experiential Education's accreditation program to review and accredit their academic programs.

Some academic programs are not accredited but still prepare students for obtaining a certification. Therapeutic recreation students are familiar with the Certified Therapeutic Recreation Specialist (CTRS) certification offered by the National Council for Therapeutic Recreation Certification (NCTRC). You should keep in mind, though, that graduation from an academic program that prepares you to sit for the examination is not a guarantee that you will meet the minimum requirements of the Council. It is always a good idea to examine the Council's requirements and to make sure that your credentials meet their requirements.

Networking Ability of the Faculty

The second area to examine in selecting a major is the networking ability of the faculty. This refers to the ability of the faculty to help you network and make the necessary connections with people who can help you find employment in the field. In a variation of the classic adage, if the academic program is *what* you know, networking refers to *whom* you know. Although professional networking is covered in chapter 6, it is also mentioned here in terms of the faculty's ability to help you develop your own professional network and professional family.

To develop a horizontal or vertical bridge into the field of your choice, you need to develop a professional network within the field. New to the field, your professional network is in its infancy. Therefore, you must rely on the professional network and contacts of the faculty in your academic program. As you develop your career, and as you become professionally active within your field, you too will develop your own professional network and, in time, will have a lesser need to rely on the network of the faculty. As previously noted, the concept is expanded in chapter 6 as part of the discussion on developing your professional family.

In chapter 2, Joe initially used a faculty member who had connections with several key people in MWR (Morale, Welfare and Recreation) to obtain an internship position in Kodiak, Alaska. As a student just entering the field, his professional network was in its infancy at best. He used the more established network of a member of the faculty in his academic program to gain entry into MWR through acceptance into its management training program. In a very short period, Joe's professional network and connections within the field increased significantly. After completing his internship, he was no longer totally dependent on the faculty member's professional network for entry into the field and for his career advancement. Although he will use the faculty member

as a resource in the future, he has begun his own professional network.

Some questions to ask in evaluating the networking opportunities provided by the faculty are as follows: What is the reputation of the professional faculty within their given field? Do they attend professional conferences? More important, do they create opportunities for students to attend and participate in these conferences? Are faculty involved in their professional organizations, and do they involve their students? Do they help place students in field experiences and internships?

Typical of many recreation, parks, and tourism programs, the faculty and students of Steve's school attended the state association's recreation and parks conference. At the conference, students are matched with professionals in the field. Steve went to lunch with the mentor he was matched with and participated in several other informal activities with him as well. He returned from the conference with a broad smile on his face. He had obtained a summer job and a future with the commission where his mentor was an administrator.

Service Learning Opportunities

The service learning opportunities provided by the program are the third area of academic preparation to examine in selecting a major. *Service learning* is the current term used for gaining hands-on, or practical, experience in the field. For example, if you want to learn to play tennis, at some point in the learning process, you actually need to play the game of tennis. You can study strategy, rules, and even how to hold the tennis racket, but at some point you must actually play the game. You need experiential learning opportunities in which you can actually do what you will eventually be doing professionally. Service learning opportunities provide these experiences.

Different academic programs address service learning opportunities differently. For example, the service learning component for doctors is referred to as their residency. Other programs include extensive opportunities in their courses and through internships and field experiences. Both approaches provide practical learning experiences. Also, many programs use extracurricular activities to provide service learning opportunities. The question to ask is, Does the program provide ample

Service Learning Resources

A quick Internet search of the term *service learning* reveals a wealth of Web sites with information and resources related to this topic. *Service Learning for Health, Physical Education, and Recreation: A Step-by-Step Guide* (Cheryl Stevens, 2008, Human Kinetics) highlights many of the better service learning resources available on the Internet. In addition, it is a particularly valuable resource for students in recreation, parks, and tourism programs because it is specifically focused on service learning projects within this subject area. It features a five-step process for planning, implementing, and evaluating service learning projects.

learning experiences of an experiential nature to prepare you for entry into your field?

Mary entered her major late in her academic career, well into her junior year. In addition, she had limited service learning and practical experiences. Having chosen her major, she applied herself academically and professionally. She was fortunate to do her senior internship with one of the best agencies in the state, where she, again, applied herself. Her learning curve during the internship was impressive.

Unfortunately, it was not quite good enough. She applied for a position with the agency, but didn't get it. Unfortunately, although she was qualified, there were more qualified applicants for the position. In the end, her late entry into the field and limited experience were not sufficient to get her the job of her dreams. Her potential employer and former internship supervisor was apologetic. However, she had to go with the more qualified candidate. Mary went to Colorado, got a job in her field, and is having a successful career.

Using Academic Experiences in Bridging

One of the most important components for positioning yourself for your career is the experiences you obtain as part of your academic preparation: courses, field experiences, summer and part-time jobs, and internships. These experiences relate to the E in the KSAEs that you are acquiring for your next job. You gain not only actual professional experience, but also networking contacts and skills that relate directly back to the classroom.

This section addresses several types of experiences you are likely to encounter during your academic career that can help position you for entry into your field. They are presented in reverse order starting with internships. Usually, internships are the culminating experience in most programs, with all of the other experiences funneling into them. Therefore, we present them first.

Internships

The internship, or similar experience, is the culmination experience in the major before making the transition into the field. In terms of positioning, the internship is probably the most important experience in determining your future in your career. Think of the progression as academic preparation, internship, and career. Quite simply, the internship is often the transition from school to the workplace. Its importance cannot be overstated. The internship builds on all of the previous experiences including field experiences, part-time employment, summer work, and service learning experiences.

Internships, or practicums as they are sometimes called, have different meanings within different programs and among different institutions. Generally, internships are intensive experiences over an extended period of time. The internship usually occurs at or near the end of the academic career. This is reflected in standard 8.30 of the Council on Accreditation standards, which requires an "Internship, full-time continuing experience in one appropriate professional recreation organization/agency of at least 400 clock hours over an extended period of time, not less than 10 weeks." Other disciplines have standards that, although different, approximate this standard in terms of the criteria required.

Internships are offered either at the end of the academic program or between the junior and senior years. There are advantages and disadvantages to both.

When the internship is offered as the culminating experience, you complete it only after completing all course work. This is the student teaching approach borrowed from most education programs. Conceptually, the internship offers a transition into the workplace. In terms of the positioning model, it is good to complete an internship at the organization that will best position you for the job you want upon graduation. It is not unusual for students returning from internships to announce that they received a job offer from the organization. Students who don't receive job offers, however, need to find another job.

You may be in a program that has you complete your internship between your junior and senior years. The disadvantage of this approach is that if the organization offers you a job, you usually need to wait until graduation before taking it. Some organizations are unwilling to wait, although others will. The chief advantage of internships at this time is that you enter your final classes ready to build on your internship experience. This infusion of experience can provide a significant contribution to the learning process.

Some programs give students the option of completing their internships either between their junior and senior years or as a culminating experience. In some majors, students complete their internships during the summer. In others, such as education, students complete their internships, or student teaching, during the fall or spring semester. The combined approach gives you some flexibility in coordinating your experience with the courses you need to complete and positioning yourself to enter the workplace.

Regardless of the approach used, the internship traditionally provides the transition from the university into the workplace. Completion of a good internship often results in a successful transition into the field.

Employment

Previously, we suggested that if you want to work there, work there. A summer job with an organization you'd like to work for is one of the best ways to gain valuable sustained experiences in the field. During each summer, except one, I worked at a summer camp. With a business degree, upon graduation, I went to work in a bank. It became

clear to me fairly quickly that my real interests were elsewhere. I decided that I wanted to become a camp director. I chose the academic route and enrolled in a master's program. Although I got sidetracked in my education for other reasons, my summer job provided me with valuable experiences and positioned me well for my eventual career. My summer employment helped me see what I wanted to do in my career.

Much like Sally Herr, Melissa was an aquatics person. She completed her undergraduate degree in the recreation and parks field and then completed her master's in an allied field. It is probably not an understatement to say that she lived and breathed aquatics. During the summers, she worked for the City of Frostburg, eventually working her way up through the ranks to pool manager. She was responsible for all aspects of the pool.

As a graduate student, in her spare time, Melissa taught all types of aquatics courses for Activities of Life, a community service program offered by the university. Her courses were popular and well attended. She obtained her Red Cross Instructor Training certification in several areas of aquatics. I am sure that my listing of her aquatics involvement here is only the tip of the iceberg of what she actually did.

Both the City of Frostburg and the Activities of Life positions were paid jobs. Although she wasn't going to make a full-time living from them, she gained valuable experiences there. When she graduated, she applied for and received a position at the University of Maryland as the assistant director of pool operations. Through her full- and part-time employment, she had positioned herself well.

Sally Herr gained two valuable experiences in aquatics through summer employment. Both of these experiences relate directly to the KSAEs she needed to attain her employment goal. First, she used her experience as a head swim coach at the Rolling Hills AFC to partially meet KSAE 6, programming (see figure 4.6). Her involvement as a swim coach helped her to meet one of the programming subsets for this KSAE. This experience led to her second experience, which also served as her internship. During the following summer, she became the assistant aquatics director at the Rolling Hills AFC. As part of her functions, she managed five lifeguards, worked with the director and executive director, and performed other functions associated with pool management. This experience assisted her in partially meeting KSAE 4, administration (figure 4.6). Sally realized that she needed another two years of administrative experience to meet the minimum requirements of KSAE 4. Regardless, her summer jobs were valuable experiences that helped her position herself for her eventual career in aquatics.

Part-time employment can be another source of valuable career-developing experiences. Because she was interested in working at an AFC, the best thing Sally Herr could do was to work at an AFC. Working at an AFC part-time during her internship gave her an understanding of the AFC culture and philosophy. Also, it helped her address KSAE 3, philosophy, because she gained an understanding of the philosophy and culture of the AFC during that time.

Some workers resent managers who are hired without ever having worked at the grassroots of the organization. Part-time work provides you with this perspective regarding the organization. As you move up the chain of command, the fact that you have experienced what everyone else in the organization has can provide valuable insights into the organization and its culture.

Practicums and Field Experiences

Practicums, field experiences, and even internships have different meanings in different programs and among different institutions. Generally, field experiences and practicums are shorter experiences conducted by students early in their academic careers. In some cases practicums are more structured and are similar to internships except that they are not as long.

The meaning of field experiences is reflected in the Council on Accreditation standards. In standard 8.29, the Council on Accreditation requires a "formal field experience(s) of at least 100 documented clock hours in appropriate professional recreation organizations/agencies prior to internship." The Council recommends a field experience of shorter duration than an internship prior to the completion of the more intensive internship. In addition, the field experience is usually associated with college credit, and it usually has some type of faculty supervision.

Like many students entering the field with limited experience, Jim knew that he wanted to work with special populations, but he wasn't sure with which group. And there were so many groups. As part of his leadership course, he did some activities at the senior center. He discovered that he didn't want to make a career of working with seniors. As part of another course, he had an experience with adjudicated youth at risk in a camp setting. Although he had a good experience, he didn't see himself working with this group either. After participating in several class activities and other experiences, he walked into the office one day with a broad smile on his face. He found the group he loved to work with, the mentally challenged. Jim had used class and field experiences to find out which special population he preferred working with.

Summer jobs can provide many valuable employment skills, including leadership, responsibility, management, and programming.

In addition, Jim determined the group he liked to work with early in his academic career. He decided to pursue an internship with the mentally challenged, which will prepare him to enter the field. In a sense, he has positioned himself well by adhering to the principle: If you want to work there, work there.

Sally Herr completed a field experience at the Veteran's Administration Center, where she gained valuable experiences working with people with disabilities. After she obtains her first job and gains several years of work experience, she will have experiences that will supersede her internship experience. In four or five years, she will most likely drop her internship experience from her resume or diminish its importance as a listing. However, given her career development at this point, this is a very valuable experience.

Volunteer Experiences

Service learning and volunteer experiences involve practical experiences and activities in the larger community that usually offer no compensation to the volunteers. They may or may not be related to class activities. Often, *service learning* and *volunteer activities* are fairly synonymous; *service learning* is simply the more modern term for volunteering. Often, these experiences are offered as part of classes. They offer a variety of experiences to help you decide what you eventually want to do. In addition, these activities help you choose an internship that will help you position yourself for the transition into the field.

Sally Herr is an adapted aquatics instructor (AAI) with the American Red Cross. As part of her training, she taught students with disabilities to swim in several programs. At least one of these programs was volunteer; it was not part of her duties at the pool where she worked. This experience has two benefits to her in terms of her future as an aquatics director. First, she gained knowledge and experience working with special populations in an aquatics setting. Second, it indicates her continued involvement in and commitment to aquatics. A potential employer will see that she is sincere about her commitment to aquatics.

PROFESSIONAL DEVELOPMENT

Professional development is often overlooked in discussions of developing a skill set. However, it is a critical element in your preparation to enter the workforce. Not only does professional development aid you in networking, but it also helps you develop the skills necessary for your next position. Following are some typical forms of professional development:

- Attend a professional conference
- Give a presentation at a professional conference
- Join a professional organization
- Work on a committee within a professional organization
- Edit a professional newsletter
- Attend management schools or in-service workshops
- Write an article for a professional newsletter or magazine
- Become a member of your local chamber of commerce
- Become a member of the Rotary

Joining a professional organization is a beginning. It entitles you to membership benefits including receiving a newsletter and access to other professionals like you. More important, it is your entry into the organization that you can help, and that can help you. Professional organizations are always looking for people to do work for them. They need people to organize workshops and contribute to newsletters. In return, they provide many of the networking opportunities discussed in chapter 6 and offer opportunities to advance yourself professionally by developing your experience and skills. However, be careful and think smart. Volunteering for professional organizations can evolve into a black hole that consumes most of your energy and takes you away from your business. Review The Volunteer Trap in the next section.

As a member, you can attend the organization's conferences. The workshops provide updates of current practices, issues, and what is going on in the field. These can be excellent sources of information that is extremely useful.

The downside of attending a conference for its content is that most of the workshops are presented by a limited number of professionals. This usually becomes evident after five or more years when you see the same faces doing pretty much the same things. This occurs at both the state and national levels. Because there is a larger pool at the national level, it usually takes longer before you experience redundancy in terms of content and people.

Most people find that their level of involvement at professional conferences changes over time. For the first couple of years, the conferee finds everything new, interesting, and exciting. But after some time, workshops and sessions become less important as involvement moves more toward social events and maintaining professional contacts. Through these professional meetings, events, and conferences, you have the opportunity to reestablish contacts with people you normally wouldn't interact with during the year.

If you are a daring person, try attending a conference that you haven't attended before. Although it may place you outside of your comfort zone, it can be exciting because you will receive a plethora of information and new contacts.

A recent graduate, Nina worked for the Department of Natural Resources (DNR). One of her responsibilities was the development of water trails within the state. In part because of her involvement, she was invited to share her knowledge and experience with the American Canoe Association, which was developing its stewardship initiative and had an interest in water trails. Nina served on the board of directors of the ACA, where she developed water trail initiatives, including a water trail program, and presented at national and international conferences. Her job with the DNR aided her professional commitment on the board of directors, and her involvement on the board aided her in performing her job. She was able to integrate these experiences and programs into her job with

the DNR. Her professional involvement led to a promotion, and to state and national recognition of the state's water trail efforts, as well as the recognition of other states and nonprofit organizations. She used her professional involvement to advance herself and her agency.

Sally Herr had attended the state conference last year so she had some familiarity with it. She attended again this year, where she met with Mr. Muncheck, the executive director of the Anytown AFC. Her meeting with him will be discussed in chapter 8 on the one-on-one interview.

The Volunteer Trap

Be careful of falling into the volunteer trap. In an effort to reduce costs, most organizations, particularly nonprofit organizations, rely heavily on volunteer help. It is very easy to become totally absorbed in the organization to the point that it consumes most of your time. It is important to weigh the benefits you will derive from your volunteer experience against the costs in time, money, and energy. Remember that you are using the organization to develop your knowledge, skills, abilities, and experiences. For this reason, try to limit your involvement to experiences that will help you acquire your KSAEs.

In the previous example, at some point Nina began to experience the volunteer trap. Her involvement on the board of directors of the ACA was beginning to interfere with her job responsibilities at the DNR. Membership on the board involved responsibilities other than her specific interests in stewardship and water trails. It involved meetings and considerable committee work involved with maintaining the viability of the nonprofit organization. Also, her responsibilities within the DNR were not diminishing; rather, with program consolidation within the agency, they were increasing. Forced to choose, Nina wisely chose to cut back her involvement on the board. Her professional involvement, however, had greatly aided her career development.

CONTINUING EDUCATION

For professionals, continuing education has become an important way to keep current with new developments in the field. In the information age, with technology and information changing rapidly, professionals must remain current. Continuing education can help you create a bridge to a new content area.

Traditionally, the term *continuing education* covers a wide range of professional activities. For example, a professional workshop or a course in a management school may be considered continuing education. Some define it as any education that occurs after graduation from college. Regardless, continuing education is a way to position yourself by developing the KSAEs you need for your next job. Following are several things you can do to continue your education:

- Attend a professional management school
- Attend a specialty school
- Take a course at a community college or university
- Attend a professional workshop
- Complete continuing education credits
- Complete an online course

VOLUNTEER ACTIVITIES

People who are out of school and working in the workplace can use volunteer and part-time experiences to develop their KSAEs. This section offers some alternatives for developing yourself after you have graduated from school so that you can build a bridge to your next job.

If you determine that you need to increase your communication skills to obtain a promotion, there are numerous volunteer activities that can help you do this. More specifically, let's assume that you want to develop your classroom teaching ability. You could approach the local college and offer to teach a course for them. Clearly, this would strengthen or build your formal classroom teaching ability. If this option is not available, you could use your presentations at professional conferences as an indicator of your ability to teach in a formal setting. If you lack this experience, you might use past experiences such as Sunday school teaching to demonstrate your ability to teach in a formal setting.

Is teaching at the local college better than Sunday school teaching? Absolutely. Does it supersede Sunday school teaching? Yes. However, if you are bridging, the Sunday school teaching opportunity may be the first step in constructing the bridge that demonstrates that you have formal teaching skills and experience. Also, it demonstrates how volunteer activities may be used to develop these competencies. Again, be careful of falling into the volunteer trap.

ACQUIRING YOUR KSAES

The heart of your developmental plan is the KSAE worksheet in exercise 5.1. Essentially, this worksheet helps you know when you have acquired each KSAE. This worksheet can be extremely sophisticated so that it captures all of the nuances of developing a plan of action, but this version was kept simple to reflect the fundamentals of the process.

Copy several blank worksheets, one for each KSAE you identified for yourself in chapter 4. If needed, break the KSAEs into their subsets; the importance of the KSAE to your career goal is a good criterion to use in deciding how or whether to subdivide it. Sally Herr's KSAE worksheets are shown in figures 5.1 through figure 5.7. Sally broke her KSAE 6, programming, into two subsets, swim team and water aerobics. She believed she needed a separate worksheet to address the development of her water aerobics skills. In contrast, she kept all her certifications in figure 5.2 together without breaking them into subsets. If she needed to complete all three certifications, she might have broken them out onto separate worksheets also. Think of your KSAEs as accordions that you can expand or compress as needed to meet your specific needs.

The worksheet in exercise 5.1 provides a convenient way to quantify your plan. It asks typical who, what, where, when, and why questions. For each of the KSAEs identified, it asks what minimum competencies you need to know to acquire it. Then it asks where and when you will obtain the competency. Finally, it asks how you will know when you have it.

Exercise 5.1

Your Plan to Obtain the KSAEs You Need

Make copies of the KSAE worksheet, enter your KSAEs from chapter 4, and develop a plan of action, using the worksheet, to obtain the KSAEs you need for your next job.

KSAE Worksheet

Name _Sally Herr_   KSAE____1____

This KSAE is   completed [   ]   partially completed [✓]   new [   ]

1. List the KSAE/subset: __*KSAE 1: Education—College degree in related field needed.*__

    KSAE/subset (a, b, c, etc.): _(not applicable)_ _____

    _____

    KSAE/subset (a, b, c, etc.): _____

    _____

2. Describe the minimum knowledge, skills, abilities, and/or experiences necessary for obtaining this KSAE or its subset.

    BS degree

    Related field (e.g., recreation and parks)

3. Describe where and how you will obtain these minimum KSAEs. If you have already done so, indicate where you have done it. If you have partially obtained the KSAE, identify how long it will take you to complete this KSAE.

    State College University

4. If applicable, describe when you will obtain the KSAE/subset.

    May 2xxx

5. Indicate how you will know that you have obtained the minimum KSAE or its subset, or if you have obtained the KSAE/subset, indicate what you have done to do so.

    BS degree in recreation and parks (i.e., related field)

    Expected graduation: May 2xxx

Figure 5.1   Sally Herr's worksheet for KSAE 1. For Sally Herr this KSAE is fairly straightforward. She is actively working toward obtaining it, and when she graduates in May, she should meet the minimum requirements of this KSAE.

Exercise 5.1

Your Plan to Obtain the KSAEs You Need

Make copies of the KSAE worksheet, enter your KSAEs from chapter 4, and develop a plan of action, using the worksheet, to obtain the KSAEs you need for your next job.

KSAE Worksheet

Name _Sally Herr_   KSAE _2_

This KSAE is   completed [✓]   partially completed [   ]   new [   ]

1. List the KSAE/subset: _KSAE 2: Certifications—Lifeguard, first aid,_
CPR/AED certifications required

    KSAE/subset (a, b, c, etc.): _(not applicable)_

    KSAE/subset (a, b, c, etc.): _____

2. Describe the minimum knowledge, skills, abilities, and/or experiences necessary for obtaining this KSAE or its subset.

a. _ARC lifeguard certificate_

b. _ARC first aid certificate_

c. _American Heart Association CPR/AED certificate_

3. Describe where and how you will obtain these minimum KSAEs. If you have already done so, indicate where you have done it. If you have partially obtained the KSAE, identify how long it will take you to complete this KSAE.

Local chapter of ARC and ambulance corps when needed

4. If applicable, describe when you will obtain the KSAE/subset.

Currently certified

5. Indicate how you will know that you have obtained the minimum KSAE or its subset, or if you have obtained the KSAE/subset, indicate what you have done to do so.

a. _ARC lifeguard certificate_   _expires July 2xxx_

b. _ARC first aid certificate_   _expires March 2xxx_

c. _American Heart Association CPR/AED certificate_   _expires March 2xxx_

Figure 5.2 Sally Herr's worksheet for KSAE 2. Because she has all three certifications, Sally decided not to break these certificates out into separate subsets. This is in contrast with KSAE 6, which she decided to break into subsets.

Exercise 5.1

Your Plan to Obtain the KSAEs You Need

Make copies of the KSAE worksheet, enter your KSAEs from chapter 4, and develop a plan of action, using the worksheet, to obtain the KSAEs you need for your next job.

KSAE Worksheet

Name _Sally Herr_ KSAE _3_

This KSAE is completed [✓] partially completed [ ] new [ ]

1. List the KSAE/subset: _KSAE 3: Philosophy—AFC experience along with experience working in a multicultural environment preferred._

    KSAE/subset (a, b, c, etc.): _(not applicable)_

    KSAE/subset (a, b, c, etc.): _____

2. Describe the minimum knowledge, skills, abilities, and/or experiences necessary for obtaining this KSAE or its subset.

One year of experience in the AFC

3. Describe where and how you will obtain these minimum KSAEs. If you have already done so, indicate where you have done it. If you have partially obtained the KSAE, identify how long it will take you to complete this KSAE.

Rolling Hills AFC, Rolling Hills, MD

4. If applicable, describe when you will obtain the KSAE/subset.

Summer 2xxx

5. Indicate how you will know that you have obtained the minimum KSAE or its subset, or if you have obtained the KSAE/subset, indicate what you have done to do so.

I have worked two summers at the Rolling Hills AFC. Although it would probably be good to work at another AFC, my experience with management was probably sufficient to familiarize me with the organizational culture and philosophy of the AFC, including working in a multicultural environment.

Figure 5.3 Sally Herr's worksheet for KSAE 3. Sally concluded that because she worked two summers at the Rolling Hills AFC, she probably has a good understanding of the AFC philosophy and culture. Also, she hypothesized that one year of experience is probably adequate for meeting this KSAE.

Your Plan to Obtain the KSAEs You Need

Make copies of the KSAE worksheet, enter your KSAEs from chapter 4, and develop a plan of action, using the worksheet, to obtain the KSAEs you need for your next job.

KSAE Worksheet

Name _Sally Herr_____ KSAE ___4_____

This KSAE is   completed [   ]   partially completed [✓]   new [   ]

1. List the KSAE/subset: _KSAE 4: Administration—Strong leadership and organizational skills: Must be able to work effectively with staff and volunteers including hiring, training, supervising, and evaluating employees._

   KSAE/subset (a, b, c, etc.): _(not applicable)_____

   KSAE/subset (a, b, c, etc.): _____

2. Describe the minimum knowledge, skills, abilities, and/or experiences necessary for obtaining this KSAE or its subset.

   Three years of experience managing lifeguards and other personnel is desirable.

3. Describe where and how you will obtain these minimum KSAEs. If you have already done so, indicate where you have done it. If you have partially obtained the KSAE, identify how long it will take you to complete this KSAE.

   Assistant aquatics director—Rolling Hills AFC   Summer 2xxx

   One summer

4. If applicable, describe when you will obtain the KSAE/subset.

   Will need to obtain this on the job or work as an assistant manager again for the summer (two years or seasons of experience) and then seek a full-time job in the fall.

5. Indicate how you will know that you have obtained the minimum KSAE or its subset, or if you have obtained the KSAE/subset, indicate what you have done to do so.

   Three years or three seasons as an assistant manager or in a similar supervisory position.

Figure 5.4   Sally Herr's worksheet for KSAE 4. Sally concluded that an aquatics director should have a minimum of three years of experience to truly meet this KSAE. Her one year of experience shows capability. In addition, it shows potential to a prospective employer.

Your Plan to Obtain the KSAEs You Need

Make copies of the KSAE worksheet, enter your KSAEs from chapter 4, and develop a plan of action, using the worksheet, to obtain the KSAEs you need for your next job.

KSAE Worksheet

Name _Sally Herr_   KSAE _____5_____

This KSAE is   completed [   ]   partially completed [✓]   new [   ]

1. List the KSAE/subset: _KSAE 5: Membership—Can actively assist in the recruitment of new members, while maintaining strong relations with current members._

   KSAE/subset (a, b, c, etc.): _(not applicable)_

2. Describe the minimum knowledge, skills, abilities, and/or experiences necessary for obtaining this KSAE or its subset.

   a. _Show a percentage increase in membership—10 percent over three years._

   b. _Maintain a turnover ratio in which 80 percent of current members renew their memberships next year._

3. Describe where and how you will obtain these minimum KSAEs. If you have already done so, indicate where you have done it. If you have partially obtained the KSAE, identify how long it will take you to complete this KSAE.

   At this point, it probably would be best to obtain on the job after graduation. I would discuss with my supervisor ways they monitor these two items. It would not be difficult to devise a method to collect the necessary information.

4. If applicable, describe when you will obtain the KSAE/subset.

   As part of my next job.

5. Indicate how you will know that you have obtained the minimum KSAE or its subset, or if you have obtained the KSAE/subset, indicate what you have done to do so.

   a. _Develop an instrument to measure an increase in membership—a 10 percent increase over three years would be desirable._

   b. _Develop an instrument to measure membership turnover. Need renewals, non-renewals, and why they left—80 percent renewal._

Figure 5.5   Sally Herr's worksheet for KSAE 5. Sally concluded that she will not be able to acquire this KSAE before entering the job market after graduation. However, by focusing on this KSAE, she has, in part, prepared herself. When she interviews, she is prepared to discuss the topic area and what she might do to recruit and maintain members based on the feedback she obtains. Also, she may refine and restructure how she measures membership. She is thinking the way her supervisor is most likely thinking, which indicates her understanding of the AFC organizational culture.

Your Plan to Obtain the KSAEs You Need

Make copies of the KSAE worksheet, enter your KSAEs from chapter 4, and develop a plan of action, using the worksheet, to obtain the KSAEs you need for your next job.

KSAE Worksheet

Name _Sally Herr_____ KSAE____6a_____

This KSAE is   completed [   ]   partially completed [✓]   new [   ]

1. List the KSAE/subset: _KSAE 6a: Programming—Able to design and implement a variety_ _of aquatics programs (e.g., swim team, water aerobics, water therapy)._

    KSAE/subset (a, b, c, etc.): _Swim team_____

    KSAE/subset (a, b, c, etc.): _____

2. Describe the minimum knowledge, skills, abilities, and/or experiences necessary for obtaining this KSAE or its subset.
   Swim team coach—minimum of one year of experience

3. Describe where and how you will obtain these minimum KSAEs. If you have already done so, indicate where you have done it. If you have partially obtained the KSAE, identify how long it will take you to complete this KSAE.
   Rolling Hills AFC, Rolling Hills, MD

4. If applicable, describe when you will obtain the KSAE/subset.
   Summer 2xxx

5. Indicate how you will know that you have obtained the minimum KSAE or its subset, or if you have obtained the KSAE/subset, indicate what you have done to do so.
   Probably completed KSAE as head swim coach at Rolling Hills AFC. (One summer may not _be considered sufficient experience.)_

Figure 5.6 Sally Herr's worksheet for KSAE 6a. Because Sally Herr had completed the swim team component of this KSAE and not the second component, she decided to break the programming KSAE into two subsets. This is in contrast to KSAE 2 on certification, which she could have easily broken into three separate subsets also. However, she chose to keep them on one form.

Exercise 5.1

Your Plan to Obtain the KSAEs You Need

Make copies of the KSAE worksheet, enter your KSAEs from chapter 4, and develop a plan of action, using the worksheet, to obtain the KSAEs you need for your next job.

KSAE Worksheet

Name *Sally Herr*   KSAE 6b

This KSAE is   completed [   ]   partially completed [✓]   new [   ]

1. List the KSAE/subset: *KSAE 6b: Programming—Able to design and implement a variety of aquatics programs (e.g., swim team, water aerobics, water therapy).*

    KSAE/subset (a, b, c, etc.): *Water aerobics and water therapy*

    KSAE/subset (a, b, c, etc.): _____

2. Describe the minimum knowledge, skills, abilities, and/or experiences necessary for obtaining this KSAE or its subset.

a. Obtain certification in water aerobics.

b. Conduct at least one class in water aerobics.

3. Describe where and how you will obtain these minimum KSAEs. If you have already done so, indicate where you have done it. If you have partially obtained the KSAE, identify how long it will take you to complete this KSAE.

Obtain certification at State College Community College continuing education class; co-teach or assist in conducting classes as part of Activities of Life class at State College University. If hired, complete the program at the new job.

4. If applicable, describe when you will obtain the KSAE/subset.

Take certification March, April, and May, 2xxx.

Attempt to co-teach course during the summer of 2xxx.

5. Indicate how you will know that you have obtained the minimum KSAE or its subset, or if you have obtained the KSAE/subset, indicate what you have done to do so.

a. Obtain certification.

b. Co-teach course.

Figure 5.7 Sally Herr's worksheet for KSAE 6b. Although Sally Herr is only three months from graduation, she can squeeze this certification in before graduation, which should aid in her job search. Not only does it help her meet her KSAE, but it shows continued commitment on her part to becoming an aquatics director.

Like many students beginning their careers, Sally Herr may only have partial completion of her KSAEs. For KSAE 1, completion of her academic degree is partial and it will be completed shortly with her graduation. For KSAE 4, she identified that she should have three years of experience managing lifeguards and other personnel. For a student starting out in their career, acquiring three years of experience is often difficult. However, her one year of experience is important since it shows that she has the capability to be an administrator. Regardless, by identifying what she should have, she can develop a plan to obtain the KSAE she needs or, in the case of experience, how to best compensate for something she doesn't have the time to develop. Sometimes being able to compensate is almost as important as having completed the KSAE.

PUTTING IT ALL TOGETHER

You need to obtain the KSAEs that will enable you to position yourself for your next position. Most people consider academic preparation the key to obtaining these KSAEs. It is important, but don't overlook professional development and volunteer experiences as ways to gain the KSAEs you need to bridge yourself vertically to a promotion or horizontally into a new field. The important thing is to acquire the KSAEs that qualify you for your next position and not to sit on the riverbank and watch the water flow by.

The problem on the *Titanic* was that by the time someone saw the iceberg, it was too late to avoid it. Had they seen the iceberg in sufficient time, they could have maneuvered the ship around it. Similarly, focusing on what you want to do three or four months before graduation is often too late to change your career course.

Sally Herr is typical of many students. During college, she gained experiences that related directly to her career goal of becoming an aquatics director. Could she have done more? Absolutely! But her academic preparation, summer employment, volunteer work, and other service learning experiences significantly strengthened the likelihood that she would obtain a job as an aquatics director. Although by her own analysis, she needs more experience, she does have the academic training and experiences that will probably get her into the field. Moreover, her analysis of what she needs to do gives her a plan to further prepare herself for the position she wants.

Simply doing a good job in your current position does not qualify you for your next job. Your next job may require a very different skill set than your current job does. For this reason, it is important to identify the KSAEs you need for your next job (see chapter 4) and develop a plan to acquire them, even if only partially. The KSAE worksheet in exercise 5.1 will help you in this task. This is how you build a bridge to your next job.

Exercise 5.1

Your Plan to Obtain the KSAEs You Need

Make copies of the KSAE worksheet, enter your KSAEs from chapter 4, and develop a plan of action, using the worksheet, to obtain the KSAEs you need for your next job.

KSAE Worksheet

Name _____ KSAE _____

This KSAE is   completed [   ]   partially completed [   ]   new [   ]

1. List the KSAE/subset: _____

    KSAE/subset (a, b, c, etc.): _____

    _____

    KSAE/subset (a, b, c, etc.): _____

    _____

2. Describe the minimum knowledge, skills, abilities, and/or experiences necessary for obtaining this KSAE or its subset.

    _____

    _____

    _____

3. Describe where and how you will obtain these minimum KSAEs. If you have already done so, indicate where you have done it. If you have partially obtained the KSAE, identify how long it will take you to complete this KSAE.

    _____

    _____

    _____

4. If applicable, describe when you will obtain the KSAE/subset.

    _____

    _____

    _____

5. Indicate how you will know that you have obtained the minimum KSAE or its subset, or if you have obtained the KSAE/subset, indicate what you have done to do so.

    _____

    _____

    _____

From *Career Development in Recreation, Parks, and Tourism: A Positioning Approach* by Robert B. Kauffman, 2010, Champaign, IL: Human Kinetics.

A Comparative Analysis of Your KSAEs

This exercise is a variation of the blank resume exercise, in that you determine a plan for how to acquire the KSAEs needed for your next job. This exercise uses the working table in figure 4.5 to determine the KSAEs required for your current job and for your next job. If you have any questions regarding how to determine your KSAEs, refer to chapter 4.

Record the KSAEs required for your current job and those that you need for your next job. Compare and contrast the two columns. If you don't have the KSAEs for your next job, what do you need to do to obtain them?

KSAEs required for the current job:

1. _____
2. _____
3. _____
4. _____
5. _____
6. _____
7. _____

KSAEs required for the next job:

1. _____
2. _____
3. _____
4. _____
5. _____
6. _____
7. _____

Exercise 5.3

Providing Feedback

This exercise is a group discussion. Chapter 4 was about think evaluation and determine your KSAEs. In this chapter, you determined how you might acquire your KSAEs to prepare yourself for future employment. Now that you know what you should be doing, discuss what you can do to prepare yourself better. Consider some of the following questions:

What could your program do to help you prepare yourself better in terms of academic preparation, professional development, and service learning and volunteer experiences? With what you know now, what would you do differently in preparing yourself? What are three things you need to do to acquire your KSAEs? Make a table listing the needs of everyone in the class. Are there any common needs? For example, is there a general consensus that everyone needs first aid and CPR certification, or does everyone need to attend a professional conference?

chapter 6

Professional Networking

How do I meet the person who will hire me?

It is said that everyone who has made it in a career has had help from other people. Instructors often help their students meet people who can help them develop their careers. Those nearing the end of their careers often note how much someone reached out and helped them at the right time in their career. Sometimes this person took on a mentoring role. This chapter introduces you to professional networking and mentoring. Both will help you make the necessary contacts within the field that will help develop you professionally.

Since the introduction of the concept in the mid-1950s, *networking* has come to mean many different things to different people. One of the earliest references to the term was in a 1954 study of a network of ties of kinship, friendship, and neighborhood in a Norwegian island parish (Barnes, 1954). From this austere beginning, it has become an important tool in positioning people for their next job on their career path.

PROFESSIONAL NETWORKING

Professional networking differs from normal networking, which tends to emphasize just making contacts. Professional networking is defined as the process of developing professional relationships that advance your career and those of the people in your network. It involves *creating visibility through participation* in professional events (Fisher & Vilas, 1992, p. 145), which includes attending networking events and creating them for others.

Professional networking is linked to professional development and has three main benefits for you and your field of work:

- It enhances your resume and career development (e.g., presenting at a conference enhances your resume).

A TALE OF TWO MODELS

Developing your professional network and taking advantage of mentors are important in both the positioning and traditional models. The first step in the traditional model is applying for the position with your resume and cover letter. The emphasis is on creating a good first impression with these two documents. Who you know may become important later in the process if you are invited for an interview.

In the positioning model, the one-on-one interview comes at the beginning of the process. It relies on your networking with the person within the organization who can hire you. This process begins with researching the organization as part of casing the joint. In addition, networking and mentors can help you with bridging and determining the knowledge, skills, abilities, and experiences needed for your next job.

In the end, you will find that networking and mentoring will greatly aid you in the traditional model also. Things don't happen in a vacuum. There is a high probability that two people will know each other and an even higher probability that two people will know a common third person. If the person reviewing your application knows you or has heard of you, she will be more likely to review your application favorably. This may result from your efforts to develop quality networking contacts or your professional family. Both are discussed in this chapter. Or, a person mentoring may be the common third person that two other people know.

- It increases your visibility among other professionals in your discipline, which greatly aids your networking. People who attend your session will tend to seek you out.

- It contributes to and enhances the profession itself by adding to its body of knowledge.

Technical competence is an underlying principle of most professional networking and of mentoring (Pines, & Aronson 1981). It is a key factor that separates professional networking from simple networking. Generally, a person who has technical competence already has the technical skills you are seeking to develop. In the recreation and parks field, technical competency may refer to a person who has programming experience. Technically competent people understand the problems of coordinating, scheduling, budgeting, advertising, and staffing because they have done it themselves. If you ask a prominent person in the field what you need to do to advance your career, you will consider their advice as more valid if they can appreciate what you are doing since they too have experienced it. Furthermore, you need to believe that they are honest and trustworthy and that they have integrity.

One way to approach networking is to identify the people who can help you acquire the KSAEs you need in order to advance your career. In chapter 4, you identified the KSAEs you need. These represent your technical competency. A variation of exercise 6.1 at the end of this chapter is to identify the people with whom you need to network based on their potential KSAEs.

Making Good Contacts

Networking is not simply knowing people; it is knowing the key people in critical positions who can help you advance your career. Stated another way, professional networking is about more than just making contacts; it is about making good contacts. Developing good networking contacts builds on the content discussed in the previous chapters.

In chapter 4, you analyzed job announcements to determine the KSAEs you need to obtain to procure your next job. The question is *Who can help you acquire these KSAEs?* You need to consider networking with these people.

In chapter 7, Casing the Joint, you will determine who in the organization you need to meet to obtain the job you seek. Once you identify whom you need to contact, you need to determine when and where you will contact this person. You may try to meet him at the work site or at a professional conference or other networking event.

In chapter 5, you addressed what you need to do to build a bridge from your current job to your next one. Bridging focuses on academic preparation, professional development, and volunteer work. Most people who are in their academic preparation phase are preparing themselves for entry into the profession. Part of that preparation is the process of developing their professional networks. You may rely on faculty to share their professional contacts in your discipline. In addition, you can attend networking events and become professionally active in an effort to develop your own professional network, remembering that networking is the process of making good contacts.

Although this chapter emphasizes developing good contacts, you don't want to overlook or dismiss the casual networking contacts provided by friends and what may seem to be more serendipitous relationships. The following two examples from the legends videotapes (see exercise 6.4) illustrate the importance of not overlooking the influence these networking contacts can have on your career (Kauffman, 2009).

Jim Peterson spent three years in the U.S. Marines upon graduation from high school and before going to college. In college, a professor introduced him to another professor through a seminar in recreation, and that's when he realized that a career in recreation might be for him.

In another example from the legends videotapes, Ira Hutchison worked as a hospital attendant at a hospital in Topeka, Kansas. He originally wanted to be a coach, but because of his color, there wasn't much opportunity for him at that time. He became close friends with a psychiatrist with whom he happened to work. Because the psychiatrist knew that Ira really wanted something more recreational, he talked to some people and got Ira into a recreational setting within the hospital, where he began his career in recreation.

AVOIDING BLACK HOLES

It is important to view your professional activities in terms of what they cost and how they benefit your professional development and network. Try to avoid black holes that consume everything that comes in contact with them. If you aren't careful, your professional activities can consume your time and energy like black holes. For young professionals the most common costs are time, energy, and opportunity. You want to maximize the benefits of your professional networking activities and minimize their costs.

CC was a graduate student in our program who took on the responsibility of organizing the Whitewater Parks and Courses Conference as a volunteer. He did an excellent job organizing the event, coordinating sessions, and managing volunteers. However, doing the organizational work for this event had a cost. He invested three months organizing this event, during which he was not able to take on other responsibilities.

When choosing where to become involved, you need to determine the benefits, or opportunities, that each activity provides as well as its costs. CC could have invested his time in something else. He might have attended several conferences, served on a professional committee, or led an outdoor trip that would have given him additional professional experience. Each of these activities would provide benefits in terms of professional development and networking. Also, they have costs, particularly in terms of his time. Because he couldn't do all of the activities, he had to choose one. Organizing the conference required a considerable time investment, but it also provided a benefit in terms of professional development and networking. He chose the conference and benefited greatly from the event.

Professional organizations need volunteers to fuel their activities. You are that fuel. For young professionals like CC, their involvement in professional activities has immense benefit in terms of professional networking, and the costs of this involvement are more than offset by the benefits.

For mature professionals, the costs of professional involvement can easily become greater than the benefits. At this point in their careers, all the players know each other. Mature professionals are no longer actively developing their professional networks. If they are interested in giving back to their profession, they may be willing to accept that the costs exceed the benefits derived. Nevertheless, such activity is a potential black hole that every professional should be aware of.

DEVELOPING YOUR PROFESSIONAL FAMILY

Think of networking as developing your professional family. As a young professional, the network you develop can last throughout your career. For this reason it is important to treat the other professionals in your network as part of your professional family rather than as consumable and expendable relationships. Professionals treat those in their networks as investments in their future. These relationships are career long, and they need replenishment to account for attrition and new people entering the discipline.

Most professions are structured like pyramids. As your career advances, and as you approach the top of the pyramid, you will find fewer and fewer people to network with. Even in large professions, the players at the top of the pyramid make up a small group of people. Either they know each other personally, or they know of each other. In addition, they are likely to be separated geographically.

Your professional family will be with you throughout your career.

As you move up the chain of command within your organization, you will find yourself dealing with fewer people in your network. In turn, as you become active within your state organization, you will find that it, too, is pyramidal in terms of its network structure. Again, as you advance within the association, you will find that you are dealing with a limited number of people. If you move from the state to the national scene, you will find the same phenomenon occurring although it may take a little longer for you to reach the top of the pyramid. Whether it is your community, the state association, or national involvement, as your career advances and as you move toward the top, you will be seeing many of the same people within your circle of associates. For this reason, it is important to treat the professionals with whom you associate, your professional network, as your professional family rather than as disposable relationships.

You should approach the development of your professional network as an investment in your future. This may not be obvious until later in your career when you look back on the other professionals with whom you have associated. Many of the contacts made at school or during your first position can last your entire professional career. If you are active in your professional organization, you will serve with many of the same people on committees, task forces, and projects throughout your career. These other professionals are your professional family.

Initially, you will rely on other professionals to help you develop your network. However, as you develop professionally, you will increasingly rely less on others and more on your own networking ability. Regardless, as people retire or leave the profession for other careers, you will need to seek new professionals to replenish your network. In addition, as you advance in your career, you will need to develop contacts with professionals who are younger than you.

Attending Networking Events

Generally, if you want to find more of something, go to its source. If you want to network, attend networking events. A networking event is an event or activity that you attend to increase your professional network and to better position yourself. These events may be either professional or social in nature. Most networking events contain both professional and social elements.

Attending networking events creates visibility through participation. By participating, you are indicating your investment and commitment. Networking includes becoming a member of a professional organization, serving on a board or committee, and attending professional conferences and events.

One of the degree requirements for students in our university program is to attend a professional conference. The professional conference is a networking event that enables them to position themselves for internships, summer jobs, or full-time positions, or to simply advance themselves professionally. The conference provides an opportunity to expand their professional networks, which will last them throughout their careers. They position themselves by meeting potential employers in an informal, or nonwork, setting. Many students use the conference to conduct one-on-one interviews with potential employers (see chapter 8).

To maximize your networking at a professional conference or other networking event, consider developing a systematic and organized plan of attack (figure 6.1). Before the conference, determine which sessions to attend for your own personal growth. Determine whom you want to meet and where you might encounter them. If you

---

Before the Conference

1. Type a one- to two-page summary of what you are currently doing: your mission, target population, goals, and so on.

2. List the people you know and hope to see again. Label them *old contacts*.

3. Page through the conference preview booklet and highlight the names of anyone you would like to meet. This can include gurus, officers, presenters, or professionals similar to you. List them under *new contacts*.

4. Write an e-mail or brief letter of introduction to people you really want to meet.

During the Conference

1. Each day, decide who to meet.

2. Catch presenters before or after their sessions.

3. If you exchange business cards, jot down some notes on the back.

4. At the end of the day, check off the people you met and decide whom you will try to meet tomorrow.

After the Conference

Send a short follow-up note or e-mail to everyone you met. Use the notes off the backs of their business cards. Enclose any materials that you promised to send.

Obtaining Professional Advice

1. Before the conference, write down the problems you would like to solve.

2. Decide who would be the best person to talk to, or what kind of person might have the information you're after.

3. E-mail that person before the conference to let him know you would like to discuss this topic with him. Usually, you can set a date and time to meet. Also, this person will look for you rather than you just looking for him.

Figure 6.1 Plan your networking activities to maximize your opportunities.

have already made initial contact with someone, e-mail her and set up a mutually agreed on meeting location. Don't leave it to chance. This theme is addressed in more depth in chapter 7, Casing the Joint.

During the conference or networking event, review the schedule or agenda. Check off those contacts whom you met and those you still need to meet. If you have collected business cards, write notes on the backs of them indicating something to remember them by or what you need to do as a follow-up after the conference.

After the conference or networking event, send an e-mail follow-up to everyone you met. Be personable and include any materials that you promised them as attachments. One of the hardest things to do is to start out a letter or e-mail to someone you have never met. You might start with: *It was a pleasure meeting you at the recent conference.* The next sentence and the rest of the message usually flow much more easily.

Networking Is a Two-Way Street

Networking is a two-way street. It is not only who you know, but who knows you. Most people attend networking events to meet other people and to increase their professional networks. However, the reciprocal is also true: Other people get to know you. In everyone's quest to increase their contacts, they often overlook this important point and forget that they, too, are being assessed as potential contacts. Networking is a two-way street in the sense that just as you want to get to know others, they want to get to know you.

Attending networking events increases your visibility. Others will conclude that you are professionally active. Even though they may not know you personally, they may know about you. Your professional participation makes you a player. Over time, people will take notice of this fact, and they will seek you out as much as you are seeking them.

Whom would you prefer to hire, someone you know, or someone you don't know? Most people would prefer to hire someone they already know. It is less of a risk. Even if they don't know you

personally, they may know about you, and that counts equally well. In addition, they already have a measure of your professional involvement and commitment. They may have seen your performance, if only indirectly. Attending networking conferences is important, not just because you network with others, but because others get to know you. It can increase your chances of being hired also.

Many people mistakenly think of networking as simply making the connection with someone who can help position them. Networking, however, is a symbiotic relationship. When you are networking, consider what you can do for others and not just what they can do for you.

Networking is a process in which you seek a relationship to gain a resource. Each person has something to offer the other person. Networking often occurs between a superior and subordinate. An employer has a need for employees, and employees bring to the table their ability to perform the job. As someone who is just entering the field, you may be a little short on experience. However, you can offer intangibles such as enthusiasm, innovation, new ideas, and excitement. These intangibles are extremely valuable to employers. Their benefits should not be understated, particularly in today's service-oriented market.

Organizing a Networking Event

Creating or organizing a networking event offers several benefits. First, it brings together experts in your profession for a common purpose. They may serve on the same committee or task force, or they may be presenters or attendees. The knowledge that you gain from their shared expertise is beneficial to you. Second, you are showcasing the professionals who participate. Because you are the driving force behind the networking event, the benefits accrue to you. Third, it is not who you know, but who knows you. As the organizer of the event, other professionals get to know who you are and your capabilities. For a young professional, the costs of organizing a networking event in terms of time and energy are more than offset by the professional networking benefits obtained. Fourth, it advances you professionally. You have created a professional event.

In the previous example, CC did an excellent job organizing and coordinating sessions and volunteers for the biannual Whitewater Parks and Courses Conference. The other professionals who attended recognized his accomplishments. They benefited from the event. It opened doors for him, and he was able to obtain employment opportunities from the experience.

Event, or Task, Mentoring

Event, or task, mentoring is when a person with knowledge, skills, abilities, and experience, but not time, mentors you as you organize a professional task or event. Unlike traditional mentoring, event mentoring begins and ends with the event or task. It can occur within or outside of your organization. The classic elements of event mentoring are as follows:

1. The mentor and protégé work together to accomplish a specific task. The relationship results in the professional development of the protégé.
2. Generally, there is a beginning and an end to the mentoring relationship. Often, however, the end can become a bit blurred as the relationship changes to a more generic form of mentorship. However, there is a tapering off in the mentoring with the conclusion of the event or task.
3. It is a symbiotic relationship in which each party has something to gain. The protégé has the time but not the expertise, and the temporary mentor has the expertise but not the time.

CC's situation is an example of event mentoring. Because I had organized a similar event, it was easy for me to assist CC. He had the time, and I didn't. I had the expertise, and he was new at organizing this type of events. It was a symbiotic experience for both of us.

Working the Room

When you attend networking events, you need to be able to work the room. Working the room is about meeting other people and engaging them. In *How to Work a Room* (2005), Susan RoAne describes the art of working the room. She notes that you need to introduce yourself, make eye contact, have a good handshake, know when and how to break into another conversation, know how to exit a conversation, and be able to pick up the body language cues of others. Two additional skills include exchanging your business cards and wearing your name tag.

Introducing Yourself at a Networking Event

Most people find meeting other people at social events unnerving and rank it among their all-time stressors. But professional networking at a networking event requires meeting people. Following are some tips for introducing yourself and interjecting yourself into the conversation.

When introducing yourself, adopt a positive attitude. Most people are shy and are intimidated about meeting new people. If you don't have a positive attitude, it will show. The best way to adopt a positive attitude is to focus on the benefits of the events. Identify why you are attending the event. Are you attending to increase your visibility among your peers, to make contacts, or because you are expected to attend? Are you positioning yourself to meet the person who can hire you? Getting clear about your intentions can awaken a positive attitude.

Concentrate on the mechanics of your self-introduction. Taking care of the mechanics will help you smooth it out. If you plan your self-introduction, no matter how nervous you are, you should be able to rattle it off smoothly and flawlessly.

When meeting someone you don't know, the first thing you should do is introduce yourself (figure 6.2). Even if you know the other person and you think she remembers you, reintroduce yourself. It will put her at ease. If appropriate, shake her hand with a firm handshake when you meet her.

The best self-introductions are energetic and no more than eight or nine seconds long. Yours should include your name and a tag line that tells the other person something about you or who you are. Smile and directly engage the other person's eyes as you deliver your name and tag

1. Ensure that your presentation, including your clothes, speech, and mannerisms, represents you in the best possible way as a statement of who you are and what you do.

2. Introduce yourself in a way that is clear, concise, and personable, and that generates interest. *Hi, I'm Sally Herr, a student in the Recreation and Parks program at State College University. Hi, I'm Sally Herr. I create outdoor programs to help adolescents reach their full potential.*

3. Have two or three conversation generators or icebreakers to which people can easily respond. Small talk is good. *How did you become involved in . . .? Can you tell me a little bit about this organization?*

4. Reintroduce yourself to people rather than waiting for them to remember you. It will put them at ease.

5. Repeating a person's name will help you remember it. Focus on her name tag. Use her name in the conversation. Look at the name again when she gives you her business card.

Figure 6.2   Use these tips to ease your self-introductions.

From D. Fisher and S. Vilas, 1992, *Power networking - 55 secrets for personal and professional success* (Austin, Texas: Mountain Harbour Publications).

line. *Hi, I'm Sally Herr, a senior in the Recreation and Parks department at State College University.* This is a simple and straightforward name and tag line. However, consider incorporating your mission statement or something about yourself. *Hi, I'm Sally Herr. I create aquatics programs to help people reach their full potential.* Sally's tag line is also her mission statement and the tag line on her business card. In addition, the tag line will stimulate conversation. *Your job sounds interesting. Tell me more about the aquatics programs that you create.*

Making Small Talk

Small talk is an important aspect of conversation. To make a good impression and initiate and maintain productive conversations, you must learn to do it well. You can start small with such innocuous topics as the weather, or perhaps some aspect of the event you're attending, such as travel to and from the event. Making a consistent effort to be well informed about current events, especially those related to professional topics of mutual interest, is a great way to elevate your small talk skills. Read newspapers, Web sites, and trade journals; listen to radio shows and podcasts. (But take care to avoid discussing controversial topics such as politics or environmental concerns.) As noted in the previous section, a tag line in your introduction can also stimulate conversation.

Exiting the Conversation

Making a gracious exit is just as important as making a good entrance. It is the last thing the person will remember of you. In general, you want to signal that you are interested in concluding the conversation and then quickly do so.

Finish what you are saying or let the other person finish. Shake his hand as you give one of the following closings. *It was a pleasure meeting you. I need to meet several other people.* This is being direct. Some people fib slightly. *It was a pleasure meeting you. I need to freshen up a little.* When you leave, generally move at least one quarter of the room away and engage someone else. Engaging someone else suggests to the person that you left for legitimate reasons and not because you were bored.

You may want to begin pointing your feet away from the person with whom you are speaking. Subconsciously, they may pick up on the cue. Also, you can glance away with increased frequency. However, be careful. Glancing away too often is considered rude because you are not focusing on the person with whom you are speaking.

Another graceful way to close a conversation is to introduce the person to someone else. Remember that most people are just as shy about meeting other people as you are. After speaking with both people for a couple of minutes, graciously exit the conversation. You are a matchmaker and have helped your acquaintance meet someone else.

Exchanging Business Cards

Your business card is a miniature resume. It gives people a concrete way to remember you. Figure 6.3 provides some pointers on the use of business cards; chapter 11 addresses the design of business cards. Be sure to bring a sufficient supply. Consider carrying your business cards in a separate folder where they are easily accessible.

If you want to give someone your card and he hasn't asked for your card, ask for his. This breaks the ice and prompts him to ask for your card. Distribute your cards selectively rather than hand them to everyone you meet. As a rule, distribute your card only to people with whom you have made a connection and developed a relationship.

Once you've collected a lot of business cards from people, they all begin to look similar. Write notes on the backs of the cards as reminders of your meetings. Consider writing any or all of the following: the date, the event, a highlight of the conversation, how you met, who introduced you, any interesting information about the person,

and follow-up actions you have taken or plan to take.

Wearing Your Name Tag

People often wear name tags at networking events. Most people place them on the left side of their chests because they are right-handed. However, you should wear your name tag on the right side of your chest. It is customary for people to shake hands with their right hands. As you do, you can easily glance at the person's name on the right side of the chest. This glance is inconspicuous and unobtrusive. If the name tag is on the left side, glancing at it requires an obvious eye motion that reveals that you don't know the person's name.

When I attend events at which people wear name tags, I mentally separate people into those who know how to work a room and those who don't by how they wear their name tags. You can use the placement of the name tag on the right side as part of your small talk when you introduce yourself.

---

1. **Create an attractive business card.** See chapter 11 for suggestions on creating your own business cards. It is a miniature resume. It is a physical remembrance of your meeting. It is your calling card.

2. **Devise a system for carrying your own and others' cards.** Many people carry their business cards in plastic folders designed specifically for that purpose. Whatever system you use, you need to be able to access your business cards quickly.

3. **Bring enough cards.** You don't want to be out of cards when you meet someone that you really connect with.

4. **Write notes on the backs of people's cards.** If you have a file of business cards, after several months all the cards begin to look the same. Consider writing on the back of the card any or all of the following: the date, the event, a highlight of the conversation, how you met, who introduced you, any interesting information about the person, a follow-up action.

5. **If you want to give someone your card and she hasn't asked for yours, ask for hers.** This breaks the ice and may prompt the person to ask for your card.

6. **Distribute your cards selectively.** As a rule, distribute your card only to people with whom you have made a connection and developed a relationship.

Figure 6.3 Make the most of your business card when networking.

From S. RoAne, 2000, *How to work a room - The ultimate guide to savvy socializing in person and online* (New York: Collins Lifestyle); D. Fisher and S. Vilas, 1992, *Power networking - 55 secrets for personal and professional success* (Austin, Texas: Mountain Harbour Publications).

PROFESSIONAL MENTORING

Everyone who is successful has had the help of others—a senior member of the organization who steered them in the right direction or a close friend who was a little further along in their career development. Most people view mentors as those who help show them the way on their career path. However, a review of the literature suggests that when people attempt to create artificial mentoring relationships or structure them within organizations, the results are less than satisfactory. It is a relationship developed between two people. It can be ephemeral such as an event, or task, mentoring, or it can be a long-term relationship developed over one's career. Mentoring is a potentially important way of developing your network and professional support system. This section provides an overview of the mentoring literature that may help you in your networking process.

Benefits of Mentoring

In general, to be successful, you need other people to assist you in your career path. A review of the literature suggests that mentoring benefits both the protégé, or person being mentored, and the mentor. People who have had mentors tend to have increased job satisfaction, faster promotions, higher salaries, and firmer career plans (Dreher & Ash, 1990; Missirian, 1982; Roche, 1979; Wright & Wright, 1987). An additional benefit is that people who have had mentors tend to have increased self-esteem and better self-images (Kram, 1988; Roche, 1979; Wright & Wright, 1987).

The mentoring literature repeatedly states that everyone who is successful has had the benefit of a mentor ("Everyone," 1978; Kram & Isabella, 1985; Missirian, 1982, Higgins & Kram, 2001). Higher salaries, faster promotions, and increased job satisfaction are defacto proof that this is true. In the information age continuing education and the development of human capital are necessary for career success. Not only must employees learn the technical aspects of their positions, but they must also learn the ropes and how to negotiate political minefields. In all fields, management must constantly train new people to take on increasingly higher levels within the organization or field. This education and training comes from people who already have the knowledge, skills, abilities, and experience. These people serve as mentors.

Mentoring Life Cycle

The mentoring needs of young professionals early in their careers differ from those of older professionals in terms of their concerns about career and family (Kram, 1983, 1988; Higgins & Kram 2001). Young professional also have esteem, competency, and networking needs. Their focus is on acquiring the knowledge, skills, abilities, and experiences they need for their future careers. Older professionals have already acquired these things and usually look at giving back by becoming mentors.

Formal mentor–protégé relationships usually go through a series of stages, or a life cycle (Hunt & Michael, 1983; Kram, 1983, 1988). Understanding the changing relationship is important for students developing their careers. The *initiation stage* is between six months and a year long; in

We've all had a mentor at some time in our lives.

this stage the roles in the relationship become apparent. The protégé realizes that the mentor has the knowledge, skills, ability, and experience that they need. Conversely, the mentor recognizes the protégé as a potential rising star. This is followed by the *protégé stage,* in which the protégé's work is recognized more as a by-product of the mentor rather than the independent work of the protégé. At some point in the relationship there is a *breakup stage.* It may occur when the protégé begins to be recognized in his own right. At this point in the relationship, the mentor often has a transitional issue in the relationship where the mentor may have difficulty recognizing the protégée as an equal. Sometimes the breakup occurs when the protégé takes another position. The last stage is the *lasting friendship stage,* in which the protégé and mentor reestablish contact and become peers.

Mentoring Needs of Women

The literature suggests that mentoring is different for women than it is for men and that mentoring relationships between the sexes are rare (Dreher & Ash, 1990; Johnson & Ridley, 2004; Missirian, 1982; Shapiro, Haseltine, & Rowe, 1978; Wright & Wright, 1987). Often, women have difficulty breaking into the old boy network. There is also the problem of platonic relationships evolving into sexual relationships. Even if the relationship remains platonic, others can perceive it as sexual.

Research indicates that mentors tend to choose protégés with whom they identify, and they tend to identify along the lines of gender, race, and social class. In addition, there are gender-based professional stereotypes to overcome; women are often expected to behave differently in the professional workplace than men. An exception to this was Dreher and Ash (1990), who reported few gender differences with regard to the amount of mentoring activities and their outcomes. However, they did find a substantial difference in income levels between men and women.

Problems With Mentoring

Mentoring can have a downside. It involves risks to both the mentor and the protégée (Fieldman, 1999; Kram, 1988; Missirian, 1982; Wright &

Wright, 1987). A mentor or protégé who fails or falls short in his performance can reflect negatively on the other and can harm his career. Also, the mentor can be accused of favoring the protégé. Conversely, the protégé may be resented by peers who do not have mentors. As noted in the discussion of mentoring stages, structurally there is a *breakup stage* during which the mentor and protégé fall into conflict as the protégé establishes her own identity within the field.

It's natural to want to emulate your mentor, but it's important to remain your own person. Missirian (1982) labeled the situation in which the protégée becomes a clone of the mentor the Pygmalion syndrome. Is your success due to you or to your mentor? As the apprentice, you are in the shadow of your mentor. You want her acceptance but also her acknowledgment that you are doing a good job. You also want others to recognize that your achievements are the result of your efforts and not your mentor's. The Pygmalion syndrome is one problem people can have with mentoring relationships.

Mentors and protégés who have dissimilar demographic characteristics and backgrounds have less successful mentoring relationships than those who do. In addition, when the relationship is forced and not voluntary on the part of both the mentor and protégé, or when either person rushes into it, it is less likely to be successful. Effective mentoring requires time for cultivation and development.

If you are fortunate to have a mentor, you are better off than if you don't. However, if you don't have a mentor, you can still be successful.

Selecting a Mentor

When seeking a mentor, consider the following qualities and mentoring functions: technical appreciation and challenge, coaching, sponsorship, protection, exposure and visibility, interpersonal relationships, counseling, and friendship. Remember, not every mentoring relationship is intense or long term, nor do they need to be. Task, or event, mentoring is an example of a limited mentoring relationship. Also, remember that the mentor will be examining you in terms of many of the same factors.

A mentor should have technical appreciation and technical challenge. To have technical appreciation, she must have the knowledge, skills, abilities, and experiences to assist you in your career development. And more important, she must be willing to pass this knowledge on to you. Like a good coach, she should guide you and help you develop your talents. She should be able to give you specific advice and strategies for acquiring your own KSAEs. This is the technical challenge portion. The mentor must push you and challenge you to reach new heights in terms of your abilities. Be careful when choosing a mentor, because many people are protective of their knowledge, skills, and abilities and are reluctant to share them with others.

A good mentor can act as a sponsor, championing you in your professional career or in the organization where you work. You need someone who will take you under his wing and help you develop your talents.

A mentor can provide you with protection. In a sense, a mentor can be considered a gatekeeper, especially if he is directly connected to decision makers or if he is a decision maker himself. He can open the gate and give you challenging assignments. Conversely, he can close the gate on those who may view you as a threat or want to retaliate against your mentor by striking out against you.

A good mentor should provide you with exposure and visibility, giving you opportunities to demonstrate your competence to senior-level people in your organization or field. This requires you to be a doer and create something of value, whether it is an activity, program, or organizational work. It is a chance for you to demonstrate your competence. You want the decision makers to take notice and advance you along your career path.

There needs to be good chemistry, or an interpersonal relationship, between you and your mentor. Your mentor needs to be a good role model in terms of attitudes, beliefs, and behavior. She must also accept you for who you are and help you develop your own identity. In addition, your mentor needs to serve a counseling role, providing emotional support and advice.

Finally, a good mentoring relationship is usually built on friendship. Friendship is the glue that holds the mentoring relationship together. At some level, you need to like your mentor and the mentor needs to like you. This doesn't mean that a mentoring relationship without some level of friendship won't work. It just makes it more problematic. As noted in the beginning of this section, everyone who has been successful has had a mentor to help along the way. Mentoring is important. However, of equal importance is not to force a relationship artificially. These relationships tend to be less than successful.

PUTTING IT ALL TOGETHER

Everyone who has made it in a career has had help from other people. The focus of professional networking is on the process of developing professional relationships that advance your career and that of those who are in your network. Although it is important to develop quality contacts that can advance your career, don't overlook more casual contacts in terms of professional networking. Whether it is networking or mentoring, the relationship is a two-way street or a symbiotic relationship. You must consider not only what the other person can do for you, but what you can do for the other person.

Professional networking is an important part of your professional development. Often, other professionals have the power to open or close the gate, advancing your professional development or retarding it. The professionals with whom you work and with whom you associate at networking events will become your professional family that will last your entire professional career. They will most likely remain part of your professional family even after you retire. This is why networking and mentoring are fundamental to your career development.

REFERENCES

Barnes, J.A. (1954). Class and committees in a Norwegian island parish. *Human Relations, 7,* 39-58.

Dreher, G.F., & Ash, R.A. (1990). A comparative study of mentoring among men and women in managerial, professional, and technical positions. *Journal of Applied Psychology, 75* (5), 539-546.

Everyone who makes it has a mentor. (1978). *Harvard Business Review, 56* (2), 89-101.

Fieldman, D.C. (1999). Toxic mentors or toxic protégés? A critical re-examination of dysfunctional mentoring. *Human Resource Management Review, 9* (3), 247-278.

Fisher, D., & Vilas, S. (1992). *Power networking: 55 secrets for personal & professional success.* Austin, TX: Mountain-Harbour Publications.

Higgins, M.C., & Kram, K. (2001). Reconceptualizing mentoring at work: A developmental network perspective. *Academy of Management Review, 26* (2), 264-288.

Hunt, D., & Michael, C. (1983). A career training and development tool. *Academy of Management Review, 8,* 475-485.

Johnson, B.W., & Ridley, C. (2004). *The elements of mentoring.* New York: Palgrave Macmillan.

Kauffman, R. (2009). Student analysis of legends videos. *Schole.* Article accepted for publication.

Kram, K. (1983). Phases of the mentor relationship. *Academy of Management Journal, 26* (4), 608-625.

Kram, K. (1988). *Mentoring at work: Developmental relationships in organizational life.* New York: The University Press.

Kram, K., & Isabella, L. (1985). Mentoring alternatives: The role of peer relationships in organizational life. *Academy of Management Journal, 28,* 110-132.

Missirian, A. (1982). *The corporate connection: Why executive women need mentors to reach the top.* Englewood Cliffs, NJ: Prentice-Hall.

Pines, A., & Aronson, E. (1981). *Burnout: From tedium to personal growth.* New York: The Free Press, Macmillan.

RoAne, S. (2005). *How to work a room: The ultimate guide to savvy socializing in person and online.* New York: HarperCollins.

Roche, G. (1979). Much ado about mentoring. *Harvard Business Review, 57,* 26-28.

Shapiro, E., Haseltine, F., & Rowe, M. (1978). Moving up: Role models, mentors, and the patron system. *Sloan Management Review, 19,* 51-58.

Wright, C.A., & Wright, S.A. (1987). Young professionals. *Family Relations, 36,* 204-207.

Zigon, J. (2005). Getting the most out of a professional conference. *Business Credit, 107* (5), 10.

Identifying People

Identify four or five people with whom you want to network. Identify the benefit of networking with them, or why you want to meet them, and where you can meet them (e.g., Sally Herr: *Mr. Smith, the aquatics director, Anytown YMCA; he can employ me; I can meet him at the YMCA. Or, I can meet Mr. Muncheck at the state conference*).

Person 1:

Who: _____

Why: _____

Where: _____

_____

Person 2:

Who: _____

Why: _____

Where: _____

_____

Person 3:

Who: _____

Why: _____

Where: _____

_____

Person 4:

Who: _____

Why: _____

Where: _____

_____

Person 5:

Who: _____

Why: _____

Where: _____

_____

Working the Room

Review the principles and practices in the section Working the Room (page 85). Working in pairs or in threes, role-play how you would make contact with and meet other people. Be sure to include your introduction, small talk and conversation, and exit.

Exercise 6.3

Networking Costs and Benefits

Identify a networking event in which you want to participate (e.g., professional committee work, conference). Identify the benefits and costs of attending this event in the table below.

Benefits	Costs
1. _____	1. _____
2. _____	2. _____
3. _____	3. _____
4. _____	4. _____
5. _____	5. _____
6. _____	6. _____
7. _____	7. _____
8. _____	8. _____

Exercise 6.4

Living Legends

On its Web site, the American Academy for Park and Recreation Administration has a videotape library of legends of parks and recreation. The library is a collection of videotaped interviews with distinguished administrators and educators who have made outstanding contributions to the field of parks and recreation. Most legends are nearing the ends of their careers and can provide valuable insights into the career paths of people who have reached the zenith of their profession. The question is, If you want to be as successful as these people by the time you reach the end of your professional career, what do you need to do? What networking and mentoring tips and insights do they offer? The current Web site for the legends library is www.rpts.tamu.edu/Legends/library.htm.

Review the Web site and the brief biographies of the legends provided and select several videos to watch. Answer the following questions for each one you watch:

1. Briefly outline the person's career path.

_____

_____

_____

_____

_____

_____

_____

2. Read between the lines. How did the person get into the field? Why did the person advance, and how did the person become a legend?

_____

_____

_____

_____

_____

_____

_____

_____

3. What stands out in this person's career path? Critical decisions the person made, or something significant the person did? What did you conclude about or learn from this person?

_____

_____

_____

_____

_____

_____

_____

_____

chapter 7

Casing the Joint

Do I know everything about the organization and the job I seek?

Casing the joint is a term used by burglars. Before they rob a house, they check it out to make sure the police will be somewhere else, the owners won't be home, they won't get shot when they enter the house, the loot will be there, and they know how to disable the alarm system. In essence, they are doing their research. They are finding out everything they need to know before the robbery so they can maximize their gain and minimize their losses.

Similarly, when you seek a job, you need to case the joint, or research the firm. You want the employer to be home, and you want to make sure the desired position is available. Also, you want the people within the organization to disable the alarm system in human resources to assist you with your eventual employment.

Conceptually, casing the joint moves from the general to the specific. It begins with researching the field. Is it growing or shrinking? What are the trends and the major challenges facing the field? You may have already done this in your course of study, discussing professionalism, trends, and issues. Researching the field gives you a context for understanding the organizations you will be considering. The next level of research is the organization. Just as the field itself provides a context for understanding the organization, the organization provides a context for understanding the position you want.

Chapter 1 mentioned the seven-step sales model. Casing the joint is essentially the survey phase in this process. The emphasis, however, is on your researching the organization rather than the organization researching you.

This chapter provides tools for thoroughly researching the field you are interested in, the organization where you'd like to work, and the position you aspire to. An extensive worksheet (exercise 7.1) takes you step by step through the process of analyzing the field, the organization, the position, and even the people you might eventually work with. The worksheet also guides you in using the information you gather to position yourself for the job you want. The information that you gain from your research will not only help you identify a good employer match for yourself, but also prepare you for a great interview whether it is the one-on-one interview discussed in chapter 8 or the formal interview discussed in chapter 9.

A TALE OF TWO MODELS

Casing the joint is an important function in both the positioning and traditional job search models. In the traditional model, researching the organization helps you determine whether the organization is where you really want to work and prepares you for the formal interview. An employer expects you to know something about the organization, and if you have researched well, you can ask salient questions that indicate you have done your homework. Just as you are flattered when someone knows who you are and what you have done, people within the organization are flattered when you know something about who they are and what they are doing.

In the positioning model, you case the joint for many of the same reasons that you do in the traditional model. You want to know more about the organization and whether you want to work there. In addition, you need to prepare yourself for the one-on-one interview, which is discussed in the next chapter. You need to answer some basic questions, such as *Whom do I need to contact in the organization, and who can hire me? How do I meet or make contact with this person? Where do I see myself potentially fitting into the organization?* Depending on the situation, you may even need to sell your potential employer on why the organization needs to hire you.

Conceptually, the key difference between the two models is how active the employer is in the job search process. In the traditional model, employers are highly active. They have identified a position that they want to fill and are in the process of filling it. In the positioning model, employers are most likely not actively searching for a new employee. This is why you may need to show them where you can fit into their organization and why they should hire you. This is why the research you conduct as part of casing the joint is so important in your job search process.

Consider the following condensed version of a cover letter to a potential employer. It illustrates why it is important to research the organization and do your homework:

I am seeking a position with your organization. As part of my research, I noted that your organization has an excellent seniors program that recently received an award at the national congress. I am interested in pursuing a career in this programming area, and I have some professional experience in programming for seniors. I would like to explore the possibility of obtaining a position in your organization in this programming area.

This brief paragraph says a lot about the person who wrote it. First, she is complimenting the organization on its excellent program. Who doesn't want to receive a compliment? Second, not only does she indicate that she has done her research, but she backs it up with an example. In a sense, the passage suggests that this person has knowledge of the field with the reference to the national congress, the organization, and its programs. Next, the person indicates her interest and experience in this programming area. And, she suggests what she can do for the organization. The last sentence merges the organization's excellent program with the writer's desire to be part of it.

It is obvious that this person has cased the joint and knows more information about the organization than someone who has walked in off the street. Perhaps she obtained the information from the organization's Web site, or perhaps she attended the national congress or read about the organization in a professional magazine. This person has an idea of how she might fit into the organization.

PLACES TO LOOK

The first step in researching an organization is to view its Web site. If the information you seek isn't on the Web site, ask for a copy of the annual report. Obtain copies of brochures and literature that the organization distributes to the public. A schedule of programs offered, for example, indicates the groups the organization serves and the services offered to these groups.

It's a good idea to search the Web sites of the local government, schools, real estate agents and listings, and other services offered in the organization's community, as well. These sites can provide a good picture of the community in which the organization operates (figure 7.1).

Background and History
- Local history
- Traditions and values
- Demographics and census information
- Major industries

Communications
- Newspapers, newletters, and other local publications
- Radio
- Television

Community Services
- Hospitals
- Juvenile services
- Public assistance and welfare department

Education
- Schools (public, private, parochial)
- Teachers
- Adult education
- Libraries and museums
- Colleges and universities
- Community colleges and trade schools

Housing
- Average size and cost of a house
- Low rent and subsidized housing
- Neighborhood structure

Recreation
- Public and community recreation department and programs
- Commercial facilities
- Parks (state, local, and federal)
- Nonprofit associations

Religious Activities
- Number and types of churches, synagogues, mosques, and other houses of worship
- Church organizations

Transportation
- Road system including interstate highways, major arteries, local roads, and city streets
- Rivers, lakes, dams, and waterways
- Train stations
- Airports

Figure 7.1 When investigating a community, consider assessing these aspects of community life.

Adapted from R. Warren, 1965, *Studying your community* (New York: Free Press), XIV-XVIII.

Often the most important source of information is other people. This may include people within the organization, former employees, other professionals, colleagues, and friends. Later in this chapter Sally Herr discusses the aquatics position she is seeking with Mr. Smith, the aquatics director at Anytown AFC. For her, any conversations with Mr. Smith are an important source of information in her assessment of the organization and in completing many of the questions on the worksheet (exercise 7.1).

When seeking information from other people, as a rule, never say anything negative about the organization or the people in the organization. It is a small world, and you can expect any comments to get back to those in the organization.

Always be prepared to be introduced to key people at any time. In Sally Herr's case, she may be chatting with Mr. Smith, the aquatics director, and he may suggest introducing her to Mr. Muncheck, the executive director. Mr. Muncheck may also walk by on his rounds, and Mr. Smith may introduce her to him. If asked about your business, be honest and forthright in your response. *I am doing some research on your organization regarding its programs and employment opportunities.* If asked how far along you are in the process, again, be honest. *I am in the early phases of my research.* If you think this would be an exciting place to work, say so. *This looks like an exciting place to work.*

CASING THE FIELD

Casing the field you expect to enter is a good place to start the research process even if you have tentatively identified an organization and a potential position within the organization. For example, are both the field and the organization going in similar directions, or are they going in opposite directions? Is the organization dynamic while the field is stagnant? Perhaps the field is dynamic while the organization is relatively static.

What is going on in the field will normally affect your career path if you decide that you need to leave the organization for any reason. Remember, people change jobs approximately 10 times in their careers. Whether the field is expanding, stagnant, or constricting will affect your career path outside the organization.

This section will help you research the field. Your course of study may have given you a good understanding of the field, but it never hurts to do a reexamination.

Determining the Trends in the Field

After reviewing the professional magazines, journals, and newsletters (question 1 in exercise 7.1), as well as articles about your field written by those outside the field, you should be able to list three to five of the major trends affecting the field today. These trends form a backdrop for the rest of your findings because, once you know the national trends, you can easily relate them to the local organization you are investigating. Also, a knowledge of the trends in the field is helpful during the interview process, whether it is the one-on-one interview described in chapter 8 or the formal interview described in chapter 9 as part of the traditional job search model.

Perform an informal content analysis of the professional magazine or journal (an example of such an analysis is shown in figure 7.2) by reviewing the last 12 months of the publication. Make a list of the title and the subject, or theme, of each article. Often, such an analysis reveals the current issues or trends. If litigation is an issue, you will find it as either a primary or secondary theme in the articles. If the magazine is organized according to themes (i.e., each issue focuses on a specific subject), analyze the themes selected.

Conduct a similar content analysis of the regular columns in the professional magazine. Often, the president of the organization or a professional writes a column in the magazine each month. A perusal of these columns can provide an excellent perspective of the issues and trends in the field.

You may have to read between the lines to determine whether your field is growing, static, or declining. Very rarely will you find direct answers to these questions. For example, a review of the last several years of *Parks & Recreation* magazine notes an emphasis on skate parks and legal liability. Generally, the articles on skate parks addressed their installation, increasing public support, and liability issues that were hindering their installation. Reading between the lines, the collective statement made by the articles suggests that skate parks were in their growth phase because the issues discussed in the articles are generally associated with a new and expanding phenomenon. In contrast, if the articles had focused on how to reinvent skate parks or convert them to other uses, that would have suggested a mature industry or one in decline.

In this exercise you may need to read between the lines and ask these questions: *Who are the readers of* Parks & Recreation *magazine? What is the primary audience or readership of the magazine—nonprofit organizations such as YMCAs, scouts, or summer camps? Manufacturers of park and recreation equipment?* When students did this as a class activity, they often concluded that the articles focused on how community agencies can work with and partner with organizations such as YMCAs and camps and on how local communities can use the equipment in their recreation and park settings. They decided that the audience of *Parks & Recreation* magazine consists of public parks and recreation agencies.

Identifying Major Issues

Identifying major issues in the field (question 2 in exercise 7.1) is a variation of determining trends. You can use your content analysis of the literature to determine the major issues facing the field. In

---

Exercise 7.1

Casing the Joint Worksheet

This worksheet asks you a series of questions to help you find out more about the field, the organization, and the position you are interested in. When you have completed this worksheet, you will have a pretty good perspective on the position you seek and its environment.

Casing the Field

1. What are the trends in the field?

Issue	Titles	Content area
January 2xxx	Ten new trends in teen programming	Program
	Liability questions and skate parks	Liability/program
	Making your aquatics program a profit center	Program/profit
	Selecting new board members	Administration
	Maximizing your annual campaign	Fund-raising

Figure 7.2 Example of an informal content analysis.

a rapidly changing world, every field is facing major challenges.

An examination of *Parks & Recreation* magazine reveals a strong concern about legal liability issues. The magazine has a regular column dedicated to focusing on such issues facing the field. Moreover, most articles address legal liability. Even though legal liability has been an issue since the 1990s, it is still an important issue in the field today.

Determining Growth Trends

Overall, you want to determine whether your field is growing, remaining static, or in decline (question 3). You can analyze growth by looking at the number of jobs available in the field, the economic impact of the field, or its market share. You will also want to look at the growth occurring in various segments of the field because not all segments grow at the same rate. Your research, including the informal content analysis of the literature, should identify these areas of growth or decline. You may want to tailor your job search to one of these growth areas, or you may want to reconsider entering a field that is in decline.

Obtaining specific information on growth trends within a specific industry is not always easy. Most trade and many professional organizations are very protective of this information and will make it available only to their membership. And to become a member, you may need to be a well-established owner of a company in that field. In addition, there is usually a cost for the information.

The situation I faced in the following example is no different from situations many students face seeking similar information. I was doing a presentation at the Whitewater Symposium titled the The Perfect Storm: Is Whitewater Facing Extinction? To support my contention that growth was occurring in coastal kayaking and that whitewater was limited by the lack of available resources or facilities, I needed data on users. Although I had some good survey data from a national survey, I needed information on boat production, which was a key indicator of whether the field was growing, remaining static, or shrinking.

Fortunately, I knew the CEO of the trade organization. He gave me a temporary password (one day), and I was able to access the information I sought. I was able to support my hypothesis that with miles of available shoreline close to urban areas, sales of recreational kayaks and sit-upon kayaks were growing at a significant rate. In contrast, whitewater kayaking was fairly static, and whitewater canoeing, my area of interest, was in a state of rigor mortis, as I jokingly concluded. Although this information is available, it is often difficult to obtain because it is guarded closely. As a student, you may have difficulty gaining this information.

As a fallback position, simply ask someone you know who may have access to this information or who has a good insight into the field. Most managers will have some idea of the trends even if they haven't examined the hard data. For your purposes, this can suffice.

Becoming a Member of a Professional Organization

Becoming a member of a professional organization makes a statement that you have a commitment to the field (question 4). Also, it entitles you to membership services, which usually include a newsletter, magazine, and membership directory. A membership directory is an excellent "who's who" of the players in the field. Many professional organizations offer discounted memberships to students.

Reviewing Major Publications

To review major publications, start with the Web site of the professional or trade organization you are interested in and expand your investigation outward (question 5). Magazines and journals offer broader-based background information. In contrast, newsletters provide the nuts and bolts of what is going on in the field. Each complements the other. In reviewing the major publications of your field, you may find that the previously discussed content analysis will assist you here also.

Researching and Attending Conferences

Attend the next annual or regional conference of your professional organization (question 6). It will provide you with increased knowledge about the field as well as excellent opportunities for networking. The organization's Web site often includes thorough conference information. A review of the topics of the sessions can reveal trends in the field. If many sessions focus on litigation, it is likely that people are interested in or worry about liability issues. Many sessions that address starting your own business may indicate that this is an important topic in the field.

Identifying Major Players

Magazines, journals, and conference presentations will give you an idea of the key players in your field (question 7). In addition, you can ask personal contacts who the key players are. However, remember that the people you ask need to have technical competency in the field. Your friends, like you, are most likely unfamiliar with the field and so wouldn't know the key players. Make a card listing facts about key players so that when you meet them at the conference, you can use these facts as part of your introduction and small talk.

CASING THE ORGANIZATION

Now that you have an understanding of the field, you can move to the next level of your investigation, the organization level. The organization that you are investigating may be quite different from the field itself. The field may be booming, yet the organization may be mismanaged or out of step with the general trends. Also, the reverse may be true: the organization may be a star in a lethargic field. The organization's management culture will also directly affect the position you seek. The following sections address what to consider when you case the organization.

Identifying the Organization's Purpose

You can begin your research by reviewing the organization's mission statement. It will usually give you an insight into the product or service it provides (question 8). A statement of purpose will suffice. Be creative and insightful in your analysis. Most people, for example, would say that General Motors produces automobiles. However, General Motors is in the transportation business.

An examination of the Maryland-National Capital Park and Planning Commission's Web site quickly reveals that it was created to develop and operate public park systems and provide land use planning services within several counties. Its purpose is easily inferred from this statement:

> M-NCPPC [Maryland-National Capital Park and Planning Commission] was created by the Maryland General Assembly in 1927 to develop and operate public park systems and provide land use planning for the physical development of the great majority of Montgomery and Prince George's Counties, and to operate the public recreation program in Prince George's County. State-of-the-art facilities and award-winning programs have been the result.

Balboa Park in San Diego provides a welcoming statement to visitors on the home page of its Web site. It is typical of most welcoming statements on many home pages. It states who they are and what they do. Elsewhere, the Web site suggests that the park provides experiences with museums, performing arts, parks, and a zoo for the citizens of San Diego as well as for visitors to their community. Although it is obviously written for the general public, with a little tweaking, it can easily be transformed into a statement of purpose. Welcome to Balboa Park—the nation's largest urban cultural park. Home to 15 major museums, renowned performing arts venues, beautiful gardens, and the San

Diego Zoo, the Park has an ever-changing calendar of museum exhibitions, plays, musicals, concerts, and classes—all in the beautiful and timeless setting of this must-see San Diego attraction.

Identifying the Clientele

In some organizations, the clientele is fairly well defined (question 9). For example, the demographics of most AFCs are fairly consistent; they cater to middle- and upper-middle-class users. Often you can infer whom the business serves from the clients or other businesses associated with it. For example, certain stores offer high-end merchandise and others offer low-end merchandise.

The Internet makes demographic information easy to obtain. By entering the phrase *demographics Prince George's County Maryland* into a search engine such as Google, you can easily navigate to the U.S. Census data for Prince George's County, Maryland, as well as other pertinent information. The "Quick Facts" provided by the U.S. Census Bureau provide a good quantitative summary of the community being served by the park and planning commission in the county.

The old-fashioned way to complete a community survey is to drive through the community. What are the sizes of the homes? Are they in good repair? When were the houses built? Examine the homes closely. Is the neighborhood rundown, or is it improving? Examine the vehicles parked in front of the houses. Are they older or new vehicles? Are they compact, mid-sized, or luxury cars? As an indication of children in the community, how many swing sets are there in the backyards? Is there a local park or playground? Are young mothers visiting the park during the day, or is their general absence a sign that they are off working?

If it is not convenient to do a drive-through survey of the community, try a Google survey using the "satellite" feature. Type in the street address of the organization in the search engine and then take an aerial view of the community. Although you may not be able to count the swing sets in the backyards, you can still get the lay of the land.

Examining the Structure

What is the administrative structure of the organization you are researching (question 10)? Generally, you will have to infer this from the structure of the Web site, its listing in the phone directory, or personal conversations with people familiar with the organization. At our university, if you have a copy of the telephone directory published each year, you also have the organizational chart of the university. The listings delineate the departments.

Knowing the structure of the organization is important for several reasons. First, it helps you determine whom you need to contact within the organization. Second, it helps you determine potential colleagues in the organization. Third, it helps you determine how the organization allocates human resources in the delivery of its programs. For example, the number of full-time personnel allocated to Youth Programs is an indication of its importance to the organization. Finally, the structure provides some insight into whether the organization is centralized or decentralized, and whether it is organized by product or service, geographically, or by function.

If it is centralized, decisions within the organization will come from above. In contrast, organizations that are decentralized give more decision-making authority to subordinates, and people lower in the organizational chart tend to have greater autonomy and control over what they do.

In figure 7.3, the titles of several of the personnel suggest that at least some departmentalization is done according to product or service (e.g., swimming pool, summer camp, teen center). Geographic departmentalization is usually noted in the title with terms such as *north, south, county, city,* and *region.* Geographic departmentalization tends to be decentralized and more autonomous. Functional departmentalization focuses on the administrative function provided (e.g., marketing, maintenance, membership, accounting). Again, this is suggested by the personnel titles in figure 7.3.

Organizations departmentalized by product or service usually note the program or service. For example, in the Web site example in figure 7.3, the titles of several of the employees suggest that at least some of the structuring was done according to product or service. In turn, this observation is reflected in the organizational chart created by Sally Herr (figure 7.4). Usually, at the program level (e.g., swimming pool, summer camp, teen center), directors have a fair amount of autonomy,

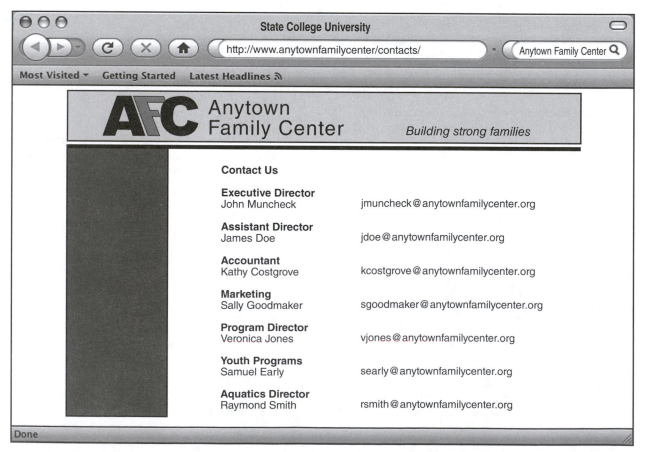

Figure 7.3   Reviewing an organization's Web site can give you insight into its structure.

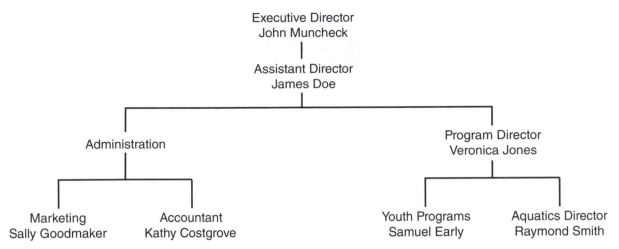

Figure 7.4 Try creating a rudimentary organizational chart based on the information you find on the organization's Web site.

even within a centralized organizational structure. This organizational chart may not be correct. However, validating and correcting the organizational structure makes for an excellent topic of discussion in the one-on-one interview. Sally's research and analysis provided her with valuable insights into the organization and its delivery system.

Identifying the Chain of Command

In most organizations, the person who would supervise you directly, or that person's supervisor, will most likely affect your employment opportunities and your ability to position yourself (question 11). This question in exercise 7.1 contains a simplified table for organizing this information. The Anytown AFC is a small organization and it was easy for Sally Herr to draw a complete organizational chart for the organization (figure 7.4). Often, you do not need to draw a complete organizational chart, particularly for large organizations. Figure 7.5 shows how Sally Herr has filled in the relevant information.

Getting a Feel for the Corporate Culture

Although this is a short question on the worksheet in exercise 7.1, it is extremely important in determining your success or failure as well as your future in the organization (question 12). The corporate culture involves the unwritten rules and behaviors of the organization and its employees. For example, are most of the employees young

people just out of college or older employees seeking retirement within the next 10 years? What does this tell you about the culture of the organization? Do they hire young people, exploit them, and then flush most of them out of the system? Or, do the young employees burn out, leave the organization, and move on to other jobs? If a large percentage of the employees are approaching retirement in the next 10 years, you may have considerable opportunities within the organization for advancement. Is the organization autocratic with a top-down management style, or is it decentralized with considerable autonomy given to employees?

This is a critical question to answer in your investigation because it will significantly affect your work environment. There may be two separate cultures in that the overall corporate culture may differ from that in the individual departments. Also, the culture can vary radically from one department to another within the same organization. However, even if a department has a culture that differs from that of the overall organization, the overall culture will still have a profound bearing on the department's culture.

Corporate culture is difficult to quantify. Regardless, give it considerable thought. Ask around and listen to what people tell you. Read between the lines of what they say.

Discerning Strengths and Weaknesses

Make a list of five strengths and five weaknesses you observe in the organization (questions 13 and 14). Examine the magnitude of each. For

Exercise 7.1

Casing the Joint Worksheet

This worksheet asks you a series of questions to help you find out more about the field, the organization, and the position you are interested in. When you have completed this worksheet, you will have a pretty good perspective on the position you seek and its environment.

Casing the Organization

11. What is the chain of command and who occupies each position? Use table 7.1 to list the position you seek and identify the next three or four people in the organizational chain of command. Also, you may need to note those below you on the chain of command.

Level	Position	Job title	Person occupying the position
1	Their supervisor:	Assistant director	James Doe
2	Their supervisor:	Program director	Veronica Jones
3	Your supervisor:	Aquatics director	Raymond Smith
4	Position you seek:	Aquatics position	????

Figure 7.5   An example of identifying the chain of command.

example, Mr. Muncheck may be a great person to work under and a leader in the field. However, this might be more than offset by an oppressive overall corporate culture within the organization.

RESEARCHING THE POSITION

Your research of the organization provides the backdrop for your research of the position you seek within the organization. In researching the position, there are two general items to look at. The first is the knowledge, skills, abilities, and experiences (KSAEs) you need in general for an equivalent position in another organization. For example, if you want to be an aquatics director, the skills set required in one community or organization won't differ too much from that of the next. The KSAEs required for similar types of positions at other aquatics facilities should be fairly similar to those required for the job you are interested in. Techniques such as bridging and think evaluation are important in determining these attributes. Next, you need to determine the specific requirements of the position you seek within the organization. Although they are usually similar to the general requirements, there may be some profound differences. The following sections address what you should look at when you are researching your desired position.

Identifying the Desired Position

Your objective is not necessarily to determine the exact position within the organization for which you are applying (question 15). It may not yet exist, or it may not be available. Your purpose is to see if there are similar positions to the one you seek, or positions at the same level. You want to determine where you can potentially fit into the organization. The better you are at articulating this to your potential employer, the easier it will be for him to actually fit you into the organization. The position may be an existing position, an adapted position, or a totally new position. Eventually, you will take this process to the next step and develop a job description for the ideal job you would like to have if you were employed by the organization.

Determining the Career Track of the Position

This question addresses the position from the perspective of career advancement (question 16). In part, this question builds on the last one. You want to know what happened to the people who were in this position before you or in similar positions. Was the position vacant because the person was promoted from within? Are people in similar positions also promoted? Do people tend to stay a year or two and then move on to other jobs, or, once hired, do they tend to stay in their jobs for the duration of their careers.

Mainlining is a term borrowed from the railroading industry and refers to fast-track positions that lead to career advancements. Positions that are *sidetracked* are essentially dead ends with no hope of promotion. In the previous examples, people who were hired and remained in their jobs are sidetracked. Generally, secretarial and clerical positions tend to be sidetracked.

Examine the career paths of people in the organization, their relative age, and turnover of people within the organization. It can be an excellent litmus test regarding what will happen once you have the job. Look at the previous people who held the job you are interested in or similar positions. What are they doing now? Did they move up in the organization? Did they move to a new position that was a promotion in terms of their career development? Or, did they leave the field because of burnout? Again, examine those people who are 10 to 15 years older than you in similar positions in the organization. If everyone in the organization is stagnant in their careers, why should you expect to be any different? Conversely, if everyone is dynamic and progressing, it suggests an environment that will foster your advancement.

View this as a continual process of collecting information. Initially, you may want to gain a preliminary assessment from your normal interactions and conversations with people outside the organization. Then, as you begin to meet people within the organization, use your normal powers of observation to address this question. Sally Herr worked in two other AFCs in the region. It was a simple matter for her, as part of her normal conversations with other workers, to obtain at least a preliminary determination of the Anytown AFC's culture. Then, when she met with Mr. Muncheck, she listened between the lines to further assess the organization's culture. When she met other people within the organization, she was continually mindful of addressing this question and the organization's culture.

Matching Your KSAEs to Those of the Position

It is vital to compare the KSAEs you possess with those required in the position you aspire to (question 17). You need to determine whether you need to acquire any knowledge, skills, abilities, or experiences specific to this organization and position. Sally Herr is interested in an aquatics position. Perhaps this organization works with a specific population such as seniors or specialized activities such as water aerobics, where expertise in these areas is required of their employees. If there are specific requirements, determine whether you need to obtain them before you are hired, or whether you can obtain them after you are hired. For example, if you need a teaching certificate, can you obtain it after you are hired, or do you need it in hand prior to your employment?

Generally, it is difficult to assess the KSAEs required for a specific job within the organization unless the organization has advertised this position or a similar position recently. You may need to rely on your general findings for similar positions within the field. Sally Herr did an assessment of other aquatics positions within the AFC system. Her findings are presented in figure 7.6. It is not unreasonable for her to assume that these KSAEs would also apply to the Anytown AFC.

CASING THE PEOPLE

Your positioning efforts can be furthered by identifying the people who will hire you and with whom you will work once you are hired. In the information age, there is a large amount of data on the Internet. Google the people in charge of

---

Exercise 7.1

Casing the Joint Worksheet

This worksheet asks you a series of questions to help you find out more about the field, the organization, and the position you are interested in. When you have completed this worksheet, you will have a pretty good perspective on the position you seek and its environment.

Researching the Position

17. What knowledge, skills, abilities, and experiences are required for this position within the field or within the organization? (Review chapter 4 to help you determine the KSAEs needed for this position.)

Do you possess the KSAE?

KSAE 1: _Education—College degree in related field needed._ [ ] Yes No [✓]

KSAE 2: _Certifications—Lifeguard, first aid, CPR/AED certifications required._ [✓] Yes No [ ]

KSAE 3: _Philosophy—AFC experience along with experience working in a multicultural environment preferred._ [✓] Yes No [ ]

KSAE 4: _Administration—Strong leadership and organizational skills: Able to work effectively with staff and volunteers including hiring, training, supervising, and evaluating employees._ [✓] Yes No [ ]

KSAE 5: _Membership—Can actively assist in the recruitment of new members, while maintaining strong relations with current members._ [✓] Yes No [ ]

KSAE 6: _Programming—Able to design and implement a variety of aquatics programs (e.g., swim team, water aerobics, water therapy)._ [✓] Yes No [ ]

Figure 7.6 KSAEs required for the aquatics positions Sally Herr is interested in.

hiring or who might be your supervisors. What articles have they written? Did they speak at rotary or other civic organizations? Were they in the newspaper? If so, why? Often, other people are an excellent source of information about the people in the organization. Remember, it is a small world, and even if they have something bad to say about the person or organization, refrain from making negative comments.

Information is power. How you use it and present it is important also. If used incorrectly, it can hurt you rather than help you. Much of the information you uncover will be background information, particularly personal information about the person and their family. If you try to impress the person who is interviewing you with information about what their children are watching on MySpace or similar Web sites, you may get a backlash. Simply let the other person tell you about her background information as part of the normal conversation. Be sure to look interested if she tells you something you already know.

Identifying the Supervisor

Usually, your supervisor will be your point of contact within the organization for the one-on-one interview (question 18). Sally Herr's supervisor would most likely be Mr. Smith, the aquatics director. He was also her initial contact within the organization.

Identifying Who Will Hire You

Don't assume that your supervisor is the person who has the authority to hire you (question 19). The supervisor may serve as your point of entry into the organization; however, the person who has the authority to hire you or grant you entry into the organization is often someone else. You need to identify this person and court him. Usually, your supervisor or point of entry into the organization will know who this person is and help you meet him.

Sally used Mr. Smith as her point of entry into the organization, but the person who will hire her is Mr. Muncheck, the executive director. Her prior relationship with Mr. Smith is noted in her e-mail to Mr. Muncheck later in this chapter (figure 7.10). Although Mr. Smith is the aquatics director, Sally's discussions with him revealed that Mr. Muncheck is responsible for all hiring in the organization. Mr. Smith may advise or make a recommendation; however, Mr. Muncheck is the person who will hire her. Therefore, Sally needs to focus her attention and research on Mr. Muncheck, the decision maker, unless he delegates this responsibility to Mr. Smith.

Researching Key People

Everyone likes compliments. Most people are impressed when you know what they have done professionally. Research key people's articles, presentations, and contributions to the field (question 20). Google the people you will meet and find out what they have done, even service to their church or community. Check their personal Web sites or blogs. Researching people will pay you dividends. In addition, it helps to make a positive statement about you. It suggests that you are interested in others, and that you are interested in people other than yourself. Insert your findings on the worksheet in exercise 7.1.

Sally Herr conducted a Google search of Mr. Muncheck. She found that he had a personal Web site. Figure 7.7 lists some of her findings from his Web site as well as from her other sources. He graduated from the same program and major she was in. He has three children. Active professionally, he presented at the state professional conference and wrote an article. When making small talk during the interview process, referencing his three children may provide a nice touch, or she may let him bring forth this information as part of the discussion. Also, the fact that he has presented at two recent conferences is important information because it suggests to Sally that she might want to meet Mr. Muncheck at the conference. This is addressed in the next section on positioning yourself.

POSITIONING YOURSELF

How will you use your research to position yourself within the organization? Now begins the transition from information gathering to making contact with the people you've targeted within the organization.

Exercise 7.1

Casing the Joint Worksheet

This worksheet asks you a series of questions to help you find out more about the field, the organization, and the position you are interested in. When you have completed this worksheet, you will have a pretty good perspective on the position you seek and its environment.

Researching the Position

20. Research the people. (Identify things that are special about the people listed in questions 18 and 19 as well as other key people. Consider articles published, presentations made, programs presented, awards won, common colleagues or friends.)

Supervisor: _John Muncheck_

Title: _Executive director_

a. _He is also a graduate of State College University. He graduated from the same program that I am graduating from . . . interesting!_

b. _He has three children. Jill is in high school, Jeff is at State College University, and Nick is in sixth grade._

c. _Published a paper in the AHPERD Journal . . . Interesting topic . . . I need to get a copy of it._

d. _Presented last year at the state conference on effective management of nonprofits._

e. _Presented the previous year at the state conference on the importance of maintaining membership in nonprofit organizations._

Figure 7.7   Sally Herr's summary of her research on Mr. Muncheck.

Reminding Yourself of Your Mission

If you have determined your mission statement in chapter 2, write it down in exercise 7.1 (question 21). If you are like most people and don't know what your mission statement is, or if you have a hard time articulating it, write your career goal instead. This is important to the positioning process because it helps you to frame your activities.

Often, people write the description of the job they are seeking as their career objective on their resume. Many publications recommend this practice when applying for positions. Although this practice is okay when applying for a specific job, you are doing yourself a disservice if you use it to answer this question. The essence of this question is to help you focus on what makes you tick, what motivates you. It is about what you are about. Try to think beyond the next job and answer the question *Why have you just gone through a lengthy research process to obtain a position in this organization?*

Sally Herr's mission statement is *To create aquatics programs to help people reach their poten-*

tial. In it she indicates her desire to work in aquatics as well as to help people through aquatics activities. Her statement goes beyond the job and addresses her mission in life.

Listing Your Contacts

Make a list of the people you know who currently work in the organization, have worked there in the past, or have knowledge of what is going on within the organization (question 22). The information you gain from these people will help you complete the previous questions on this worksheet. For example, they can help greatly in helping you determine the culture of the organization. These people can help you determine whom you should contact within the organization and who is the key person you need to approach for a job. Add additional sections to this question if you have more than four people.

Writing a Job Description

This exercise will help you focus on the position (question 23). In chapter 8, when you are developing your individual job description, you may use the description you create here or a variation of it (figure 7.8). One of the following four situations will occur:

1. The position you propose is exactly what the employer has in mind. If you have researched the organization well, you may describe a position that meets their needs exactly. Although this is unlikely, it is great when it happens.

2. They will reject your job description out of hand and offer you one of their own.

3. You merge what you desire with what they offer to create a negotiated position.

4. They reject your proposal and terminate the process.

Exercise 7.1

Casing the Joint Worksheet

This worksheet asks you a series of questions to help you find out more about the field, the organization, and the position you are interested in. When you have completed this worksheet, you will have a pretty good perspective on the position you seek and its environment.

Positioning Yourself

23. Based on your investigation of the organization, write a brief job description of the position you want in the organization. Is it the same as or different from the one you wrote in question 15? (This is important because it gives you a place to start.)

    1. *Requires lifeguard, first aid, and CPR certificates.*

    2. *AFC experience along with experience working in a multicultural environment preferred.*

    3. *Strong leadership and organizational skills: Able to work effectively with staff and volunteers.*

    4. *Can actively assist in the recruitment of new members, while maintaining strong relations with current members.*

    5. *Develop or coordinate a water aerobics program or coach the swim team.*

Figure 7.8 Sally Herr's preliminary job description.

By creating a job description, you now have a place to start and can frame the parameters of the position you want. Also, you are designing the position in the context of an actual organization. This makes the job description more than just interesting and hypothetical; it is also feasible.

Planning to Contact Your Target

This is the who, what, where, and when question. Confirm who you want to contact about a position, and plan where and when to make the contact (question 24). The Sally Herr example is illustrative of this process. Based on her discussions with Mr. Smith, the aquatics director, and others, Sally identified Mr. Muncheck as the person with whom she needs to meet regarding a position. She identified in her research of Mr. Muncheck that the state conference might be an ideal place to meet with him. If meeting at the conference is acceptable to him, the *when* will also become finalized. A plan is beginning to take shape.

Sally decided to e-mail Mr. Muncheck (figure 7.10). She used the standard three-paragraph format described in chapter 12. In the introductory paragraph, she stated her business and indicated that she had discussed this with Mr. Smith, the aquatics director. The second paragraph is her sales pitch. It indicates what she can do for the organization. Compare how her statement parallels the KSAEs delineated for this position (question 17 and figure 7.6). She addressed each of the KSAEs in her e-mail, if only briefly. Her research paid her dividends. She wrote based on knowledge, not on supposition. Her third paragraph suggested her desired course of action, which is to meet with him at the conference. Again, this reflects her research.

Mentioning that she had discussed her career opportunities with Mr. Smith may serve Sally in several ways. First, it may result in Mr. Muncheck approaching Mr. Smith about her. Second, it is common courtesy to let Mr. Smith know that she is using him as her entree. Third, by informing everyone of what she is doing, Sally demonstrates that she is on the ball. Finally, if Mr. Smith is going to be less than supportive of her, it is better to know this up front so she can deal with it. There is nothing worse than having someone kill your application behind the scenes.

Mr. Muncheck consulted with Mr. Smith and replied to Sally (figure 7.11). He is attending the conference and suggested a time and place to meet. Also, he wanted more information and requested

---

Exercise 7.1

Casing the Joint Worksheet

This worksheet asks you a series of questions to help you find out more about the field, the organization, and the position you are interested in. When you have completed this worksheet, you will have a pretty good perspective on the position you seek and its environment.

Positioning Yourself

24. Indicate whom you want to contact in the organization regarding a position, where you want to contact this person, and when you will do it.

Who: *John Muncheck*

Where: *The state conference seems like a good place. He has presented two years in a row and is likely to attend this year.*

When: *Need to e-mail him.*

Figure 7.9 Sally's preliminary plan to contact Mr. Muncheck.

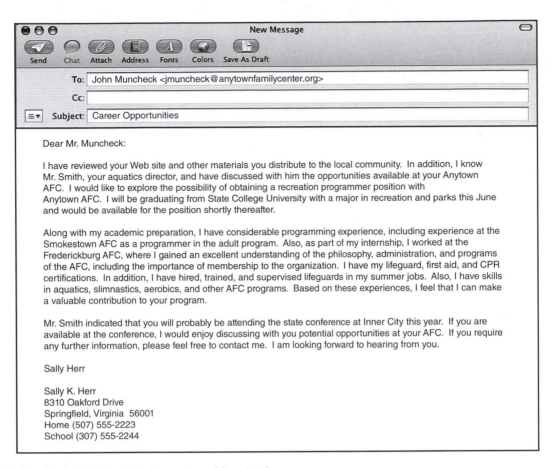

Figure 7.10 Initial e-mail from Sally to Mr. Muncheck.

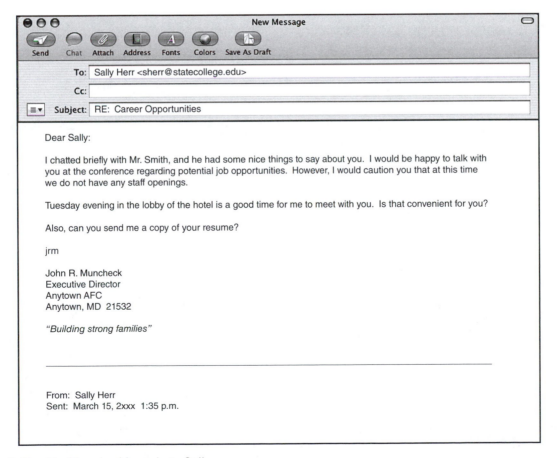

Figure 7.11 Mr. Muncheck's reply to Sally.

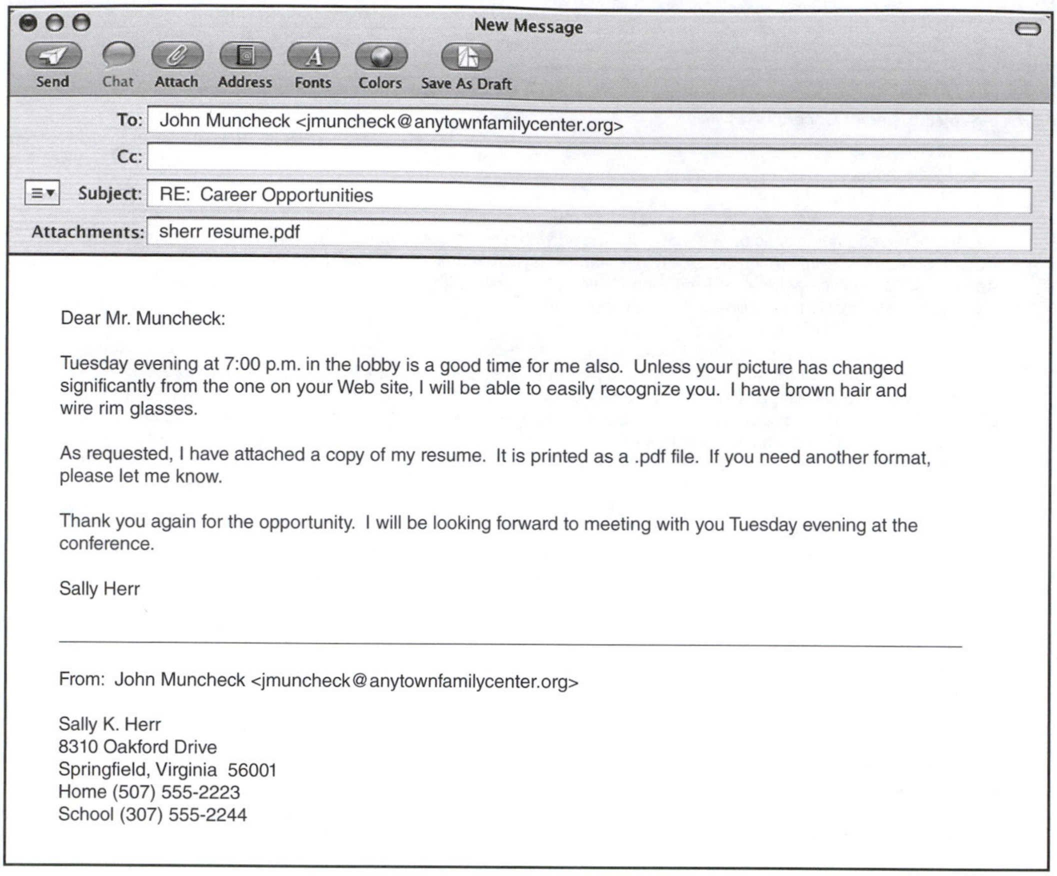

Figure 7.12 Sally follows up with Mr. Muncheck.

her resume. Sally confirmed the meeting time and place (figure 7.12). She cautiously interjected some humor by saying she will recognize him by his Web site photograph (this comment also has the effect of further proving that she has done her homework). In addition, she sent him her resume as requested. Often, the employer won't ask for the resume until further along in the process. However, Mr. Muncheck has read about Sally's KSAEs in the second paragraph of her first e-mail, which was extremely informative.

Shortly before the conference, Sally sent Mr. Muncheck a confirmation e-mail about their meeting (figure 7.13). This was prudent on her part. First, she made Mr. Muncheck look good. He is a busy person, and quite frankly, Sally is not high on his priority list. Her e-mail served as a reminder and a reconfirmation of the meeting. It also indicated that she is responsible and will do things that will make him and the organization look good. Mr. Muncheck replied in a typical businesslike e-mail that was short and to the point

(figure 7.14). However, if he is any type of executive director, he didn't miss the message conveyed by Sally's correspondence. She indicated that she is responsible, that she will attempt to make him look good, and that she has a sense of humor. She did this simply through her correspondence.

Sally and Mr. Muncheck confirmed a meeting time and place. They are now ready to meet in a one-on-one interview at the state conference. The stage is set for the next step in the process, the one-on-one interview, which is covered in chapter 8.

PUTTING IT ALL TOGETHER

The chapter began by asking whether you know everything about the organization and the job you seek. As a general rule, the more information you can accumulate about the organization, the better. However, it is important to put this information in perspective. As you collect information, you will also unearth issues and problems with the

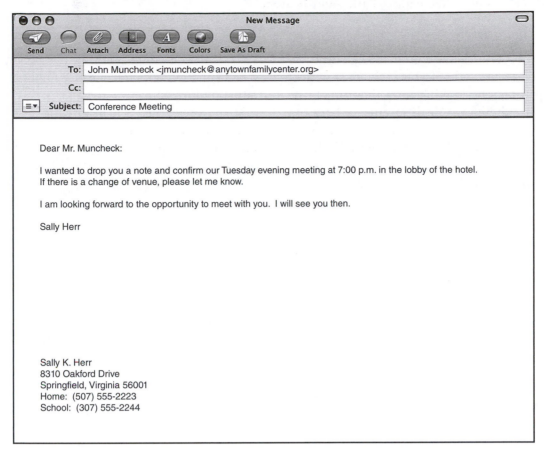

Figure 7.13 Sally reminds Mr. Muncheck of their meeting.

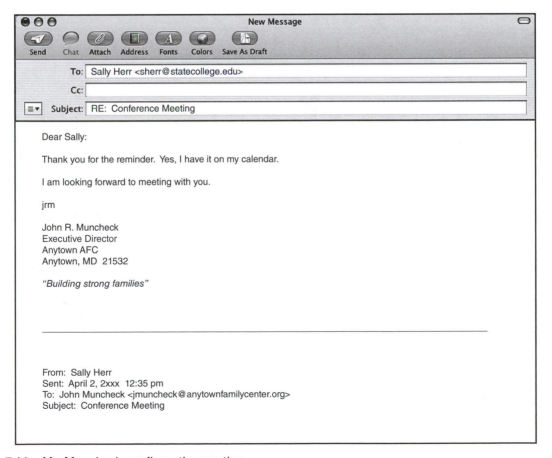

Figure 7.14 Mr. Muncheck confirms the meeting.

organization and the potential job. There is no perfect place to work. If you look for a perfect place, you may be looking for a long time. It is important, therefore, to differentiate between normal circumstances associated with any organization and those that can potentially harm you. Weigh the information collected in terms of who you are, where you are going, where the organization is going, and your needs. Sometimes a bad situation for someone else might be a good situation for you.

To be forewarned is to be forearmed. The information you collect on the field, the organization, and the job help you to be forearmed. It's always good to case the joint.

Exercise 7.1

Casing the Joint Worksheet

This worksheet asks you a series of questions to help you find out more about the field, the organization, and the position you are interested in. When you have completed this worksheet, you will have a pretty good perspective on the position you seek and its environment.

Casing the Field

1. What are the trends in the field?

   a. _____

   b. _____

   c. _____

   d. _____

   e. _____

   f. _____

2. What are the major challenges or problems in the field?

   a. _____

   b. _____

   c. _____

   d. _____

   e. _____

   f. _____

3. What are the areas of major growth in the field?

   a. _____

   b. _____

   c. _____

   d. _____

   e. _____

   f. _____

4. Are you a member of a major professional or trade organization servicing this industry?

   [ ] Yes   [ ] No

From *Career Development in Recreation, Parks, and Tourism: A Positioning Approach* by Robert B. Kauffman, 2010, Champagn, IL: Human Kinetics.

List them here:

a. _____

b. _____

c. _____

d. _____

e. _____

f. _____

5. Did you review the major publications in the field (e.g., magazines, journals, newsletters)?

[ ] Yes   [ ] No

List the ones reviewed here:

a. _____

b. _____

c. _____

d. _____

e. _____

f. _____

List three things you learned or observed in the magazines or journals (e.g., predominant areas of interest or focus, trends, issues).

a. _____

b. _____

c. _____

6. Where is the next annual or regional conference of the organization servicing the field?

Conference: _____

Dates: _____

Location: _____

List three things you want to accomplish at the conference (e.g., visit the booth of the organization or attend the presentation of a person you want to contact):

a. _____

b. _____

c. _____

From *Career Development in Recreation, Parks, and Tourism: A Positioning Approach* by Robert B. Kauffman, 2010, Champagn, IL: Human Kinetics.

List three people who can help you find out more about the organization(s) in which you are interested (identify where and when for each person):

a. _____

b. _____

c. _____

7. Who are the major players in the field? (Magazines or journals may suggest these people.)

a. _____

b. _____

c. _____

d. _____

e. _____

f. _____

Casing the Organization

8. What product or service do they provide? (Try writing this as a one-sentence mission statement.)

_____

_____

_____

_____

9. To whom do they provide this product or service? Who is their clientele? (Depending on the size of the organization, you may need to list several groups or limit the focus to the group that interests you.)

_____

_____

_____

_____

10. How is the company organized? (Use the company's telephone directory to determine its organizational chart. Most companies list people by departments in the phone directory. Also, the Web site's structure usually parallels the company's organizational structure.)

[ ] **Centralized**   In a centralized organization everything is controlled and run by the central organization. Small organizations and businesses located in one building or at one site are inherently centralized.

[ ] **Decentralized**   Geographically organized organizations tend to be decentralized. Often product- or service-structured organizations are also, particularly when the product or service

From *Career Development in Recreation, Parks, and Tourism: A Positioning Approach* by Robert B. Kauffman, 2010, Champagn, IL: Human Kinetics.

is located at different sites. In decentralized organizations, people located down the organizational chart tend to have greater autonomy and control over what they do

[　] **Product or service**　Organized by products or services. (e.g., youth program, swimming program, teen program)

[　] **Geographic**　Organized by geographic regions (e.g., north, south, county, or city)

[　] **Function**　Organized by functions (e.g., maintenance, administration, marketing)

[　] **Other (specify):**

_____

_____

_____

11. What is the chain of command and who occupies each position? Use the table below to list the position you seek and identify the next three or four people in the organizational chain of command. Also, you may need to note those below you on the chain of command.

Level	Position	Job title	Person occupying the position
1	Their supervisor:		
2	Their supervisor:		
3	Your supervisor:		
4	Position you seek:		

12. What is the company's culture? (Is it a young or mature staff? How long have the employees been in their positions? Is there a lot of turnover in employees? Do the employees seem happy or unhappy? What is the management style of the supervisor?)

_____

_____

_____

_____

_____

_____

13. List five strengths of the organization.

a. _____

b. _____

c. _____

d. _____

e. _____

From _Career Development in Recreation, Parks, and Tourism: A Positioning Approach_ by Robert B. Kauffman, 2010, Champagn, IL: Human Kinetics.

14. List five weaknesses of the organization.

a. _____

b. _____

c. _____

d. _____

e. _____

Researching the Position

15. What position are you seeking? (from question 11, if applicable)

a. [ ] New position   [ ] Existing position

Is the person retiring? Is the position currently vacant? Was the person fired or terminated? Was the person promoted? Did the person leave for another job?

_____

_____

_____

_____

b. If an existing position, indicate the person and his or her title.

Person: _____

Title: _____

c. Write a job description of an existing position within the organization that is most like the position you seek. (This job description should be an existing position within the organization. It can be for the person in the previous item. This position may be the same or modified to the position you desire in question 23.)

_____

_____

_____

_____

_____

_____

16. Is this position mainlined or sidetracked within the field or within the organization?

[ ] **Mainlined**   Are the people who occupy similar positions in the organization advancing quickly within the organization? Did people use this position to obtain other positions outside the organization that were equivalent to a promotion?

[ ] **Sidetracked**   Do the people who occupy similar positions in the organization seem stagnant within the organization or field?

From *Career Development in Recreation, Parks, and Tourism: A Positioning Approach* by Robert B. Kauffman, 2010, Champagn, IL: Human Kinetics.

17. What knowledge, skills, abilities, and experiences are required for this position within the field or within the organization? (Review chapter 4 to help you determine the KSAEs needed for this position.)

_____

_____

_____

_____

_____

_____

Do you possess the KSAE?

KSAE 1: _____ [ ] Yes   No [ ]

KSAE 2: _____ [ ] Yes   No [ ]

KSAE 3: _____ [ ] Yes   No [ ]

KSAE 4: _____ [ ] Yes   No [ ]

KSAE 5: _____ [ ] Yes   No [ ]

KSAE 6: _____ [ ] Yes   No [ ]

Casing the People

18. Who is my supervisor? (from question 11)

    Person: _____

    Title: _____

19. Who is the person who will hire me?

    Person: _____

    Title: _____

20. Research the people. (Identify things that are special about the people listed in questions 18 and 19 as well as other key people. Consider articles published, presentations made, programs presented, awards won, common colleagues or friends.)

    Supervisor: _____

    Title: _____

    a. _____

    b. _____

    c. _____

    d. _____

    e. _____

    f. _____

From _Career Development in Recreation, Parks, and Tourism: A Positioning Approach_ by Robert B. Kauffman, 2010, Champagn, IL: Human Kinetics.

Hirer: _____

Title: _____

a. _____

b. _____

c. _____

d. _____

e. _____

f. _____

Colleague 1: _____

Title: _____

a. _____

b. _____

c. _____

d. _____

e. _____

f. _____

Colleague 2: _____

Title: _____

a. _____

b. _____

c. _____

d. _____

e. _____

f. _____

Colleague 3: _____

Title: _____

a. _____

b. _____

c. _____

d. _____

e. _____

f. _____

From *Career Development in Recreation, Parks, and Tourism: A Positioning Approach* by Robert B. Kauffman, 2010, Champagn, IL: Human Kinetics.

Positioning Yourself

21. Write your mission statement here. If you are unsure of it, write your career goal. (e.g., "To create out-door programs to help adolescents reach their potential." Avoid describing the next job you want.)

_____

_____

_____

_____

22. List here people you will contact to gain more information about the organization. (These are people who currently work in the organization, have worked in the organization, or have knowledge of what is going on within the organization. This is part of your research before contacting the key person in the organization.)

    Person 1:_____

    Person 2: _____

    Person 3: _____

    Person 4: _____

23. Based on your investigation of the organization, write a brief job description of the position you want in the organization. Is it the same as or different from the one you wrote in question 15? (This is important because it gives you a place to start.)

_____

_____

_____

_____

_____

24. Indicate whom you want to contact in the organization regarding a position, where you want to contact this person, and when you will do it.

    Who:_____

    Where: _____

    When: _____

From _Career Development in Recreation, Parks, and Tourism: A Positioning Approach_ by Robert B. Kauffman, 2010, Champagn, IL: Human Kinetics.

Introductory E-Mail

For this exercise, you will need a friend or colleague. After you have completed the worksheet in exercise 7.1, write an introductory e-mail similar to the one in figure 7.10. Give a copy of the completed worksheet to your friend or colleague, who will play the employer. This will help in the role-playing and assessment of your e-mail. You may want to review the three-paragraph e-mail format in chapter 12. Remember to integrate your research into each of the paragraphs. Once you are finished, reverse roles with your partner.

chapter 8

The One-on-One Interview

Who within the organization can hire me?

You have spent considerable effort and energy positioning yourself to meet the person you hope will hire you. As part of bridging, you may have become professionally active. The person you want to meet may be at a conference you are attending or may serve on a committee with you in your professional organization. In addition, you have applied networking principles to help position yourself. By doing all this, you have set the stage to approach the person in the organization who can hire you. The next step in the job search process is the one-on-one interview.

The term *one-on-one interview* is derived from the book *One-on-One: Win the Interview, Win the Job* (Pettus, 1981). Pettus's thesis is simple: "Nobody has ever gotten a job offer of any kind, at any salary, at any point in history without first having that one-on-one meeting known as the interview" (p. 6). Although his book was framed in the context of the traditional job search model, his point is appropriate for the positioning model as well. You won't get hired without first having an interview with someone in the organization. However, what is more intriguing about the use

of the term is that it also captures the desire of everyone who has ever searched for a job to be the only applicant applying for the position. Who would not prefer a job search in which they are not competing with anyone else for the job?

The one-on-one interview is an interview with the person you hope will hire you. Although it may be formal, more often it is an informal, casual meeting. Its purpose is to engage the person who can hire you, work with that person to design a position for you within the organization, and if possible, close the deal and receive a job offer. In this sense, the purpose of the one-on-one interview is closely linked to the seven-step sales model. And, as its name implies, you are the only job prospect.

In chapter 7, Sally Herr identified Mr. Muncheck, the executive director of the Anytown AFC, as the person she needed to contact. She e-mailed him and suggested meeting with him at the state conference. They established a time and place to meet at the conference. Now Sally will take the next step in the positioning process and meet with Mr. Muncheck in a one-on-one interview.

A TALE OF TWO MODELS

The traditional and positioning job search models are moving in opposite directions in this chapter. In the traditional model, the interview process comes toward the end of the job search process. This is because the organization has determined its employment needs, developed a job announcement that reflects those needs, and then advertised the position to attract the largest possible cadre of qualified applicants.

The traditional job search process is characterized by the terms *sort* and *select*. Applicants apply for the position. Like a large funnel, the employer sorts through the applications and narrows the pool to three to five applicants, who come in for interviews. From the employer's perspective, the interview process is a sign that the end of the search process is at hand. The employer uses the interview process to compare and contrast the semifinalists and to sort them to determine the finalists. It is a formal process in which the employer asks most of the questions. The questions are known by both the applicant and the potential employer. Each side knows what the other side will ask, and both have prepared for the questions using the countless books written on interview questions. In a variation of this process, the employer may skip directly to a mass interview of a lot of applicants. Regardless, the emphasis is still on sorting applicants and selecting the finalist. This type of interview is covered in chapter 9.

In contrast with the traditional model, in the positioning model the interview usually comes at the beginning rather than at the end of the job search process. Because you have approached the potential employer, the communication is between you and the organization. You have no competitors for the position—hence, the term *one-on-one*. From the employer's perspective, the first task is to determine your suitability. Does she like you, and can she use you? Once she has determined your suitability, she determines how she is going to employ you or make your employment happen.

In the traditional job search model, the employer develops the job description and job announcement early in the process, before meeting the job candidates. In the positioning model, the candidate and employer will often work together in the one-on-one interview to develop a mutually acceptable job description. This occurs toward the end of the process rather than toward the beginning. Because of these fundamental differences in the approaches of the two job search models, this chapter addresses the one-on-one interview and the tasks associated with it. The formal interview is covered in chapter 9.

This chapter incorporates the seven-step sales model into the one-on-one interview process. Next, it provides some background skills including a primer on dress, seating arrangements, and engaging in conversation. The chapter concludes with Sally Herr having a productive and successful one-on-one interview with Mr. Muncheck and being offered a job at the Anytown AFC.

THE SEVEN-STEP SALES MODEL AND POSITIONING

The positioning model uses the seven-step sales model. This basic sales model has been used in every aspect of sales ranging from retail sales to consulting. The model was introduced in chapter 1. Because the majority of the seven-step sales model is applicable to the one-on-one interview, the model is discussed in depth in this chapter.

The seven-step sales model has been modified and adapted to meet many types of settings and uses. The basic steps in the model are to identify your prospect, engage the decision maker, survey, design, propose, close the deal, and follow up.

1. Identify Your Prospect

Most likely you have already identified your prospect in chapter 7, Casing the Joint. This is the person in the organization who can hire you or introduce you to the person who can hire you. In addition, you may have already identified where you will meet this person. It may be at her office or at a neutral site. Sally Herr arranged to meet Mr. Muncheck at the state conference. Depending on circumstances, this phase may come quickly. You may be introduced to someone at a conference or other networking event and find yourself in the middle of a one-on-one interview.

2. Engage the Decision Maker

In the second step, you need to engage the person who can hire you. Depending on circumstances, you may need to go through other people to reach the actual decision maker. Often, you may already know the person you are contacting because you have networked with him on a previous occasion or perhaps you have previously worked for him. Even if you know the person, your first contact is usually through e-mail, a phone call, or a meeting. If you use e-mail, consider using the pointers outlined in chapter 12. Remember, your e-mail might be the first impression the decision maker has of you.

For most people using the positioning model, engaging the decision maker as part of the one-on-one interview is often their first formal contact with someone within the organization. It implies that you have done your homework regarding the organization. Although you are not expected to know everything, you are expected to know something about the organization and the job you seek. You have done this. You have cased the joint.

3. Survey

Normally, the third step in the seven-step model is to survey the organization to determine how you might be able to fit in. If you have cased the joint, you have already completed a significant portion of the survey process. During the one-on-one

Do you really want to work here?

interview, you may have the opportunity to supplement your earlier survey.

Most likely you are ready to move quickly to the design step. It is important to remember that the survey step is your opportunity to analyze the situation. In the design step, you will need to know the employer's needs. For this reason, it is extremely important that you listen to what your potential employer is saying because you need to adapt your strategy if you hope to design a proposal based on the employer's needs as well as your own.

4. Design

In the design step, you develop your job description and a job announcement in conjunction with your potential employer. Even if the employer eventually uses an off-the-shelf job description and job title and offers you the job, this step is still important because it may determine the evolution of your job. Unlike the predetermined job description used in the traditional interview described in chapter 9, the individualized job description described here reflects an effort by both you and the employer to best use your talents within the organization.

Often, in the positioning model, a formal job description doesn't exist. In the one-on-one interview, you and your potential employer can create an individualized job description that meets both of your needs. There is usually a great deal of flexibility in the process because the employer has not formally identified a position to be filled. As such, he may be willing to tailor the position to fit you. The individualized job description helps you and the employer reach a mutually beneficial conclusion.

Sally Herr's story reflects the design process. During his one-on-one interview with Sally, Mr. Muncheck decided he wanted to hire her. He considered how she could be of use to their aquatics program. Although in the end, he used the standard AFC job description to hire Sally, he added water aerobics as part of the position, a reflection of the design process.

5. Propose

In the positioning model, the job description and job announcement are the products of the design phase. Whether it is an off-the-shelf job description or your job description, it reflects the combined efforts of you and the employer to reach common ground. At this point in the process, if all has gone well, the employer offers you the position you have designed. There should be few surprises, and the process should move quickly to the next phases, closing the deal and then following up.

6. Close the deal

Because there is now a formalized job description and job offer, you should be ready to accept the proposal when offered or shortly thereafter. If there are still points of disagreement, concerns, or items to be resolved between you and the employer, they should be identified and noted by both parties. Be honest and disclose anything that might prevent you from saying *yes* and closing the deal. This is not the time to be playing the field, unless you have previously indicated this to the employer. Not closing the deal at this point may be considered an act of poor faith. If the proposal is as designed, you should be ready to move to a speedy conclusion and close the deal quickly.

It is not uncommon for this phase to occur after the meeting or interview. The employer may have the power and authority to hire you on the spot and may offer you the position during the interview. However, in most cases the employer must do some groundwork back at the office to finalize the proposal and close the deal.

In Sally Herr's example, Mr. Muncheck didn't finalize the offer until after the conference. He needed to make sure the position was feasible, and he wanted to check with Mr. Smith regarding the position. In a sense, he was buying some time. It is only natural. Also, he wanted to keep Mr. Smith in the loop and include him in the process.

7. Follow Up

Whether you close the deal during the interview or afterward, you want to follow up with the employer. Even if you are not hired, it is proper etiquette to follow up with a thank-you letter or e-mail. Some publications recommend that you write a handwritten letter. There is no question that this is a nice touch. But it's perfectly acceptable to follow up by e-mail, and Sally Herr did just that. Because she had already done all her communications by e-mail, her e-mail response in figure 8.1 is appropriate.

The process leading to her hiring occurred in several e-mails and letters. Mr. Muncheck offered her a job after June 10th in an e-mail (figure 8.2). She replied and accepted the position in an e-mail (figure 8.3). Because formal business is usually done by letter, Mr. Muncheck backtracked and indicated in an e-mail to Sally that she would be receiving a letter to that effect from him (figure 8.4). Except for some minor modifications, the letter in figure 8.5 uses the same text as the previous e-mail (figure 8.2). Sally responded with a letter accepting the position (figure 8.6).

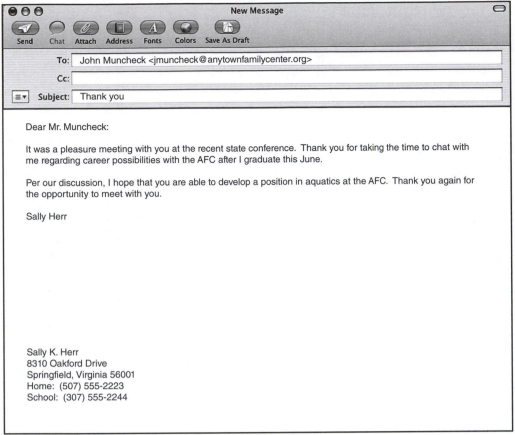

Figure 8.1   Sally's thank-you e-mail.

New Message

Send   Chat   Attach   Address   Fonts   Colors   Save As Draft

To: John Muncheck <jmuncheck@anytownfamilycenter.org>

Cc:

Subject: Thank you

Dear Mr. Muncheck:

It was a pleasure meeting with you at the recent state conference. Thank you for taking the time to chat with me regarding career possibilities with the AFC after I graduate this June.

Per our discussion, I hope that you are able to develop a position in aquatics at the AFC. Thank you again for the opportunity to meet with you.

Sally Herr

Sally K. Herr
8310 Oakford Drive
Springfield, Virginia 56001
Home: (507) 555-2223
School: (307) 555-2244

This is a simple but effective thank-you e-mail. First, Sally thanks Mr. Muncheck for the meeting. Second, she reminds him of her situation and when she will be available. At this point in the process, he will probably remember anyway. Third, she unobtrusively reminds him to follow up on the position after the conference. The importance of this point cannot be overemphasized. Fourth, as discussed, she alludes to the position and its creation.

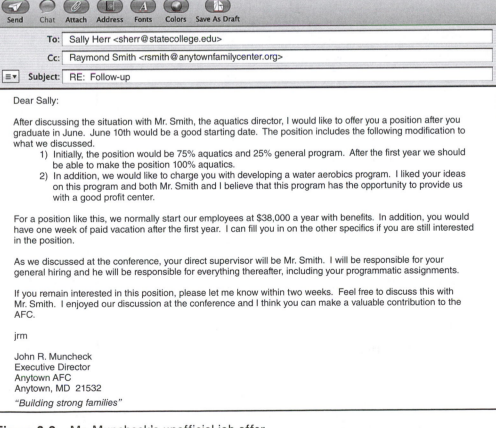

Figure 8.2   Mr. Muncheck's unofficial job offer.

New Message

Send   Chat   Attach   Address   Fonts   Colors   Save As Draft

To: Sally Herr <sherr@statecollege.edu>

Cc: Raymond Smith <rsmith@anytownfamilycenter.org>

Subject: RE: Follow-up

Dear Sally:

After discussing the situation with Mr. Smith, the aquatics director, I would like to offer you a position after you graduate in June. June 10th would be a good starting date. The position includes the following modification to what we discussed.
   1) Initially, the position would be 75% aquatics and 25% general program. After the first year we should be able to make the position 100% aquatics.
   2) In addition, we would like to charge you with developing a water aerobics program. I liked your ideas on this program and both Mr. Smith and I believe that this program has the opportunity to provide us with a good profit center.

For a position like this, we normally start our employees at $38,000 a year with benefits. In addition, you would have one week of paid vacation after the first year. I can fill you in on the other specifics if you are still interested in the position.

As we discussed at the conference, your direct supervisor will be Mr. Smith. I will be responsible for your general hiring and he will be responsible for everything thereafter, including your programmatic assignments.

If you remain interested in this position, please let me know within two weeks. Feel free to discuss this with Mr. Smith. I enjoyed our discussion at the conference and I think you can make a valuable contribution to the AFC.

jrm

John R. Muncheck
Executive Director
Anytown AFC
Anytown, MD 21532
"Building strong families"

Mr. Muncheck is offering Sally a position. He provides most of the basics she needs to know to move it to conclusion. This includes the salary, starting date, and responsibilities. In this respect, this is a fairly standard e-mail.

It is fairly clear to Sally that Mr. Muncheck wanted to iron out some internal issues before offering her a position. He wanted to check with Mr. Smith regarding how they could create the position and to include him as part of the process. This is good administration on the part of Mr. Muncheck.

Mr. Muncheck offers Sally a standard position with two modifications. The first is a shared duty, which suggests an internal accommodation that they made to create the position. The second is an accommodation of Sally's skills and interests.

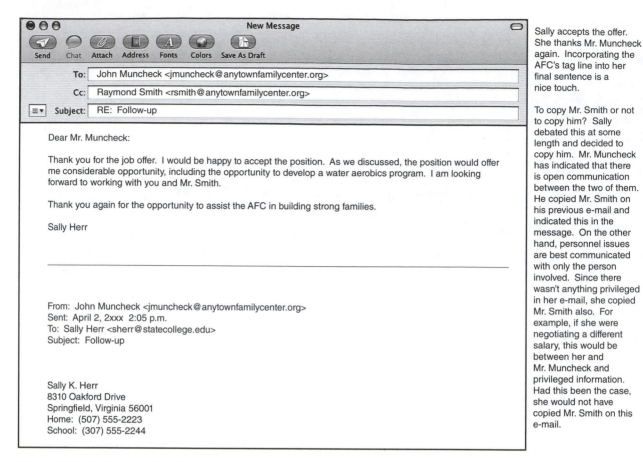

Figure 8.3   Sally's unofficial acceptance.

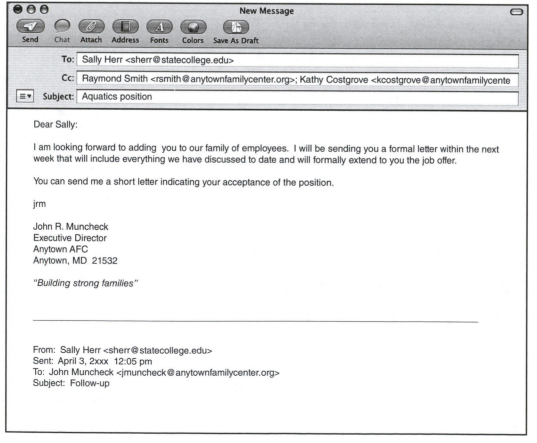

Figure 8.4   Mr. Muncheck's follow-up e-mail.

Anytown AFC

Building strong families

April 10, 2xxx

Ms. Sally Herr
8310 Oakford Drive
Springfield, VA 56001

Dear Ms. Herr:

This letter is a follow-up to my e-mail of April 2, 2xxx. After discussing the situation with Mr. Smith, the aquatics director, I would like to offer you a position after you graduate in June. June 10th would be a good starting date. I am offering you the position with the following modifications to what we discussed.

1. Initially, the position would be 75 percent aquatics and 25 percent general programs. After the first year we should be able to make the position 100 percent aquatics.

2. In addition, we would like to charge you with developing a water aerobics program. I liked your ideas on this program, and both Mr. Smith and I believe that this program has the opportunity to provide us with a good profit center.

For a position like this, we normally start our employees at $38,000 a year with benefits. In addition, you would have one week's paid vacation after the first year. I can fill you in on the other aspects if you are still interested in the position.

As we discussed at the conference, your direct supervisor will be Mr. Smith. I will be responsible for your general hiring, and he will be responsible for everything thereafter including your programmatic assignments.

If you remain interested in this position, please let me know within two weeks. Feel free to discuss this with Mr. Smith. I enjoyed our discussion at the conference, and I think you can make a valuable contribution to the Anytown AFC.

Sincerely,

John R. Muncheck

John R. Muncheck
Executive Director

cc: Raymond Smith
    Kathy Costgrove

Figure 8.5 Mr. Muncheck's official offer.

April 15, 2xxx

Mr. John R. Muncheck
Executive Director
Anytown AFC
Anytown, MD 21532

Dear Mr. Muncheck:

Thank you for the job offer. I am happy to accept the position. As we discussed, the position would offer me considerable opportunity, including the opportunity to develop a water aerobics program. I am looking forwad to working with you and Mr. Smith.

Thank you again for the opportunity to assist the AFC in building strong families.

Sincerely,

Sally K. Herr

Sally K. Herr

Figure 8.6 Sally's acceptance letter.

THE SEVEN-STEP MODEL AND THE ONE-ON-ONE INTERVIEW

In the positioning model, circumstances will dictate how many of the seven steps will actually occur during the one-on-one interview. The actual interview may cover all or just one or two of the steps. Typically, identifying the prospect and surveying are performed as part of casing the joint; closing the deal and following up occur after the actual meeting. The following two examples show the variability and flexibility of the process. In addition, the role reversal in the second example shows the robustness of the general process.

Remember from chapter 2 that Bud was a graduate student who used networking events and professional development to position himself as a camp director in Maine. He attended the American Camping Association conference with the specific purpose of networking and pursuing camp director positions. Using a bulletin board at the conference designed to link people looking for positions with those seeking to hire people, he met with Steve, the owner of a small private camp in Maine.

Bud contacted Steve at the conference, and they arranged to meet in the lobby of the hotel. Because this was their first contact, they spent some time on the survey step exploring each other's backgrounds. Bud wanted to know background information on the camp, and Steve wanted to know more about Bud's background and capabilities. As part of the survey step, they addressed many of the items listed in exercise 7.1 in chapter 7, Casing the Joint.

At some point, their conversation moved into the design phase. They discussed the role and responsibilities of the camp director including staff recruitment and supervision, programming, and maintenance. In addition, they discussed the relationship of the camp director and the owner. One item they discussed that is not normally included in a job description was a potential buyout program in which Bud would gain equity and eventual ownership of the camp.

The one-on-one interview was successful. They both knew that the final proposal would need more discussion and work. They had laid out a basic game plan. Bud would need to visit the camp, and Steve would need to conduct a background investigation to make sure Bud was the person he said he was. They would need to formalize contracts and sign them. Regardless, they were on their way to consummating and closing the deal. Eventually, they did. The process started with the one-on-one interview in which Bud was the only contender for the position. It ended with Bud becoming the camp director.

The next example, also from chapter 2, demonstrates the flexibility and variability of the one-on-one interview. Katie did her internship with the park and planning commission. Then she took a lesser position in the commission until the desired position at the new recreation center became available. In terms of the positioning model, her example demonstrates a role reversal in which Joe, Katie's supervisor, initiated many of the steps in the seven-step sales model.

As she was approaching the end of her internship, Katie had a routine meeting with her supervisor, Joe. Although the meeting started out as routine, it quickly evolved into a one-on-one interview. Joe knew that her internship was coming to an end, that she was graduating, and that she would soon be looking for a full-time job. He was impressed with her performance and the contributions she made helping to develop the new recreation center. Also, he had done some preliminary investigations with his key people regarding hiring her on a contractual basis.

Joe initiated the one-on-one interview. They quickly confirmed her current situation regarding graduation and her future. In addition, Joe confirmed Katie's desire to remain with park and planning, if the opportunity became available. Because she already worked there and had a good understanding of the commission, they were ready to move to the design step.

Quickly, Joe entered into the design step. He outlined the position he had envisioned for Katie in the commission. It was a lesser position than her qualifications suggested. However, it was a full-time position in the commission. She would gain additional experience, and she had someone in the organization to champion her so that when the job came open at the new recreation center, she was well positioned to obtain it.

Joe and Katie discussed the position and what it entailed. They even discussed her career path. They were in general agreement regarding the job and how it could help her career. If they hadn't already moved into the proposal step, they were ready to do so. Although in principle they closed the deal, they stopped short of officially doing so. Joe needed to do some more work on his end, mostly paperwork.

Katie left Joe's office with a job virtually in hand. Knowing that Katie was interested, Joe completed the paperwork and finalized the steps needed to place her in the job. Her one-on-one interview with Joe had started out as a routine meeting. It had a different twist to it because it could be argued that Joe had targeted the prospect, Katie, and then engaged her. In addition, he had done most of the work required for the survey and design phases. Nevertheless, this one-on-one interview was Katie's first big step in her career.

THE INDIVIDUALIZED JOB ANNOUNCEMENT

In the design phase of the seven-step sales model, you develop a job announcement that is suitable to both you and your potential employer. In the positioning model, a formalized job description and job announcement most likely don't exist. Remember, the positioning model is unlike the traditional model, in which the employer has already determined the job description and prepared a job announcement. For this reason you will need to develop a job description and announcement for the position. It is the logical conclusion of the process.

In some cases, the potential employer has loose requirements for the position and is essentially just looking for the right person. When she finds this person, she attempts to design the position around the abilities and interests of this person. Even in this case, a job description and announcement serve to focus the discussion on the required basics of the job.

As part of casing the joint, you developed a job description for the position you seek within the organization (question 23 in exercise 7.1). If you did it correctly, it should be fairly close to what your potential employer would write if she were conducting a traditional job search. Simply, it provides you with structure and a model for designing or modifying a position in conjunction with your potential employer. The need for the individualized job announcement is illustrated by the Bud and Katie examples. Because Bud is negotiating with the owner of the camp, his need for it is obvious. He needs the structure it provides because neither he nor the owner has developed a job announcement. Katie's need is a little less obvious because Joe has developed a position for her. Most likely, Joe is adapting an existing job description and attempting to modify it to accommodate Katie's abilities. Regardless, the individualized job announcement provides her with a focus in her discussions with Joe.

Figure 8.7 lists the items normally included in a job announcement. Support resources and evaluation were added (they are not traditionally included in a job announcement) because they may be important to your success in your new job.

• **Job description.** A job description lists the responsibilities and duties of the job. Job descrip-

tions obtained over the Internet or from other sources can provide models on what to include. More important, you should use the KSAEs that you determined from analyzing job announcements and from your response to question 17 in exercise 7.1 to formulate your job description. Simply list the KSAEs, or, if you like, write a paragraph that incorporates your KSAEs as you did in that exercise.

• **General responsibilities.** General responsibilities include your job duties. Your response to questions 15 and 23 will help you list your duties. Often, the employer is plugging you into an existing position or is adapting an existing position to accommodate you.

• **Supervisor.** Who is your supervisor? Question 18 in exercise 7.1 provides an initial answer to this question. As you conduct your one-on-one interview with your potential employer, you may need to update your findings based on additional information you receive.

• **Salary/compensation.** Most people don't like to discuss what they earn. However, even if you are reluctant to discuss salary and benefits as part of the one-on-one interview, you will need to determine your salary and any benefits associated with the position at some point in the process.

• **Support resources.** To perform your job, you need support resources. The question is whether you will provide these yourself or whether the organization will provide them for you. Office

---

Job description

General and specific responsibilities of the position

Supervisor

Salary/compensation

Support resources: office, computer, Internet access, administrative assistance, etc.

Evaluation, promotion opportunities

Beginning date

Termination date (if applicable)

Figure 8.7 Individualized job announcement.

space, telephone, and administrative support are usually provided by the organization. Although a cell phone, computer, specialized computer programs, and travel funds are usually provided by the organization, you may find that you are expected to provide these items yourself, particularly if you want an upgrade of any of these items. If you want any special items to help you work more efficiently, the general rule is to negotiate for them as part of the initial negotiations process. If you wait until after you are hired, you are less likely to obtain them.

• **Evaluation and promotion.** Unless there is something unique that you need to negotiate as part of your employment, evaluation usually becomes a concern after you are employed. Regardless, your future in the organization is determined, in part, by how your employer evaluates you. The same is true of advancement and promotion. For this reason, it is never too early to begin thinking about evaluation. During your interview, you may want to ask about how the employer evaluates performance, as well as typical career paths for people in similar positions to yours.

• **Beginning and ending dates.** You will need to determine when you will begin work and, if applicable, when the position ends. Often, contractual positions, temporary positions, consulting positions, and internships have ending dates.

DRESSING FOR SUCCESS

People will make judgments about you within a minute of meeting you based largely on how you dress. Historically, dress has been associated with social class and status, but today, people are often free to dress however they choose—including dressing in a fashion that is above their actual station in life. This is a common practice among people applying for jobs. How you dress is extremely important to how you present yourself during your one-on-one interview, formal interview, or meeting with your potential employer. This section provides some guidance on dressing for these situations. This section looks at the effect of the setting on how you dress, and on dress considerations (style).

Formal Dress

Some meetings with potential employers require that you dress well. In such situations, men should wear conservatively cut suits and ties, and women should also wear conservative business attire. Both men and women should avoid excessive jewelry and overly dramatic hairstyles. Generally, darker-colored clothes command more authority than lighter colors. Black commands the most authority.

Business Casual

The business casual style used in many workplaces can serve you in a variety of settings including many one-on-one interview situations. If you were a man meeting Mr. Muncheck in the hotel lobby rather than Sally Herr, business casual would probably be your choice of dress, as it was for Sally.

Sally decided to dress conservatively and slightly more formally than would normally be required by the situation. This is a planned rather than a casual meeting even though it will occur in an informal setting. She selected a navy blue blazer, white blouse, and beige skirt along with pumps.

Suggestions on What to Wear

What you wear depends on the setting in which you are meeting the potential employer. This is more of an issue for the one-on-one interview than the traditional interview. Because the traditional interview is more formal, it's almost always appropriate to dress formally for it. Formal dress might also be appropriate for a one-on-one interview if you are meeting the potential employer at the workplace. However, formal dress would most likely be out of place at a professional conference where everyone dresses casually. Katie's one-on-one interview at park and planning started as part of a routine meeting with her supervisor, Joe. Because her normal dress was casual, she dressed casually for her meeting.

The first general rule, or suggestion, for dressing to meet a potential employer is: It is better to overdress than to underdress. If you can, dress so you can shed articles (for example, a suit coat or tie) to dress down if the situation is less formal than you expected.

The second rule is: Dress equal to or slightly better than the person with whom you are meeting. You need to think about not only where you will be meeting, but whom you will be meeting and why. For example, if you are meeting at a professional conference, you know that most people will be dressed casually, so it's a safe guess that you would be overdressed in a suit. Also, it would depend on the circumstances under which you meet the potential employer. If you are anticipating a casual meeting with the employer, dress slightly better than others at the event—for example, if people at the event will be dressed casually, you can dress business casual.

Sally Herr's meeting with Mr. Muncheck was very different from a casual meeting with someone in which the discussion evolves into examining job options. They are meeting in the lobby of the hotel for the express purpose of discussing job opportunities. Because of the elevated formality of the circumstances, her dress should be more formal than casual.

It is your responsibility to assess the situation and select the appropriate dress, and the overdressing rule of thumb will never fail you in this regard. For example, when we were interviewing candidates for the presidency of our institution, the search committee concluded that the appropriate dress for the formal interview process was business casual for both the search committee and candidates. In retrospect, this dress code was more applicable for the search committee. If a candidate had shown up for the interview in a sports coat and open shirt (no tie), there is little doubt that, even though the committee had indicated otherwise, the more casual dress would have reflected negatively on the candidate. It was the responsibility of the candidate to appropriately assess the interview setting and select the correct dress, even if told otherwise. Again, when in doubt, dress for the situation, even if the potential employer suggests otherwise. You can always dress down at the interview if necessary.

The third rule for dressing for an interview is: If in doubt, ask about the appropriate dress. Then, follow the second rule and dress equal to or slightly better than what was indicated. Normally, you will have enough concerns about the interview, and you don't want to worry about how to dress. In a sense, it takes this element off the table because you have agreed on the way to dress.

SEATING ARRANGEMENTS

When meeting with someone, you generally want to select a seat that facilitates conversing. Four potential seating arrangements are shown in figure 8.8; note the tone or atmosphere that each arrangement tends to promote. Sitting at a right angle or at a near right angle tends to facilitate conversing. This enables you to chat with the other person, and you can both survey anyone walking by. In the cooperative arrangement, the chairs can be slightly tilted toward each other, which makes it easy to talk. This seating arrangement can work on a large couch on which people sit with a slight angle toward each other. As a general rule, if given a choice, choose a cooperative seating arrangement.

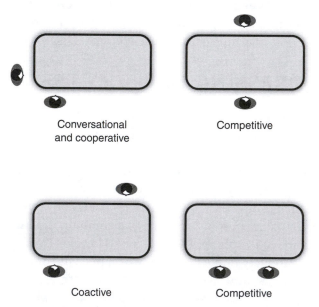

Figure 8.8 Different seating arrangements tend to promote different conversational dynamics.

Reprinted, by permission, from T. O'Connell and B. Cuthbertson, 2008, *Group dynamics in recreation and leisure: Creating conscious groups through an experiential approach* (Champaign, IL: Human Kinetics), 121.

STARTING THE CONVERSATION

Sometimes starting the conversation is the hardest part of the interview. The following points, which are adapted from Roberts' discussion of the seven steps of the sales model (2007), will help you to engage the potential employer in your one-on-one interview. Start with a smile, introduce yourself, and set the scene with the purpose of your interview. As with any meeting between two people, the opening may include small talk about family, mutual contacts, or the weather.

- **Smile and be relaxed.** Draw confidence from the fact that you are well prepared. You know a lot about the organization. As an outsider, you may even have a fresh perspective and even a vision of their needs that they have not yet considered. However, more important, the one-on-one interview is more of a discussion and conversation. It isn't the one-sided interview associated with the traditional model, which is presented in chapter 9.

- **Introduce yourself.** Introduce yourself to the potential employer and state your business. This is a courtesy to the other person. *Hello, I'm _____. I would like to explore an [internship, job position] with you today.* Even though the potential employer may know this from your efforts to set up the meeting, it is still appropriate to begin with your name and the purpose of the meeting.

- **Set the scene.** In addition to explaining the purpose of your interview, you want to quickly begin to infuse information about the organization into the conversation. Because it is important to meet your potential employer's needs, focus on what is important to the employer and the organization. *My review of the Internet reveals that your program is exemplary. I would like to explore [doing my internship, working] with your organization.* Flattery is good. However, be prepared for the follow-up question from the employer asking you why you think the program is exemplary. Rattle off a quick list of items from your research, and you will be quickly into the next step in which you are surveying your and the employer's needs.

- **Ask how much time you have.** This is a courtesy and helps you avoid an abrupt termination of the interview or unsettling body language as your potential employer begins looking at his watch, signaling that time is running short. Also, it lets you know the amount of time you have to move the one-on-one interview through as many of the sales steps that you and your potential employer deem appropriate.

- Depending on the relationship with your potential employer, or if you know that you have limited time, you may want to consider addressing the time issue earlier in the process. You may even want to address it when setting up the meeting.

- **Use skillful small talk.** Small talk is the icebreaker. It includes the trivial niceties about the family, mutual acquaintances, and the weather that people use to initiate any meeting, particularly if they haven't seen each other for a period of time. Small talk doesn't directly advance the purpose of your one-on-one interview, but it establishes a relationship with the other person through common experiences. Be sure that you spend some time on these niceties, but not too much. It is your responsibility to sense when you need to move on to the task at hand.

PUTTING IT ALL TOGETHER

The one-on-one interview is the culmination of the positioning model. It incorporates several or all of the steps in the seven-step sales model. Unlike the interview in the traditional model, the interview in the positioning model normally comes toward the beginning of the process, not at the end. Also, unlike the traditional model, which emphasizes sorting candidates and selecting a finalist, you are the only person who has applied for the job. The one-on-one interview reflects a paradigm shift to the positioning model from the traditional model.

The one-on-one interview is the culmination of an extensive amount of work and research on your part to position yourself for your next job. You have examined job descriptions to determine the knowledge, skills, abilities, and experiences that you need and developed a bridge to this job by acquiring those KSAEs. You have cased the joint. Then, using the one-on-one interview, you have approached the organization and engineered, with the cooperation of those in the organization, the job you are seeking.

Sally has successfully positioned herself for her job with the Anytown AFC. With the assistance of others, she determined the job she wanted and the KSAEs she needed, cased the joint, and then determined how to meet Mr. Muncheck, the person who could hire her. Then, using a variation of the seven-step sales model, she successfully completed a one-on-one interview with Mr. Muncheck. Together, they engineered an aquatics position that would benefit both the Anytown AFC and Sally. They sealed the deal shortly after the one-on-one meeting. She has the job she sought. Congratulations are in order for her.

Chapter 9 returns to the traditional model and provides tips and tricks for the traditional interview process. The two models complement each other. Although the positioning model will assist you in many situations, you may still be subject to the interview process associated with the traditional model. Chapter 9 provides a primer for this type of interview.

REFERENCES

Pettus, T. (1981). *One on One: Win the Interview, Win the Job.* New York: Random House.

Roberts, J. (2007). Seven steps of the sales process. *RTO Online.* Retrieved from www.rtotradeshow.com/content/Contributor/Jay_Roberts/SevenStepsIn theSalesProcess.asp.

Exercise 8.1

Seating Arrangements

In this exercise you will examine how people seat themselves in public settings. Go to a place where people congregate and interact with each other (e.g., a cafeteria, the student lounge, or even the library). From a safe distance observe people's behavior. Note where people sit at tables and whether they are conversing, competing, or co-acting (sitting in close proximity but not interacting) with each other. You may want to copy the following form.

1. Diagram the seating arrangement. Note where the people are sitting in relationship to each other.

2. Person 1: [　] Male　　[　] Female

   Person 2: [　] Male　　[　] Female

3. Describe the behavior of people you observe.

   Are they conversing? [　] Yes　　[　] No

   Explain:

   _____

   _____

   _____

   _____

   _____

Are they competing? [　] Yes　　[　] No

Explain:

_____

_____

_____

_____

_____

Are they co-acting? [　] Yes　　[　] No

Explain:

_____

_____

_____

_____

_____

The Good Listener

Think of someone in your organization or group whom you consider to be a good listener. Describe what this person does to make him or her an effective listener. Is there anything this person does that you should be doing?

_____

_____

_____

_____

_____

_____

_____

Exercise 8.3

Perfecting Your Greeting and Introduction

In this exercise you will perfect your greeting and introduction with others. Your objective is to get your introduction down to a science so it is natural and flawless. For best results, video record this exercise.

For this exercise, one person takes the role of the employer and the other person takes the role of the job hunter. It is a quick exercise, so repeat it until your greeting and introduction are smooth.

During this exercise, avoid critiquing nuances in behavior. Consider keying in on some of the following points: Do you make good eye contact? What kind of handshake do you give? How is your posture? Look for smoothness from the handshake to the verbal greeting, and consider eye contact. Your objective is to create an introduction that you can execute flawlessly without much thought about what you are doing.

Exercise 8.4

Writing Your Individualized Job Announcement

Write a job announcement for the next job you want. Focus on the job description and job responsibilities sections. List here your items for each of these sections. Next, indicate whether there are any major differences between what you seek and what the employer is likely to offer. Consider using the job announcements you found on the Internet in the previous chapters (exercise 2.5). Also, consider using the information you found in exercise 7.1 regarding casing the joint. You have already identified the job description and the chain of command, including your potential supervisor.

Individualized Job Announcement

1. Job description (Review questions 15 and 23 on the Casing the Joint Worksheet, exercise 7.1. You may want to insert it here if it hasn't changed.):

_____

_____

_____

_____

_____

_____

_____

2. General and specific responsibilities of the position:

_____

_____

_____

_____

_____

_____

_____

3. Supervisor:

_____

4. Salary/compensation:

_____

_____

_____

_____

5. Support resources, including office space, computers, Internet access, administrative assistance:

_____

_____

_____

_____

6. Evaluation and promotion opportunities:

_____

_____

_____

_____

7. Beginning date: _____

8. Termination date (if applicable) : _____

Employer's Perspective

1. Examine your individualized job announcement from the perspective of your potential employer. If the employer has a stock job description, write it here:

_____

_____

_____

_____

_____

_____

_____

2. Compare and contrast your job announcement with the employer's and note any changes you should make in yours.

_____

_____

_____

_____

_____

_____

_____

The Formal Interview

How should I prepare for a traditional interview?

This chapter focuses on the interviewing process associated with traditional interviews and the types of questions you will be asked during the interview. It complements the discussion of the one-on-one interview in chapter 8. Even if you have positioned yourself, you may still be subjected to the traditional interview process. This may be because the employer is required to conduct a formal search, or because you may apply for a job that you see advertised through traditional channels. Topics covered in this chapter include tips on face-to-face interviews, the types of questions you might encounter, phone interviews, and inappropriate and illegal questions.

STRATEGIES

The three general strategies discussed in this section can help you with the formal interview process. The first is to be yourself. This strategy focuses on things you should do as part of your interview including being conversational and avoiding monologues. The second strategy is to talk to your talking points or, more accurately, your KSAEs and how they meet the KSAEs required by the job. The third strategy, the reversal, involves taking control of the situation in the interview, especially turning a weakness into a strength. The discussions of these

strategies in the following sections also include suggestions and strategies for addressing specific questions during the interview.

Take most of the suggestions and strategies on how to answer the questions as simple suggestions. Don't overanalyze your responses. Second-guessing your responses can adversely affect your performance. If the interviewer analyzes your answer in terms of psychological ramifications, there is not much you can do about it. On the other hand, he could be asking the question because he simply wants to know something about you. Or, perhaps he was asked this question when he was hired, and he thought it was a good question.

Most interview questions and their responses are scripted. It may become clear to you as you read through this section that the formal interview is like a minuet with the employer, in which each partner in the dance knows what the other partner is going to do. The classic example of this is the question, *What are your weaknesses?* The employer asks you this question knowing that in your response you will most likely note an inconsequential weakness, or show how you turned a minor weakness into a strength. To answer otherwise could reflect badly on you. Not following the expected script is like stepping on your partner's feet. It is important to know the

A TALE OF TWO MODELS

The traditional job search process is a funneling process in which the employer starts with a large number of applicants and narrows the list down to one finalist, who is offered the job. The formal interview is a step used in the process to eliminate candidates. In addition, the traditional model tends to be more formal than the positioning model. The employer asks most of the questions, which the candidate can anticipate if he has done his homework. Each side is relatively prepared for what the other side will do. This chapter minimizes the surprises you might encounter in a traditional, formal interview.

In contrast, the one-on-one interview in the positioning model (discussed in chapter 8) has a different focus because it normally occurs at the beginning rather than at the end of the job search. Because the interview is one-on-one between you and the employer, it tends to be less formal and more conversational. Because of the fundamental differences between the two interview types, the same question asked in a traditional interview may have an entirely different context and purpose in a one-on-one interview. For example, in the traditional job search model, the question *What training or qualifications do you have for this job?* helps the employer sort through the applicants to determine who best meets the job requirements listed on the job announcement. In the positioning model, the employer might ask a variation of this question to assess your knowledge, skills, abilities, and experiences (KSAEs) to determine where she might use your talents within the organization.

script so that you can do the dance well in the formal interview.

Being Yourself

Generally, trying to be someone or something you aren't will be obvious to those interviewing you. This section offers some points to help you be natural in a formal interview. You need to be positive, practice active listening, avoid monologues, focus on what you can do for the employer, and try to keep your personal life out of the conversation.

Always be positive during the interview. Whatever you say should move the agenda forward in a positive fashion. Remember, if you speak ill of someone not present, the interviewer may wonder what you might say about her later behind her back. This is true even if you already work there and are going through the formal interview process to obtain the job you already have. Save your shop talk for after the interview, and always be positive.

The first few seconds set the tone of the interview. A lot of evidence suggests that people formulate an opinion of you within the first few moments of meeting you. Make eye contact, stand erect, smile, shake hands if applicable, stand up as people enter the room, and sit down after they sit down.

Practice active listening. When asked a question, pause for a moment. Slow yourself down and counteract the effects of the initial surge of adrenaline. Try counting mentally (e.g., *one thousand and one, one thousand and two*) before giving your answer. Make eye contact with the person asking the question. Then make eye contact with one or two other people if it is a group interview. Smile. Feel relaxed. Collect your thoughts. Now give your response.

When answering questions, try to avoid lengthy monologues. Give clear and succinct answers. If your interviewer asks a question that requires a monologue, make one or two of the most important points. The interviewer can always ask a follow-up question if she wants more. The following is a good example: *Tell me briefly about your career history and how it has prepared you for this position.* Often, this is the first request you will receive. Ten minutes into a detailed chronology of your career history, someone on the search committee may realize the mistake and cut the monologue short so he can ask questions during the 45-minute interview. If asked this question, discuss your last job or perhaps your last two jobs and how they prepared you for this position. A good alternative is to discuss the job that has best prepared you for this position. You should consider doing this even if the interviewer doesn't ask the question this way.

Focus on what you can do for the employer. What you have done is all well and good, but in the end it is all about what you can do for this organization. There is nothing wrong with telling the interviewers about the KSAEs you have. If that is all you do, though, then you may fall short. The question is, How can you convert what you have done to assist your potential employer? *As part of my last position, we did this [insert the type of] special event.* This is what you have done. Now you can say: *I know that you have done a similar type of special event.* This becomes your transitional statement for your next statement, what you can do for them. *Have you considered doing this as part of what you are doing?* Not only are you addressing what you can do for the organization, but you are also making the interview more conversational because you are getting the interviewers to respond.

Try to keep your personal life out of the discussion. Remember to focus on the job and on job performance. Avoid a slip of the tongue that could imply the wrong conclusion about you, such as, *That was a wild party.* Or, *I was able to apply what I learned from the 12-step program to my work environment.* Both of these responses suggest something about your personal life. The second question invites the obvious follow-up question regarding whether you or someone you were close to was in the 12-step program.

Talking to Your Talking Points

Talking points help you to focus your comments and to deliver a coherent, succinct, and consistent message. The first approach in talking to your talking points is to determine your strengths and then speak to them. Assume that you determine the following strengths as your talking points:

1. I am creative, innovative, and able to follow through on implementing my ideas in the workplace.
2. I have perseverance.
3. I work well with other people.
4. I am a good director of my organization.

During the interview, the interviewer says, *Tell me about your greatest success.* You respond by telling her about a program that you developed (*creative and innovative*). You note how you worked your proposal through the bureaucracy (*perseverance*) and how you *worked successfully with other people* to implement the program. By implementing the program, you imply that you are a *good director.* If the interviewer asks, *What has prepared you for this job?* you can answer by talking directly to point 4, that you are a good director.

A second approach to using talking points is to review the job description and list the KSAEs required for the position. Condense this list to four or five of the most important items. Use these as your talking points. For example, if you want to be a CEO of a YMCA. you need the following:

1. A bachelor's degree
2. YMCA Senior Director status
3. Financial and budget experience
4. A demonstrated ability to raise funds
5. An ability to develop membership
6. Community relationships
7. Program development experience
8. Previous CEO experience

The first two and last items (items 1, 2, and 8) don't lend themselves to talking points. Either you have a bachelor's degree, Senior Director status, and previous CEO experience or you don't. The remaining KSAEs form your talking points. When someone on the search committee says, *Tell me briefly about your career history and what led you to apply for this position,* you can discuss your last position as a YMCA CEO, emphasizing your accomplishments by noting that you *increased membership* by 20 percent (point 5), *increased* United Way and external *fund-raising* by 15 percent (point 4), and balanced the *budget* and created a fund to buy new equipment every three years (point 3). In talking about who you are and what you have done, you have emphasized why you are a good candidate for the job. You have talked directly to the KSAEs needed for the job.

Using a Reversal

Wrestlers sometimes use a technique called a reversal. Your opponent is dominating. He has you facedown on the mat and is moving toward a pin and winning the match. You make a move that reverses the situation. Now you are in the dominant position over your opponent. His face is now in the mat, and he may face potential pinning. You have turned, or reversed, a potential loss and disaster into a winning situation.

In the interview process, a reversal is about turning a weakness into a strength. It turns a gotcha question into something you did well. *What are your weaknesses?* This and its many variations are designed to trap you with self-incrimination. The classic approach is to turn or reverse a weakness into a strength. It is a good approach too. For example, you may respond as follows: *In high school, I had poor writing skills. After considerable work and assistance, I overcame my weakness, and as evidenced by my numerous articles, I eventually turned this weakness into what most of my colleagues consider a strength.*

An alternative approach to answering this question is to trivialize your response. Pick something benign and present it as your weakness. For example, you love chocolate, you have a sweet tooth, or you like a good cup of coffee in the morning. Who doesn't? Although the reversal is generally a better approach, most interviewers are so used to the trivial response that they won't blink twice if you use this technique. Regardless, be careful that your response is really trivial and that you don't inadvertently fall into one of the traps of the three-doors situation discussed later in this chapter, in which you duck the question or offer something that diminishes the interviewer's view of you.

TYPICAL QUESTIONS

The first group of questions discussed are of a general type and are normally asked of most interviewees. Interviewers use these questions to find out who you are and how you might fit into the organization. Other questions are more procedural and help move the interview process forward.

Career History

Often, the interviewer will begin the interview with the following question or a variation of it: *Tell me briefly about your career history and what led you to apply for this position.* It is a good opening question. It serves as an icebreaker. It is also an easy question to answer. It provides a brief background for those who are interviewing you and have not thoroughly read and examined your application package. Brevity is important; do not give your life history.

This question lends itself to a lengthy answer that can easily extend for 8 to 10 minutes. Be disciplined even if the interviewers aren't. Select your two most recent jobs and explain how they led you to apply for this position, or select the two most significant positions that you had in terms of preparing you for this job. Your focus should be on why you are prepared for this job, and implicit in your answer is why you are the best candidate for the job. This is the correct way to answer this question even if the interviewers didn't specifically ask you to say how your history has prepared you to work for them.

Training and Qualifications

The question, *What training/qualifications do you have for this job?* helps the interviewers find out more about who you are and what you have done. In addition, it indirectly focuses on your qualifications for the job.

Brevity is important; do not give your life history.

Try a talking points response. You have cased the joint and you know what KSAEs are required for the position. Rattle off a couple of your KSAEs that directly relate to the qualifications required for the job. Key to answering this question is your knowledge of the KSAEs required for the job, and your ability to meet them.

Why You Want to Work There

Interviewers will often ask, *Why do you want to work here?* Because you have cased the joint, this should be an easy question to answer. To enliven your answer, imagine the interviewers have asked, *What excites you about this job?* You should be excited about the job, and you should be able to rattle off two or three things that excite you about this job. Again, be succinct.

When answering this question, focus on what you can do for the organization. People answering this question tend to emphasize what they want rather than what they can do for the organization. Many will explain how this job will advance their career. To avoid answering this way, consider this response: *The job announcement lists that you are looking for an individual with the following qualifications [list some of them here]. I believe that my training, education, and professional experiences have prepared me well for this next step in my career, your position.* Even though the focus is on your development, you have linked what you are doing to the qualifications they are seeking.

When answering the question of why you want to work for the organization, emphasize motivation factors and avoid hygiene factors. In general, hygiene factors focus less on what you are going to do in your job and more on the work conditions, hours, comp time, and salary. Poor work conditions, salary, and hours lead to job dissatisfaction. However, good work conditions, salary, and hours don't result in job satisfaction. In contrast, the programs you create are a motivational factor and tend to lead to job satisfaction. The following responses are typical of hygiene factors:

- The job is close to home.
- The salary is good.
- I need the job.
- The hours are good.

If you were the employer, would you hire someone who gave these as her primary reasons for wanting to work for you? Probably not. In contrast, focus on what the business community calls motivation factors, which tend to facilitate job satisfaction. The following responses address motivation factors:

- I like to create programs for people.
- I really enjoy working with this clientele.
- I like recreational programming.
- I want to work for a leader in the field.

Finally, when addressing why you want to work for the organization, emphasize its strong points:

- Your organization is one of the premier organizations in the country.
- Your firm is a leader in the field.
- I want to be part of an organization that is innovative, creative, and highly productive [choose relevant adjectives], and that offers me the opportunity to contribute to its growth.

Your Ideal Job

Your answer to the request to describe your ideal job can reveal a lot about who you are and what you plan to do. Following are some things the interviewers can glean from your response to this question:

- Your career goal.
- How ambitious you are. They may be able to imply from your answer whether you are upwardly mobile or focused more on hygiene factors (e.g., salary, work conditions, time off, or living close to home.
- Whether you are focused on your long-term career development or simply your next job. Neither response is necessarily incorrect.
- Whether you have set realistic goals for yourself. The emphasis here is on *realistic*. A corollary of this is whether the job you seek is a logical step in your career path or you are merely seeking a lateral move.
- Whether you want to work with people or things, and whether you focus on service to others or your accomplishments.

As we said earlier in this chapter, don't overanalyze the possible conclusions the interviewers may derive from this question. Second-guessing yourself will detract from your response. Remember, they may simply be interested in knowing your future goals and not much else. When focusing on your ideal job, you should be realistic in terms of who you are, your skill set, and the position you are seeking. Be honest.

If you want to interject some humor into the interview, tell the interviewers that your ideal job is the one you are applying for. If they decide to question you further, try a response that incorporates your talking points. *The job announcement indicates that you are looking for an individual with the following qualifications [list some of them here]. I believe that my training, education, and professional experiences have prepared me well for this next step in my career, your position.*

A variation of the ideal job question is, *What is the best job you have had?* This question attempts to focus on what you want to do in the future by looking at your past. The safe route is to choose your current or a recent job and focus on how that job has prepared you for the position for which you are applying. Choose attributes of that job that are similar to those of the one for you are applying for, and emphasize their importance to both jobs.

I had a young colleague who said that his best job and also his ideal job was one he had in graduate school. Think for a moment about what this statement says to his current employer or to a future employer. Would you want to hire this person as part of your team? Probably not. This person is living in the past and is implying that anything he does in the future will be less than what he has already done.

Consider this variation of the ideal job question: *What would you like to be doing five years from now?* The obvious answer is that you will be happily employed with them. This is not an unrealistic answer because in many jobs you spend the first two years learning the job and then you implement your new programs during the next three or four years. After five or six years, many think that it is time to move on to a promotion or different job.

Relocation and Travel

Questions of relocation and travel are staple interview questions. *Would you relocate if necessary?* This is really a question about your knowledge of the job requirements, and it seeks to determine whether you are willing to perform the job. If you have properly cased the joint, you should already have a pretty good idea of the job requirements. If the job requires travel, are you willing to travel? If it requires you to work evenings and weekends, are you willing to do so?

Your response to this question is simple. It is a *yes* said convincingly. Saying *no* indicates that you are not willing to do the job and will invariably disqualify you from consideration. Furthermore, you should not have applied for the position in the first place knowing that this was a job requirement. Your research of the organization and the position should have revealed that it requires possible relocation, travel, or working evening and weekends.

For some questions, there really should be no surprises from either party.

Occasionally, an employer will throw you a left curve. Once, I went through an entire interview in which the interviewers made no mention of the graduate coordinator position included in the position. It wasn't listed on the job announcement, either. I was just about ready to leave for the airport when they asked me if I would be willing to be the graduate coordinator. My pregnant pause was not so much an indication that I wouldn't do it, because I would have, but rather, a reaction to their waiting until the end of the interview to spring this totally new job responsibility on me.

Surprises on this question and its variations are generally not a good idea for either party. Interviewers ask this question to make sure that you understand the requirements of the job and that you are willing to perform the job as required.

Length of Service

As in marriage, the norm is "till death do us part!" Like marriage, the perception among many employers is that you will stay with their organization forever. Unfortunately, the divorce statistics suggest otherwise. Also, because most employers don't like doing job searches, they have in the backs of their minds that they don't want to go through the search process again anytime soon. Knowing this, there are several ways to approach the question *How long will you stay with the organization?*

Suggesting a time period toward the upper end of what the employer considers acceptable is generally considered safe. This is based on the history, norm, or responsibilities of the position. For example, many occupations are revolving doors, and everyone knows it. Often, social workers and Boy Scout executives progress through a predictable life cycle in terms of their length of service. They enter the profession idealistic and wanting to help people. They become frustrated because their ability to help others is limited or because of the time demands of the job. After about four to six years, many suffer burnout and leave the profession.

Be realistic when you answer this question (e.g., six years). Suggesting too short or too long a time period may be viewed as unrealistic or perhaps suggest that you don't understand job mobility within your field.

Ask the interviewers what they consider a normal length of time for a new employee to stay with the organization. This will help you negotiate the discussion of what you both consider an acceptable length of employment. You may also want to be prepared by researching beforehand how long people tend to stay in similar positions in other organizations.

On the one hand, if the employer hires you, he has an investment in you. On the other hand, you have a career path to follow. Also, if you stay too long in the job, your productivity will plateau. Most employees spend their first year learning the job and their second year starting to make changes. If you leave after your second year, the employer won't obtain a reasonable return on his investment in you. During years 3 through 5, you tend to be highly productive. If you indicate that you will not leave until after five years, the employer gets an acceptable return on his investment.

The following question is a variation that often has direct implications on how long you will stay with the organization, particularly if you are a new college graduate: *Do you have plans to continue your studies?* Most employers will initially focus on whether you will leave their organization in pursuit of a degree full-time. But, the question suggests other important attributes about you. Do you seek to improve yourself? Are you a lifelong learner? Do you know what you need for your credentialing, and are you going to obtain it? Are you reasonably ambitious and upwardly mobile? Do you know how to advance your career and bridge yourself to the next level? A follow-up question on your part is, *Do you pay for or reimburse employees for continuing their studies?* Again, your response should be reasonable in terms of your career path and job requirements.

Strengths

The question, *What are your strengths?* and its variations are a staple in the formal interview. You should be able to quickly list several of your strengths. Be sure to tailor your answer toward the KSAEs required for the job and listed in the job description. You should know the KSAEs for the job from having cased the joint and reviewed the job announcement. Also, remember that your strengths and KSAEs can form the basis of your talking points.

Recreational Activities

Sometimes a seemingly insignificant question can reveal a lot about you. This is the case with the question, *What is your favorite recreational activity, and how has it affected your career?* Your response to this question can give a trained interviewer valuable insight into who you are. Are you a workaholic, or do you have balance in your life? Do you indicate that you are a loner because you take walks by yourself? Perhaps you suggest that you are a joiner because you volunteer your time, or a team player because you play team sports? Are you competitive? If so, how much? Do you seek active recreation (e.g., walks in the park or sports) or more passive recreation (e.g., watching TV or movies)?

Why They Should Hire You

Toward the end of the interview, interviewers often ask you why you think they should hire you (or a variation of this question). This question gives you a chance to summarize your skills and sell yourself. This should be an easy question to answer. You have already answered its component parts. It merges your response regarding your training and qualifications and your motivation. In addition, it relates to your response about your ideal job. If the question comes toward the end of the interview, view your answer as a summative statement of your qualifications. You may be asked one of the following variations:

• What can you do for us?

• If you were a member of this search committee and were asked to summarize why we should hire you, what would you say?

Consider a two-part response to this question. In the first part briefly review your KSAEs in terms of the most important ones listed in the job description. Two or three KSAEs should suffice. This part of your response addresses what you know and what you have done. In addition, it indicates that your skill set matches that necessary for the job. Remember, they have reviewed your resume and you probably have already addressed your KSAEs in the interview, so be brief and don't belabor the points. Your intention is to make the connection in their minds between your skill set and their job requirements.

Next, you want to address why you want this job. It is not enough to be qualified; you have to want it also. This is your chance to sell yourself. Focus on what excites you about this job. If you do this, your body language will also communicate your excitement about the job to the interviewers. Practice your response to this question beforehand, so you can hit a home run when asked in the interview.

References

Increasingly, employers are contacting references rather than relying on letters of recommendation. Written letters of recommendation are generally considered of little value because no one is going to write negative comments about someone else in this age of litigation. How to present your list of references is covered in chapter 10. The issue for you at this time is whether the interviewers can contact your references.

Many people list references at their current place of employment, and they don't want anyone there knowing that they are applying for another position. If there are any references you don't want contacted, you should indicate this to the potential employer during the interview. Usually, people are reluctant to have the search committee contact their current place of employment. One solution to this problem is to negotiate at what point in the search the employer can contact your references. If you become one of three or four finalists, you should be sufficiently into the process to feel comfortable about their contacting any sensitive references. You could also grant them permission if you are a finalist. An alternative is to offer additional references who are not at your current place of employment.

Your Questions

At some point in the interview you will probably be asked if you have any questions of your own. You can use the questions identified in exercise

7.1. Compared to the one-on-one interview in the positioning model, the traditional interview usually allocates less time for your questions. Because you may have only 5 or 10 minutes at most to ask one or two questions, you should be prepared.

Most publications suggest that you ask a cogent question that indicates your knowledge of the organization during this phase of the interview. In fact, not asking a question often reflects negatively on your candidacy. There is a good reason for asking a question. It shows your interest in the organization. Figure 9.1 has a list of questions you might ask, unless, of course, all the questions have been addressed. In that case, you need to know how not to ask a question in such a way as to reflect positively on your candidacy.

If at the end of the interview you feel that all your questions have been answered, you will want to avoid asking a question without it reflecting negatively on your candidacy. Consider the following situation. The face-to-face interview is near the end of its allotted time. The interviewers have answered most of your questions during this interview and other meetings you have had. They ask you if you have any questions. Try rattling off a couple of the items listed in figure 9.1 as the basis of your response. This suggests competence on your part. You don't need to list all the factors, just enough to display your knowledge. Also, it shows discretion. You can then compliment your interviewers on their thoroughness, explaining that they have covered all of the issues associated with the job. With this response, you have avoided having to

- Are there trends affecting your organization that we haven't discussed?
- What do you see as the major challenges or problems facing your organization?
- What do you see as the major growth areas for your organization?
- Of which major professional organizations are you a member, and which of these would you recommend that I join to help advance the organization?
- Where is the next annual or regional conference? Do you attend?
- Are you planning any new products or services in the future?
- Are you planning to extend your services to any new clientele?
- Is there anything else that I need to know about how the company is organized?
- What do you consider to be the major strength of the organization?
- What do you think is the biggest weakness of the organization?
- What types of things would you expect me to be doing within the organization five years from now?
- What is the projected career path over the next five years for someone in this position?
- Are there any other skills and experiences you would like the person you hire for this position to have?
- Who is the supervisor for this position?
- I realize that in the interview process you can't always meet everyone you need to meet. If I am hired, is there anyone else in your organization who I should meet and get to know?

Figure 9.1 By the time your interview draws to a close, you'll want answers to these questions.

ask a question. Try a variation of the following response:

> *I am not sure that I need to ask any questions. You have addressed the major challenges facing your organization. I have a good idea how the program is growing in the next several years. We discussed the strengths of your program. We discussed typical career paths, and I have a good idea of what a new employee needs to do to advance within the organization. Although I could go on, in reviewing my checklist, we have done a good job covering all aspects of the job, the organization, and job requirements.*

Such a response accomplishes three things. First, you indicate that you have a good grasp of all of the aspects of the position. Second, you compliment the interviewers on doing a good job of covering all the aspects of the position that you need to know about. Flattering the interviewers is a good thing. Third, you just created a win–win situation in which both you and the interviewers look good, and you did it without asking them a question.

QUESTIONS FOR RECENT GRADUATES

If you are just graduating from college, you are in a unique position compared to people who have been in the job market for a while. Although you may not have the job experience other candidates have, you can sell yourself by focusing on other experiences that have prepared you for the job you want.

What Are Your Greatest Accomplishments?

In general, there are two ways to approach this question: by addressing work-related accomplishments or by addressing personal accomplishments. Work-related accomplishments are preferred. Normally, if you did something that really stands out, by all means use the example. However, consider picking work-related accomplishments that relate directly or indirectly to the job for which you are applying. You know what the KSAE requirements are for the job. Select a program or event that relates directly or indirectly to one or more of the KSAEs.

Your answer to this question may suggest certain things about you to the interviewer. For example, do your accomplishments center around people, things, or achievements? Contrast the following accomplishments in terms of what they imply about the person saying them:

- My greatest accomplishment was helping a colleague achieve his lifetime goal.
- My greatest accomplishment was earning $100,000 last year.
- My greatest accomplishment was being selected as the commencement speaker based on my academic and professional accomplishments.

The first emphasizes people, the second emphasizes materialism, and the third emphasizes awards and achievement. If your greatest accomplishment was being selected as the commencement speaker because of your academic accomplishments, you might want to consider a follow-up response in which you emphasize how you helped others or implemented a program.

Next, be careful to suggest that your greatest accomplishments are still in front of you and not behind you. Do you think the organization wants to hire a has-been or someone in the twilight of her career? Using the service award example, you can easily tweak this toward the future by suggesting that you hope to do the same for them.

Although a work-related accomplishment is generally preferred, personal achievements tell a lot about who you are, what you have done, and your level of motivation.

- I hiked the Appalachian Trail from Maine to Georgia.
- I helped to build my parents' house.
- I was the first person in our family to graduate from college.

Each of these examples reveals goal achievement, perseverance, overcoming obstacles, and seeking new tasks, particularly if you follow it with a short story about what you did.

For recent graduates, a variation of the accomplishment question is *What honors did you earn?* If you haven't earned any honors, list your significant accomplishments. Obviously, use accomplishments that are close to honors, if possible. Another accomplishment question is *Which school activities did you participate in?* Again, focus on activities that have resulted in accomplishments, and state your accomplishments.

Who Had the Greatest Influence on You?

Everyone who has been successful has had a mentor at some point in his or her career. Other people provide an important source of learning. When asked about a person who had the greatest influence on you, mention a person who influenced you or acted as a mentor. As a rule, choose one person and provide a brief reason. You might choose a teacher, supervisor, or parent. If you have worked for a while, you can use a former boss or supervisor who served as a mentor. You could say, *My professor taught me a lot about this field*, or, *I learned a lot about management from my former supervisor.*

TRANSITION QUESTIONS

Transition questions focus on why you are leaving your job or why you have left previous jobs. For students graduating from school, the answer to this type of question is self-evident and usually poses few problems. In this discussion, we will start with the worst-case scenario, being fired, and work backward.

You could be asked this question in an interview: *Were you ever fired or forced to resign?* The more moderate version of this question is *Why are you leaving your current job?* Before discounting this discussion as not applying to you, ask yourself if there is a job listed on your resume that you had for a year or less or one you left on less than good terms? This question and its more mild variation are important questions for any job

hunter to address. The interviewers might ask, *Why are you planning to leave your current position?* Or, perhaps *I see on your resume that you worked for this organization for only one year. Did you leave on good terms?* This question is even more subtle: *This job looks like a lateral move. Was it, and if so, why?* All of these questions are designed to ascertain whether you have left a job on less than ideal circumstances.

One reason for leaving a job is that the job had a natural conclusion. You finished your internship. It was a part-time job. Perhaps it was a summer job as a camp counselor. Or maybe it was a contractual position in which you filled in for another person on leave. All of these terminations are easily explained and easily understood by the interviewer.

A second reason to leave a job is that the new job is in essence a promotion or a logical next step in your career path. This is usually self-evident in terms of the job title listed on the resume. An assistant camp director who becomes a camp director suggests a promotion and the logical next step in a career path. This new position is easily explained to and understood by the interviewer.

A third reason to leave your current job is that you were fired or asked to resign. Or, perhaps you made a lateral move because you had a conflict with your supervisor, or you faced a hostile work environment and needed to leave for self-preservation. In both of these cases, you left your job on less than a satisfactory basis. If you have faced this type of situation, there are two things you should do: avoid speaking ill of your previous employer, and move the conversation to a more positive issue as soon as you can.

Whatever you do, do not speak ill of your previous employer. If you do, the interviewer will conclude that you will speak ill of him too if a similar situation occurs. Conversely, by acknowledging that a problem existed and by not speaking ill of the previous employer, the interviewer will conclude that you are discreet. This is a good thing. At some point, everyone has hard times or a bad employer. This is a natural occurrence, and most employers understand. Try one of the following replies: *We had a difference of opinion*, or, *It was a hostile work environment,* or, *They did some unethical things.* The interviewer may want to probe into why you had a difference of opinion or why it was a hostile work environment. Who wouldn't want to know more? Whatever you do, go no further. To do so will potentially speak ill of you. You have acknowledged that you were fired, terminated, or left on less than satisfactory terms. That is all the interviewer needs to know. To say more is to suggest that you may not be discreet. By not saying more, you avoid breaking the unwritten rule of not speaking ill of your previous employer.

Your next task is to move the conversation quickly into your reversal and explain what you learned and why this experience makes you the person to hire. Your task with the reversal is to turn this insurmountable negative into a positive. What did you learn? Why are you a better person and a better employee as a result? How has this incident motivated you to succeed? Has it given you a sense of humility? Do you have a sense of proportion in your life regarding the importance of work and what you do? Often, people who have had some misfortune make better employees because they understand who they are, what they want to do, how to get there, and that everyone is fallible. Think of what you learned and why this adversity has made you a better person. Emphasize these attributes and how they prepared you for this job. Many people go through their careers and never face this type of adversity. It can be a positive for you if you approach it correctly.

GOTCHA QUESTIONS

A gotcha question is any type of question designed to put you on the spot. For example, *What are your weaknesses?* is a mild gotcha question. The three-doors question and *Have you ever been fired or forced to resign?* are both gotcha questions. A reversal works well with gotcha questions, helping you turn a negative into a positive. In some cases, you can provide a trivial response. For example, if you respond to the weakness question by saying that you talk a lot on the phone or chew gum, you trivialize your response. However, be careful that you don't enter door 1 or 3 in the three-doors question described in the next section.

Weaknesses

This question, and its variations, is a classic gotcha question and your typical response is to use a good reversal. The following response to the weakness question uses a reversal to turn a weakness into a strength. Also, the further the weakness is in the past, the less relevant it is. *In high school, I had a concern about my writing ability. However, I concentrated on writing articles and other documents, and now most of my colleagues consider writing ability a strength of mine.*

Controversial Issues

Your interviewers may ask you what you think about a controversial issue. They might ask you what you think about a political figure, a new policy, or any controversial issue. A variation of this question is to ask you a question about an issue that on the surface may not seem controversial, but is. The interviewers are trying to determine more about you, your beliefs, and your political opinions. This question is often asked at a social event associated with the interview process rather than during the formal interview. Try to avoid answering this type of

Spinning negatives into positives is an important skill in interviewing.

question directly, but don't flatly refuse. Saying, *I am not going to answer this question* would be too confrontational. By deftly sidestepping the question, you suggest to the interviewers that you are discreet and will focus on the job and not extraneous issues once you are hired.

Try speaking over the issue without supporting one side or the other. With this approach, you merely acknowledge what is already known, that there is an issue and that it is significant. The following response to the immigration issue suggests that it is an important issue and that it is significant to the future of the country, and it does so without taking sides: *Immigration is an important issue facing the country today. It is hard to say which side is correct. However, I think that we can all agree that it will significantly influence the country's future.*

Another approach is to gently direct, or nudge, the conversation back to the job and its requirements. *As much as I would like to comment on this issue, I would suggest that the issue is to determine my ability to objectively perform the criteria as outlined in the job description.* This approach can be used with the previous response if the interviewers persist after you have talked over the issue.

Your Best Work

Interviewers sometimes ask a question like this: *Have you done the best work you are capable of?* Even if you have done your best work in the past, who would ever admit it? Doing so is a form of interview suicide. Usually, this question is not much of a problem for young professionals just out of college. Their careers are still rising. However, this question becomes more of an issue the longer you have been in the workforce, the longer you remain in your existing job, and as you begin to approach retirement age.

The best response to this question is to look toward the future. Do a reversal. Pick something the organization is doing that really excites you, and tell the interviewers why you want to be part of it. *One of the reasons I am interested in this job is your excellent youth program. I am interested in being a part of this program.* This response suggests that your best work is still in front of

you. Or, suggest something that you might do for them. *I noted on the Web site that you have an outreach program. Have you considered trying [insert a new idea]?* Again, the focus is on what you can do for them and on the future. That is always where you want to be in terms of your responses.

Management Style

Interviewers may ask, *What is your management style?* or ask you to provide examples that illustrate your management style. This is one of those questions that can have multiple layers of analysis depending on the background of the people asking the question. If you are a younger job hunter who has not yet been a manager yourself, the interviewer may ask, *What type of management style do you prefer from your supervisor or boss? Why?* Your answer to this question will reveal your fit within the organization.

One approach suggests that there are four functions of a manager: *planning, organizing, directing,* and *controlling.* These functions are relatively easy to remember and can serve as a good basis for your answer whether you are a manager and indicating how you manage or analyzing the management style you prefer.

- *Planning* involves trying to anticipate the future, setting goals for performance, and identifying what needs to be done within the organization.

- *Organizing* involves the manager's ability to bring resources together to produce goods or services. These resources include people, funds, materials, facilities, and whatever else is needed.

- *Directing* refers to managing employee efforts to bring together the resources to produce the goods and services. *Hands-on, delegation, micromanaging,* and *task-* and *relationship-oriented behavior* are terms associated with how the manager directs the employees.

- *Controlling* involves the evaluation and feedback process to determine whether the goods and services are being produced as desired.

The following passage suggests how you can use the four management functions to craft a response to the question of what management style you prefer from your supervisor or boss.

I like a manager who anticipates what we need to do and sets realistic goals for me and our unit [planning]. I like a manager who provides me with good directions so that I am on task when doing my job [directing]. Also, I like a manager who provides the necessary resources for us to do our jobs [organizing]. Last, I like a manager who lets me know when I am doing things correctly, and when I'm not, tells me in an appropriate way [controlling].

THREE-DOORS QUESTIONS

Some questions require that you choose carefully how to respond. The name of this type of question is a takeoff on the old parable in which you must choose one of three doors; one door leads to life and the other two doors lead to death. In this context, if you choose door 1 to answer the question, you are disqualified for the job because you indicate by your answer that you don't have the experience; you lack the

necessary competence. Door 3 disqualifies you because, although your answer indicates that you have the experience, you reveal something about yourself that has the interviewers shaking their heads in disbelief. Door 2 suggests that you have the experience and competence, and that you handled the situation well.

Consider an outdoor leadership position that requires candidates to lead groups of 10 to 12 students on backcountry trips. Candidates are asked this question: *What was the worst accident you ever had? What caused it, and what did you do to rectify the situation?* Behind door 1 is the answer that you never had an incident. This suggests that you have no experience or perhaps, worse, that you are lying. It is a given that anyone who has extensive backcountry leadership experience will have encountered some type of incident or mishap in his or her career.

The third door leads to disaster also. In this case you describe an incident that sounds horrific to the interviewers. Unfortunately, the incident acts like a boomerang that circles back and suggests that your unsafe acts directly contributed to the accident. The interviewers begin to shake their heads in disbelief. Rhetorically, they ask themselves, Who would want to hire this person?

Behind the second door lies your correct answer. However, there are potential pitfalls here also. There are two parts here that you need to address. The first is what led to the situation, and the second is what you did to correct it. Choose a situation and solution that won't boomerang back on you and reflect negatively on your conduct. Remember, if you don't answer with some type of accident, you are back to door 1. In this case, a good incident to use is one that wasn't foreseeable. For example, describe a situation in which someone became ill through no fault of yours, and then describe how that person was evacuated from the backcountry.

When answering three-doors questions, you want to do three things. First, you want to avoid door 1, which suggests that you don't have the necessary minimum competency or expe-

Choose the right door.

rience. Next, you want to avoid door 3, which suggests that you screwed up. Third, you want to choose door 2. Door 2 requires you to select a response that is reasonable in terms of the position for which you are applying and doesn't reflect negatively on you. In addition, you need to describe how you resolved the situation. On the surface, the three-doors type of question seems complicated. However, once you are able to identify it, you should be able to address it easily.

The three-doors question is actually a very common question. *Describe a critical management problem you had, and what you did to solve it.* Substitute *personnel, budget, safety,* or *marketing* for *management problem;* the question remains essentially the same. Here are some other examples: *Describe something you did wrong. What was its impact and outcome? What kind of decisions do you find most difficult to make?* If you haven't handled a management problem, done something incorrectly, or made a difficult decision, you are liable to open door 1, revealing that you don't have the minimum experience or competencies. At the other end, your response may suggest that you screwed up so badly that, again, your competence is called into question. In this case, you cite a management problem that, had you been a good manager, would never have happened. Remember, anyone who has performed a job has had to solve problems. However, a good manager puts out brush fires, not forest fires. Choose examples that open door 2. Your examples should be reasonable in terms of your responsibilities. They should be discreet or appropriate, and they shouldn't boomerang back on you negatively.

If you are applying for a position that requires some type of decision making, you can expect this version of a three-doors question: *What kind of decisions are the most difficult for you?* Behind door 1, you admit that you don't make any difficult decisions. Behind door 3, you admit that you participated in a situation that was so severe that it calls into question the decision you made, even if it was a decent one. Choose door 2. However, remember that it, too, is not without peril. Personnel, financial, or programming decisions are always difficult. Consider your response to this type of question before the interview, and select an example that is somewhat benign in its implications.

INAPPROPRIATE OR ILLEGAL QUESTIONS

As noted in this chapter, the traditional employment process is designed to sort and select applicants. It is an elimination process that requires the employer to discriminate among candidates. The question is how. In general, questions that are protected by the law and that don't relate to the KSAEs listed in the job description are inappropriate or illegal questions. These include questions about family and gender, age, religious orientation, or national origin. The following are several illegal or inappropriate questions about religion or national orientation that you may encounter: *What is your religion? Where or when were you born?*

Generally, questions about family and children are inappropriate. In addition, they have no relationship to your job performance. *Do you have any children? Do you plan to have any children?* This type of question can occur quite subtly. The employer may say casually, *We have really excellent schools.* Your reply may reveal whether you have children. Asking you where your spouse works may reveal whether you are married and is therefore inappropriate. Asking before you are hired whom they should notify in case of emergency is another way to get information about your marriage status.

As a rule, the employer is not allowed to ask you these questions. However, you may initiate the question. If you ask the interviewer about the schools, the question is not inappropriate, and she can respond. If you volunteer that you have children and have need for day care services, the interviewer can respond.

The interviewers may ask you illegal or inappropriate questions out of innocence or ignorance, or knowingly. The issue for you is how to handle the question. Essentially, you have three options. First, you can answer the question. For example, if you are asked a question about your family or children, you might say, *I have two children who are the love of my life. They make me happy to go to work each day.* You might consider just the first sentence. The second sentence may sound as if they are your motivation for working rather than the work itself.

Next, you can refuse to answer the question. You might say, *Are you aware that this may be an inappropriate question?* or, *I believe this may be considered an inappropriate question.* Most interviewers will pick up on the fact that they may have stepped out of bounds and move on to a different line of questioning.

If the interviewers persist with the question, you can simply indicate that it is an inappropriate question and that it is inappropriate for you to answer it. Try to be tactful and nonconfrontational. However, if they persist, this may not be possible and you run the risk of being confrontational and losing your chance at the job. You have the option at this point of acquiescing and simply answering the question. In a sense, you are back to your first option.

If the interviewers are smart and want to discriminate against you based on race, religion, family status, or some other inappropriate factor, they will usually be more subtle about it. They will not call attention to the issue because to do so would flag a lawsuit. Instead, they will find some legitimate criteria to use to discriminate against you. For example, they may rank your experiences lower than others to simply eliminate you from the pool of applicants.

PHONE INTERVIEWS

Increasingly, employers are moving toward phone interviews as part of their job search process. Usually, they use them to screen applicants before inviting several finalists on site for formal interviews.

The phone interview offers employers several advantages. It reduces their travel costs because conference calls are relatively inexpensive. In an increasingly global economy, people are applying from across the country for all types of jobs. Employers can spread a wider net in an attempt to find the best candidate for the job. They can interview more people at this step than they would otherwise in an on-site interview, and they can do it fairly inexpensively. Also, rather than bring in three or even four finalists, they can sometimes cut the list of finalists for the on-site interview down to two. Sometimes they may even decide to bring in only one candidate as the finalist.

Following are some suggestions to help you prepare for the phone interview.

Review Interview Strategies

Before your interview, consider dressing as if you were actually doing an on-site face-to-face interview. The first few seconds of the conversa-

Prepare yourself for a phone interview the same way you would for an on-site interview.

tion set the tone for the interview. Be relaxed, happy, and comfortable. Always give positive responses that speak positively of others and that are positive in tone. Do your homework and know everything there is about the organization. Avoid monologues, listen actively to what the interviewers say, be conversational without getting too personal about yourself, and tell them what you can do for them. As with a face-to-face interview, be sure to follow up after the interview with a thank-you letter.

Avoid Using a Speaker Phone or Cell Phone

You want to sound the best you can in a phone interview. It may not be your fault if you don't sound natural or your voice seems distant over a speaker phone, but it can still affect the interviewer's impression of you. The same is true of a cell phone that is losing signal and begins to break up. The result is that the interviewers are making their decision based on extraneous factors rather than on your competence and qualifications. Be prudent and use a land line if one is available. If all you have is a cell phone, make sure that the battery is fully charged, that you have good reception, and that it has a good quality sound.

Expect the Same Questions

Expect your phone interview to include many of the same questions you would encounter in a face-to-face interview. *Why do you want to work here? What are your strengths and weaknesses?* It is the format that has changed, not the questions. Review the earlier discussions of questions to prepare yourself for a phone interview.

Expect a Different Format

As familiar as people are with using the telephone, they may find telephone interviews awkward because they don't do them on a regular basis. Voice counts for everything. Inflection, mood, attitude, and body language are all inferred from your voice and what you say. For this reason, phone interviews tend to be less conversational than face-to-face interviews.

Attend to Time Issues

Normally, the interviewer will call you on the phone. Your watch and theirs may not be synchronized. They may call a minute or two before or after the designated time. A busy signal or an unanswered call is not a good way to start the telephone interview, so be prepared to begin the interview 5 to 10 minutes before the appointed time. Most people are understanding regarding the difficulties associated with making a predetermined connection on the phone. If they call back immediately after receiving a busy signal and get ahold of you, most people will write it off as an unfortunate inconvenience. Nevertheless, try not to make them wait.

A common problem you may have with phone interviews results from differences in time zones. Generally, you will know if there is a time zone difference, but if you aren't sure, ask. Note the differences in your correspondence or conversations with the potential employer. A common practice is to mention the time zone as part of your correspondence. *I will expect your call at 9:00 a.m. Eastern Time.* Also, remember that 9:00 a.m. is an early-morning interview on the East Coast. However, for someone on the West Coast, it is an extra-early 6:00 a.m. interview. Most people will accommodate you and reschedule the meeting for a more convenient time.

Eliminate Distractions

A radio playing in the background is a distraction during a phone interview. Typing on your computer keyboard can usually be heard over the phone and suggests that you are not concentrating on the conversation. Chewing gum influences your speech and is usually a distraction. Obviously, eating on the phone is a distraction. If you have a cup of coffee, indicate this to your interviewers: *Good morning. I am sitting here with my morning cup of coffee, ready for your questions.* You can use the coffee cup as a prop to help you during the interview. Your statement serves as an icebreaker in the conversation and provides some levity. Also, it serves as a reminder to everyone that the phone interview is a different interview format. Your morning coffee can also give you a pause in the conversation that allows you time to collect your thoughts before answering. *That is an excellent question. Let me take a sip of my coffee before answering.* It provides some brevity and, like an icebreaker, it personalizes you. Also, your comment lets them know that you are sipping your coffee. Remember, they are not there to see this for themselves.

Listen, Speak, Listen, Speak, and Be Succinct

In a phone interview, only one person can speak effectively at a time. The format encourages you to listen to the question and then to respond. It is very easy for people to speak over others, particularly if the interviewers are a group. Often, the interviewers will compensate for this and let you speak until you are finished. If you ramble, they will generally not interrupt you. Because you are not in the room, they may even be making comments on the side along with accompanying facial expressions. For this reason you need to give shorter answers and be even more succinct than you would in a face-to-face interview. A face-to-face interview tends to be more conversational, whereas a phone interview can easily tend toward a monologue. Be succinct.

Use Notes If You Want

Because you are not in the room with the interviewers during a phone interview, you are free to have notes in front of you. Write down your talking points and any key points you want to make in response to the questions you might be asked. List one or two points that you want to make in response to each of the questions in this chapter. Spread your notes on the table in front of you where you can quickly glance at them when answering questions and avoid turning any pages. If you rustle papers, the interviewer will hear it over the phone and become suspicious of what you are doing. If they ask you if you are using notes, by all means indicate that you are. Turn it into a positive. Respond that you know you need to be

succinct in your answers because of the nature of telephone interviews. Ask them how well you are doing. You should be doing well because you have prepared yourself.

FOLLOWING UP

After you have completed your interview, remember to send a follow-up letter to the interviewers. This includes formal interviews as well as phone interviews. It is always good etiquette to send a thank-you letter. Because most organizations list their personnel on their Web sites, this information is usually easy to obtain. A formal letter is fine, as is an e-mail, particularly if you have been having a lot of e-mail communications with the person. Try a handwritten card to each of the interviewers. Consider including something that is unique to each person. This gives them something to remember you by, it personalizes you and the interview, and it is simply a nice touch.

PUTTING IT ALL TOGETHER

Although the structure of the formal interview is one of sorting through the candidates, eliminating them, and selecting a finalist, remember that the interviewers are human. They want to know who you are, what you know, and whether you are someone with whom they would enjoy working. There are only so many questions they can ask you. If you spend five minutes on each of the questions presented in this chapter, you have already easily filled an hour interview. Be honest and reasonable in your answers. And, by all means, know why you want to work for the organization. If you don't know why you want to work there, and if you aren't excited about the job, what you say in the interview probably won't matter. Conversely, if you know why you want to work there and what excites you about the job, the interview will probably fall into place and go smoothly.

Mock Interview

This is the traditional mock interview. It can be either a one-person or small-group interview. Everyone will need to agree on the job description prior to the exercise. Generally, choose a job that is agreeable to the job hunter. You can use sample questions discussed in this chapter—insert those that the interviewers plan to ask on the following evaluation sheet. The group may need to meet prior to the interview and agree on the questions they will ask during the interview. The job hunter should not know the questions they will ask.

	Impressive	Good	OK	Poor	Score
Question 1:	4	3	2	1	
Notes on 1:					
Question 2:	4	3	2	1	
Notes on 2:					
Question 3:	4	3	2	1	
Notes on 3:					

(continued)

From *Career Development in Recreation, Parks, and Tourism: A Positioning Approach* by Robert B. Kauffman, 2010, Champagn, IL: Human Kinetics.

	Impressive	Good	OK	Poor	Score
Question 4: _____ _____ _____	4	3	2	1	
Notes on 4: _____ _____ _____					
Question 5: _____ _____ _____	4	3	2	1	
Notes on 5: _____ _____ _____					
Question 6: _____ _____ _____	4	3	2	1	
Notes on 6: _____ _____ _____					
Question 7: _____ _____ _____	4	3	2	1	
Notes on 7: _____ _____ _____					

From *Career Development in Recreation, Parks, and Tourism: A Positioning Approach* by Robert B. Kauffman, 2010, Champagn, IL: Human Kinetics.

	Impressive	Good	OK	Poor	Score
Question 8: _____ _____ _____	4	3	2	1	
Notes on 8: _____ _____ _____					
				Total Score:	

Post Interview

Evaluate the interviewee on the following questions.

1. Did the candidate answer the questions?

_____

_____

_____

_____

2. Characterize the candidate's conversation. Was it animated, bland, monotone?

_____

_____

_____

_____

3. Reflect on the candidate's body language. Describe it. Did the person seem friendly? Personable? Aloof? Distant? Were there any good or bad mannerisms in the person's speech or in what the person said? How was the diction?

_____

_____

_____

_____

After the exercise the interviewee can reflect on the formal notes of the interviewers. Is there congruence or incongruence between them? In addition, the interviewers should discuss among themselves what they learned from the interview process.

From *Career Development in Recreation, Parks, and Tourism: A Positioning Approach* by Robert B. Kauffman, 2010, Champagn, IL: Human Kinetics.

Mock Phone Interview

This is essentially the same exercise as the previous one except it is a phone interview. You will need two offices or rooms with telephones. They don't need to be next to each other. At the designated time, conduct a phone interview for a position that both parties have agreed on prior to the exercise. Generally, choose a job that is agreeable to the job hunter. Use a speaker phone on the employer's side. As in exercise 9.1, you can use sample questions discussed in this chapter, inserting the ones the interviewers plan to ask on the following evaluation sheet. The group may need to meet prior to the interview to agree on the questions they will ask during the interview. The job hunter should not know the questions they will ask.

	Impressive	Good	OK	Poor	Score
Question 1: _____ _____ _____	4	3	2	1	
Notes on 1: _____ _____ _____					
Question 2: _____ _____ _____	4	3	2	1	
Notes on 2: _____ _____ _____					
Question 3: _____ _____ _____	4	3	2	1	
Notes on 3: _____ _____ _____					

From *Career Development in Recreation, Parks, and Tourism: A Positioning Approach* by Robert B. Kauffman, 2010, Champagn, IL: Human Kinetics.

	Impressive	Good	OK	Poor	Score
Question 4:	4	3	2	1	
Notes on 4:					
Question 5:	4	3	2	1	
Notes on 5:					
Question 6:	4	3	2	1	
Notes on 6:					
Question 7:	4	3	2	1	
Notes on 7:					

(continued)

From *Career Development in Recreation, Parks, and Tourism: A Positioning Approach* by Robert B. Kauffman, 2010, Champagn, IL: Human Kinetics.

	Impressive	Good	OK	Poor	Score
Question 8: _____ _____ _____ _____	4	3	2	1	
Notes on 8: _____ _____ _____ _____					
				Total Score:	

Post Interview

Evaluate the interviewee on the following questions.

1. Did the candidate answer the questions?

_____

_____

_____

_____

2. Characterize the candidate's conversation. Was it animated, bland, monotone?

_____

_____

_____

_____

3. Reflect on the candidate's manner. Did the person seem friendly? Personable? Aloof? Distant? Were there any good or bad mannerism in the person's speech or in what the person said? How was the diction?

_____

_____

_____

_____

After the exercise, the interviewee can reflect on the formal notes of the interviewers. Is there congruence or incongruence between them? In addition, the interviewers should discuss among themselves what they learned from the interview process.

From *Career Development in Recreation, Parks, and Tourism: A Positioning Approach* by Robert B. Kauffman, 2010, Champagn, IL: Human Kinetics.

Exercise 9.3

Talking to Your Talking Points

Develop four or five talking points on your strengths. Pick several of the questions in this chapter and answer them using your talking points.

Question 1: _____

_____

_____

_____

_____

Question 2: _____

_____

_____

_____

_____

Question 3: _____

_____

_____

_____

_____

Question 4: _____

_____

_____

_____

_____

Question 5: _____

_____

_____

_____

_____

chapter 10

You and Your Resume

Does my resume reflect who I am?

Before reading this chapter, consider completing exercise 10.1 at the end of the chapter. In exercise 10.1 you assess the resumes used in this chapter to determine what you like and what you don't. It will provide a good starting point regarding your preferences. Also, it will be interesting to see if any of your opinions regarding resume construction change after reading this chapter.

In the traditional job search model, the resume is usually the first thing the employer sees in your application package. She hasn't met you yet, and she has not yet invited you for an interview. This is all she knows about you. For this reason, essentially, you are your resume. Therefore, you need a dynamite resume. In the positioning model, the resume generally comes later in the job search process after the one-on-one interview in which the employer meets you and formulates an opinion of you. Its use is more supplemental to the process, or you might use it as part of the one-on-one interview to help stimulate conversation alone or as part of your portfolio. Because it may only be needed later in the job search process, the resume is of less importance in the positioning model than in the traditional model. Even though a resume may not be as important in the positioning model, you still want it to be dynamite.

In your arsenal of communication tools the resume is still one of the most important tools.

Although it may have a lesser role in the positioning model than in the traditional model, it is still important. This chapter provides helpful tips for constructing your resume. In addition, it presents several design principles to help you present your resume as an art form.

DESIGN PRINCIPLES

This section addresses both traditional and new design principles. By addressing these principles in the construction of your resume, you will be able to create a resume that communicates what you have to offer while also reflecting your unique characteristics. When you have completed your resume, you can evaluate it by asking questions based on these design principles. Is your resume designed as a sales instrument? Does it focus on your future? If you placed it on the wall next to a picture of yourself, would it be a good representation of you? In addition, many of these principles can also be applied equally well to your other communication tools including your portfolio, business card, and even e-mails.

Selling Yourself

The traditional purpose of your resume is to sell yourself to the potential employer. View your resume as a one- or two-page sales instrument.

A TALE OF TWO MODELS

The resume typifies the differences between the traditional and positioning model. Most publications emphasize the need for a "bulletproof" resume. Why? In the traditional model, the resume is an employer's first impression of you. To the employer, it *is* you. This amplifies its importance.

In the traditional job search, the resume takes on mythical importance. If there is a misspelled word, the employer might conclude that you aren't thorough. If there isn't enough white space, they might get the impression that you are unorganized. If they haven't met you, the adage that you are your resume is a truism.

In contrast, in the positioning model, the resume is less important. It is given to the employer later in the process, if at all. Usually, e-mail communications and the one-on-one interview are your first encounter with the employer in the positioning model. By the time the employer views your resume you have already developed a dialogue, and the employer may already have formed an impression of you.

Does this mean that the resume is not important in the positioning model? No, it just isn't as important as it is in the traditional job search. It is another tool in your job search.

Everything that you place in this limited space should put you in a better light or sell you better to the potential employer. As a general rule, you should consider everything you include in your resume through this prism. For example, you may wonder whether you should include references on your resume. Ask the question, Does including a list of references sell you better to the person reviewing your resume, or could you use the space better with something else? The issue is not merely about presenting references, but about whether they will enhance your resume as a sales instrument. Review the section on endorsements later in this chapter. Because space on your resume is limited, a quote from your references on your capabilities may be a better use of this space.

Focusing on Your Future

Most people write their resumes or portfolios with a focus on the past. However, as a sales instrument, your focus should be on the future and your next job. Rather than reporting what you have done, your resume should tell the potential employer what you can do for him. For this reason, you should tailor your resume to address specific jobs and clientele.

Separating Yourself From Others

The questions that you need to address are What makes you special and separates you from everyone else? Did you increase sales? Did you receive a commendation? Did you increase productivity? Did you do something new? Your resume should communicate what makes you special and different from everyone else.

Drawing a Word Picture

Whether you use bulleted items or paragraph descriptions, choose your words carefully when you describe yourself. Don't assume that the reader understands what you have done. For example, compare the following two bulleted items that depict your skills:

- Demonstrated excellent leadership skills.
- Supervised five lifeguards as an assistant pool manager.

Which one depicts the skills you have? Most people like some specifics with the word pictures that you draw of yourself.

Paying Attention to Form

The sample resumes in this chapter all use the same content—it's the *presentation* of that content that differs from resume to resume. Exercise 10.1 at the end of this chapter lets you decide this principle for yourself. If you rate the resumes differently in terms of acceptability, you will agree that form does count.

Making a Good First Impression

The first impression of the person who reviews your resume influences how that person views your candidacy. Practice the five-second rule. Glance at your resume for five seconds; then look away. What do you remember? List these items. Do these items suggest good things such as skills, honors, or accomplishments, or do you remember a bunch of meaningless dates? Does your first glance suggest that you are a winner?

Collectively, the information presented says a lot about who you are and your motivation. Conversely, misspelled words, poor structure, excessive use of the word *I*, or poor grammar can reflect negatively on you.

Being Selective About What to Include

Your resume is not a job application that requires you to list everything about your past employment. If you had a lousy job, you don't need to list it on your resume. If you have experiences that supersede earlier experiences, you need not include the earlier experiences. After students obtain their first full-time job, they often delete many of the part-time and volunteer positions they had in college, which they used to obtain their first full-time job. Two or three years of full-time employment supersedes these part-time and volunteer experiences. For example, after Sally Herr has been employed as an aquatics director, she can delete the substitute teacher and recreation assistant experiences from her resume because they are no longer necessary.

Keeping It to One or Two Pages

Some experts suggest that a one-page resume is more effective than a two-page resume. Others favor a two-page resume over a one-page resume. Take your choice. Either format is acceptable. The two-page resume gives you more room to present

You get only one chance to make a first impression.

your knowledge, skills, abilities, and experiences (KSAEs). Some human resources personnel who review job applications prefer one-page resumes because they are easier to critique. Again, the choice is yours. When you develop your resume, if you find it gravitating to a page and a half in length, either cut it down to one page or expand it to two pages. Don't have an overstuffed one-page resume that should really be a two-page resume (see resume 10.6 on page 191). Conversely, be careful not to have a two-page resume that should have obviously been a one-page resume.

REVERSE CHRONOLOGICAL AND FUNCTIONAL APPROACHES

Generally, there are two approaches to resume construction, the reverse chronological (resume 10.1, page 186) and the functional resume (resume 10.2, page 187). The reverse chronological approach emphasizes dates and when you did things, whereas the functional approach emphasizes what you did.

Reverse Chronological Approach

In the reverse chronological resume, the emphasis is on your jobs and the dates when you did things. Generally, it provides a good narrative of your history. You present the information much as you would if you were filling out a job application, with the most recent information first. Generally, if you are advancing along a predictable career path, the reverse chronological order is good for showing your career progression.

Job recruiters often like the reverse chronological format because they can quickly assess your weaknesses. Because it is date oriented, they can easily determine whether you stayed in a position too briefly or too long. If there are employment gaps, this format will quickly reveal them. For college students this usually doesn't pose a problem. Students are expected to have employment gaps.

The reverse chronological resume also helps employers determine your age. Add 23 to the date someone graduated from college, and you probably have a pretty good approximation of that person's age. How old do you guess Sally Herr is from the information in resume 10.1 (page 186)?

She hasn't yet graduated, so she is probably close to 23 years old.

Functional Approach

The focus of the functional resume is on your skills and accomplishments rather than on event dates. Generally, it suggests what you can do for the employer. Items may be listed by their impact or by their job title. For example, you may present your most impressive item first, the second most impressive item last, and then fill everything else in between. Since reviewers tend to focus on the first and last item on a list, this approach highlights your top two experiences. The items in resume 10.2 (page 187) are actually listed in reverse chronological order. This is not readily obvious because the emphasis is on the position title and not the dates of employment.

In its purest form, the functional resume does not include the employer, job title, and dates. However, the less substantive information you have on your resume, the more skeptical a potential employer will be about what you have actually done (e.g., *I have demonstrated leadership skills, I have good interpersonal skills*). Anyone can make broad statements like this. Most people want you to demonstrate that you have the skills. In contrast to the pure form, resume 10.2 (page 187) provides ample substance for the reviewer.

A review of the research suggests support for both approaches to resume construction. Human resources people tend to prefer the reverse chronological resume, whereas professionals in the field tend to prefer the functional resume. When doing an initial quick review of the resumes, reviewers tend to rate functional resumes higher than reverse chronological resumes. This is understandable because they tend to pick up on your skills and abilities rather than your dates of employment. Did you rate resume 10.2 (a functional resume, page 187) higher or lower than resume 10.1 (a reverse chronological resume, page 186)? Your rating of these two formats may provide you with some insight into which you prefer.

PARTS OF YOUR RESUME

Remember that a resume is a sales instrument, not a job application. What you include on your resume is what sells you to the employer. It is your choice what to include. You may be tempted to include some items because of general convention or because you believe everyone else expects you to include them. For example, people often include the phrase *References are available upon request* for this reason. The phrase is really not necessary, because everyone knows that in the traditional job search approach, you will probably be required to submit references at some point in the process.

Normally, your name and address are listed first at the top of the page. The order of the remaining items on the resume is discretionary. For example, a new graduate may list education first. However, 20 years later, when her experiences are more ger-mane to her career, she may list her experiences first and her education later.

Recently, there has been a trend toward one-page resumes. In general, your resume should not be more than two pages long. Don't be tempted to shrink the font size, reduce white space, and eliminate effective "word pictures" to fit everything onto one page. Conversely, you don't want to try to expand your limited information into a two-page format.

Name, Address, and Contacts

List your name and address at the top of your resume. Examine the headings in figure 10.1, *a* through *h*, and see if there is one that you

---

Sally K. Herr
8310 Oakford Drive
Springfield, Virginia 56001
Home: (507) 555-2223
School: (307) 555-2244

OBJECTIVE

Seek an aquatics director position in a community or nonprofit setting

Figure 10.1*a*   Centered heading with name not emphasized.

Sally K. Herr
8310 Oakford Drive
Springfield, Virginia 56001
Home: (507) 555-2223
School: (507) 555-2511
e-mail: skherr@statecollege.edu

OBJECTIVE

Seek an aquatics director position in a community or nonprofit setting

Figure 10.1*b*   Centered heading with no unifying line.

Sally K. Herr

8310 Oakford Drive   School: (307) 555-2244
Springfield, Virginia 56001   Home: (507) 555-2223

OBJECTIVE

Seek an aquatics director position in a community or nonprofit setting

Figure 10.1*c*   Split heading with no unifying line.

(continued)

Sally K. Herr

8310 Oakford Drive Springfield, Virginia 56001	School: (307) 555-2244 Home: (507) 555-2223

OBJECTIVE

Seek an aquatics director position in a community or nonprofit setting

Figure 10.1*d*   Split heading with unifying line.

Sally K. Herr
8310 Oakford Drive
Springfield, Virginia 56001
Home: (507) 555-2223
School: (307) 555-2244

OBJECTIVE

Seek an aquatics director position in a community or nonprofit setting

Figure 10.1*e*   Right-justified heading with unifying line.

Sally K. Herr
8310 Oakford Drive
Springfield, Virginia 56001
Home: (507) 555-2223
School: (307) 555-2244

OBJECTIVE

Seek an aquatics director position in a community or nonprofit setting

Figure 10.1*f*   Left-justified heading with unifying line.

Sally K. Herr

8310 Oakford Drive Springfield, Virginia 56001	Home: (507) 555-2223 School: (307) 555-2244

OBJECTIVE

Seek an aquatics director position in a community or nonprofit setting

Figure 10.1*g*   Heading with name overemphasized.

8310 Oakford Drive
Springfield, Virginia 56001
Home: (507) 555-2223
School: (307) 555-2244

Sally K. Herr

OBJECTIVE

Seek an aquatics director position in a community or nonprofit setting

Figure 10.1*h*   Balanced heading.

particularly like or reflects your personality. The centered format is conservative, and research suggests that professionals rank it higher than a right- or left-justified heading (Kauffman & Peckins, 1990). Try using a font for your name that is two sizes larger than the rest of your text. Set it bold also. Be careful about making your name too large and drawing too much attention to yourself (resume 10.5, page 190). Some references suggest listing only one address, the one where you want correspondence sent. Consider including your home phone number, office (school) phone number, cell phone number, e-mail address, and fax number. If you don't want to be called at home or on your cell phone, don't include them on your resume.

Objective or Career Goal

Take a look at your resume. If you are a college student with a lot of diverse experiences, using an objective may help unify your information. If you are switching career paths and need to focus on where you want to go rather than where you have been, you may find the use of a career objective useful. Conversely, if you find that your career path is fairly linear, that it is fairly clearly presented in your resume, and that your experiences are consistent with the job you are seeking, you may conclude that including a career objective is redundant and not necessary. Examine the resumes at the end of this chapter and determine for yourself whether including the objective helps to focus Sally Herr's resume.

If you choose to include an objective, the best strategy is to paraphrase the job announcement. Some research suggests that job recruiters tend to

prefer seeing their job announcement at the top of the resume (Harcourt & Krizan, 1989; Helwig 1985; Toth, 1993). However, inclusion of a paraphrased job announcement is predicated on the traditional model, in which you are applying for an advertised position.

In the positioning model, there is no formal job announcement. You will develop an individualized job announcement as part of the one-on-one interview process, or the employer will use a standard position and fit you into it. Although you can't include an adapted job announcement as your objective, you can include a generalized objective. Remember, you have cased the joint, so you have a good idea of the position you are seeking. Also, remember that because the employer will probably receive your resume later in the search process, having a specific career objective is of less importance than it is in the traditional job search process. In terms of the positioning model, Sally Herr's career objective is a fairly good generalized career objective. In addition, it unifies her resume with a common focus, and it positions her well for the aquatics position she is seeking.

Experiences

Examine the resume examples in exercise 10.1 to see how they list experiences. Before listing yours, you must first determine whether you prefer the reverse chronological or functional approach. Next, determine what you want to call this category on your resume, and whether you want to split your experiences into subcategories. Some category titles and subcategories to consider are *career experiences*, *work experiences*, *paid experiences*, *volunteer experiences*, or *professional experiences.* Or, consider simply listing your experiences under the title *experiences* and include both paid and unpaid experiences. Again, choose a heading that best fits your needs.

Compare how resumes 10.2 and 10.4 (pages 187 and 189) address the *experiences* category. The primary difference between these two resumes is that in 10.2, the experiences were split into two sections, and in 10.4, they were presented as one section. Do you think you should separate or combine your experiences? View the two resumes in terms of the principles of repetition and balance. Most people prefer resume 10.2 over resume 10.4.

Finally, you need to determine how you want to present your information. Do you prefer the bullet approach (resumes 10.1 and 10.2, pages 186 and 187)? If so, be careful not to bullet everything on your resume. Overusing bullets can minimize their ability to emphasize what is important. Do you prefer a paragraph format (resumes 10.3 and 10.4, pages 188 and 189)? If you use this format, notice that the sentences are incomplete, and the subject, *I,* is implied. A common mistake is to repeat *I did this* and *I did that.* Well, of course you did—it is your resume. The constant use of *I* on your resume draws too much attention to yourself. You might decide that you prefer the simpler listing format used in resume 10.5 (page 190).

Awards, Honors, and Accomplishments

Noting your accomplishments is an important way to differentiate yourself from everyone else. What awards and honors have you received? What accomplishments have you achieved? These can be included as a separate item if you have several of them, or they can be listed under *professional and work experience.*

Listing your formal awards or honors is obvious. However, don't overlook accomplishments that are less obvious. For example, in the resume examples, Sally Herr was an All-American and coached a swim team that won first place. Not only are these accomplishments, but they suggest that she is a quality person, a winner. If you increased sales or membership by 20 per-

cent, note this on your resume. If you solved a problem or grew a program, indicate this on your resume. Listing your responsibilities on a resume is generally nothing more than writing a job description. Noting your accomplishments differentiates you from everyone else. This is important.

Education, Certifications, Licenses

Education is more important for a college graduate than it is for someone who has worked 10 years in the field after graduation. If you are a recent college graduate or are about to graduate, you may list your education in a prominent place on your resume because of its relative importance. Later in your career, as you gain additional experiences, you may move education to a less prominent position on your resume. Listing graduation as *expected graduation* solves the problem of listing something that hasn't happened yet. Make sure your certifications are current, or list the dates for which they are current so that you don't list a noncurrent certification as current. Students often wonder whether to list the courses they have taken. The answer is, maybe. If your experiences are weak or if people may have a hard time understanding the curriculum in your major, you might consider listing the courses taken to indicate the rigor of your program. For example, most people will have an understanding of the course work required in engineering or business. However, integrated science and technology is a new major that most people wouldn't equate with being similar to engineering. Listing a sampling of your courses might help communicate the rigor of your program to others.

Affiliations

Listing your professional affiliations can aid in implying your professionalism and connections in the field. Normally, they should be consistent with your career development and the job you are seeking. In the case of Sally Herr, her affiliations would be included on the second page of her resume.

References

Before listing your references on your resume, ask yourself whether listing someone else on your resume will help to sell you better to the reviewer. Could you better use the space to present other information that sells you? If you provide complete information on your references, do you want people contacting your references? Most people list references at the end of their resume, which says something about their overall importance. Most also list the names and addresses of their references without phone numbers. If they are interviewed, they will need to provide complete information. As previously noted, the phrase *References are available upon request* is really not necessary, because everyone knows that in the traditional job search, you will probably be required to submit references at some point. Finally, consider using endorsements instead of listing references. They are described in the next section.

An alternative preferred by many people is to list references on a separate page (figure 10.2). This saves space and allows you to use discretion, providing your references only to those you want to have them. Also, you are being prudent by not widely distributing information about your references. Use the same heading on your reference page that you did on your resume.

If you decide to list references on your resume, consider listing five, including their names, addresses, and contact information. A nice touch is to indicate the relationship of the reference to you. A simple *former instructor* or *previous employer* is usually sufficient. Also, if there is someone you don't want contacted without your permission, indicate this here also. Often people don't want their current employer to know they are looking for a job unless they are a serious finalist. There is a trend to require five references because employers may succeed in contacting three of them. This is better than requesting three references and contacting only one. Also, if you have five references available, you can cut these down to three for a given employer. This is easier than expanding a list of three references to five.

Consider the following etiquette suggestions regarding your references. Ask the individual whether you can use him as a reference. Listen closely to his response and read between the lines in trying to assess his enthusiasm toward you. If he gives you a lukewarm response, you may not want to use him as a reference. Describe the type of job you are applying for and give the individual a copy of your resume. This does four things. First, it suggests that you are thorough. Second, it helps your reference fill in information gaps about you. Third, it helps to fill in longitudinal gaps. Often students request a reference two or three years after leaving school. Your resume helps bring your reference up to date regarding what you have done. Fourth, it helps your reference to write more definitively. Instead of hedging on their description of an experience he kind of remembers, he can look at your resume and remember and report more accurately what you did.

Endorsements

Consider using an endorsement as an alternative to listing references on your resume. A quote or two from your references can extol your qualities. Your resume is a sales instrument. Juxtapose these endorsements with simply listing Mary Jones or John Smith as references on your resume. As with your references, you must receive prior permission from your endorsers to use their endorsement. Nothing would be more embarrassing than to have Mary Jones exclaim, "I don't remember saying that!" when contacted by your potential employer. It will submarine your candidacy very quickly also. Although the endorsements in figure 10.3 are written for inclusion in a portfolio, they provide an idea of how endorsements can be integrated into your resume.

Personal Data

Be careful about including personal data on your resume. Height, weight, marital status, and religious affiliation are obvious examples of personal data not to include. Less obvious examples include clubs, sports, fraternity and sorority membership, and work experiences that imply

Sally K. Herr
8310 Oakford Drive
Springfield, Virginia 56001
Home: (507) 555-2223
School: (307) 555-2244
e-mail: skherr@statecollege.edu

REFERENCES

Dr. Mary Jones

Assistant Professor	Faculty advisor
Recreation and Parks Management	Student Recreation and Parks Club
State College University	
University Park, MD 20742	
office: (307) 555-1212	
cell: (307) 555-2121	
e-mail: mjones@statecollege.edu	

Mr. John Smith

President, Board of Directors	Former employer
Rolling Hills AFC	
132 Swimming Pool Lane	
Rolling Hills, MD 22232	
office: (307) 555-3332	
e-mail: john_smith@rollinghillsswim.org	

Dr. William Bandicott

Director of Student Life	Supervisor
State College University	Resident assistant
University Park, MD 20742	
office: (307) 555-4323	
e-mail: wbandicott@statecollege.edu	

Mr. Ralph Dewey

Principal Supervisor	
Springfield High School	Substitute teacher
Schole Lane	
Springfield, VA 22232	
office: (507) 555-6235	
e-mail: rjdewey@shs.edu	

Dr. Jane Doe

Professor, instructor, and advisor
Recreation and Parks Management
State College University
University Park, MD 21740
office: (307) 555-5553
e-mail: jdoe@statecollege.edu

Figure 10.2 Consider listing your references on a separate page.

Sally K. Herr
8310 Oakford Drive
Springfield, Virginia 56001
Home: (507) 555-2223
School: (307) 555-2244
e-mail: skherr@statecollege.edu

ENDORSEMENTS

"As a coach, Sally took a losing team from the previous year and won first place in the regional tournament."

John Smith
Board of Directors
Rolling Hills AFC

"As a president of the Student Recreation and Parks Club, Sally conducted some of the best programming that we've ever had."

Mary Jones
Faculty Advisor
Recreation and Parks Club

I would like to use this endorsement page as a model for my resume.

_____ Strongly agree

_____ Agree

_____ Disagree

_____ Strongly disagree

Figure 10.3 Personal endorsements can be an effective substitute for references.

an affiliation. For example, Sally Herr listed that she was an All-American swimmer. Swimming is a relatively innocuous activity and probably won't reflect negatively on her. In contrast, a sport such as rugby might imply that the person is a ruffian who parties a lot. Fraternities and sororities can provide extremely valuable learning and growth experiences. However, some people have a dislike for them that may influence their impression of you. You need to look at the experiences you include on your resume through the prism of others' perceptions. Use your experiences to present yourself positively.

YOUR RESUME AS AN ART FORM

Your resume is an art form. It creates a visual sensation that has meaning to the viewer. When reviewers do an initial review of your resume and derive a first impression of it, they are, in part, viewing your resume as an art form. If you completed exercise 10.1 as suggested at the beginning of this chapter, you may have already concluded this for yourself. With some minor variations, all the resume examples in this chapter use the same content. What we are considering is form over function. The presentation of your material is as important as the content. The following principles provide a primer to help you analyze your resume as an art form.

When people view a photo or read a document, their eyes move diagonally from top left to bottom right. This is true even in cultures in which people are taught to read from right to left. Unless something else attracts the eye, such as a large white space in the middle of the resume, upon initial glance, people will see your name at the top of the resume and move downward. Glance at resume 10.2. Do you find your eye moving toward the name and address from the top left. Your eye movement is also helped by the white space in the top left corner, which attracts the eye.

Black text unites to form a *shape*, usually a rectangle. The absence of text also creates a shape called white space, or void. White space is generally more attractive than black space because the eye is initially attracted to white and not black.

Resume 10.6 (page 191) was purposely designed to show the effect of having little or no white space. Even so, it is still defined by the white space between the sections, although there isn't a lot of it.

In resume construction, a line is used to divide sections, or to unite two or more elements such as in a split heading (see resume 10.3, page 188). Compare figures 10.1c and 10.1d (pages 177 and 178) to see how a line can unite split elements in the heading. In addition, when two parallel lines are used in close proximity in a header, they can imply a shape (figure 10.1h, page 179).

Draw a line, or axis, down the middle of your resume. Does the mass of black on the left seem to balance the mass of black on the right? If it does, your resume has *balance*. Compare resumes 10.1, 10.2, and 10.5 on pages 186, 187, and 190. Most resumes presented in this chapter are reasonably balanced.

Repeating objects or similar shapes creates a predictable pattern. In resume design, partitioning the name and address, education, and experience sections creates repetition and a pattern. When listing job experiences, the text creates a shape and the listing of items creates *repetition*. When the elements are similar in size and shape, their repetition creates a *rhythm*, much like the staccato rhythm created by a picket fence. Look for a disproportionate amount of text in one section that makes it seem to dominate, or stand out against, the other listings. This breaks up the rhythm of the listings. Compare resume 10.2 (page 187) with resume 10.4 (page 189) and see whether you agree.

Emphasis is created by focusing the reader's eye on certain elements in your resume. Underlining, boldface, italics, all capital letters, and hanging paragraphs are useful techniques for highlighting and emphasizing your items. Research indicates that resumes that emphasize key elements or accomplishments are rated higher than those that don't (Kauffman & Peckins, 1990). Did you rate resume 10.2 (page 187) higher than resume 10.4 (page 189)? On resume 10.2, did your initial quick review reveal All-American, or Head Swim Coach?

It is important to emphasize your name on your resume. Several headings are provided in figure 10.1 (pages 177-179). Normally, you want to draw attention to yourself, but not too much attention. Consider making your name two font sizes larger than the text used elsewhere. Compare the headings in figure 10.1 and determine which you like and which you don't like.

Texture refers to how a visual object "feels." Does it feel rough or smooth, coarse or soft? More important, texture is also visual. When you look at the resume, does it look as if it is rough, smooth, coarse, or soft?

The elements of your resume are viewed not only in isolation, but also in how they come together to create the total picture. This is called *unity*. How they are put together creates a sense of harmony. It refers to the gestalt, or the sense of wholeness, created by the resume. Pin your resume on the wall and view it from a couple of feet away. What is your impression? How does it look as a whole? Try this with any of the resume examples. For example, are resumes 10.1 (page 186) and 10.2 (page 187) nice but lack pizzazz? Does the use of lines in the resume in figure 10.3 (page 188) provide a nice touch, and are the lines discreet, not drawing too much attention to themselves or dominating the resume visually? Is resume 10.4 (page 189) too bland? Does the name on resume 10.5 (page 190) dominate too much? Does resume 10.6 (page 191) look cluttered, and do you tend to view it as a single mass? This should help you understand the need to focus on the presentation of your resume just as much as you do on its content.

PUTTING IT ALL TOGETHER

You are your resume. Whether you are positioning yourself in a one-on-one interview with a potential employer or applying for a traditional job as part of a national search, you need a good resume. In the traditional job search, your resume is generally the first thing the employer sees. Unless he knew you prior to the job search, everything he knows about you will be from your resume. In a real sense, you are your resume. In the positioning model, the resume generally comes later in the process and is more supplemental. Regardless, it is still important to have a good resume that accurately reflects who you are.

REFERENCES

Harcourt, J., & Krizan, A. (1989). A comparison of resume content preferences of Fortune 500 personnel administrators and business communication instructors. *The Journal of Business Communication, 26* (2).

Helwig, A. (1985). Corporate recruiter preferences for three resume styles. *The Vocational Guidance Quarterly, 34* (2), 99-105.

Ireland, S. (2006). *The complete idiot's guide to the perfect resume.* New York: Alpha Books.

Kauffman, R.B., & Peckins, S. (1990). You and your resume (Part II)—Form over function. *Employ, XVI* (9), Ashburn, VA: National Recreation and Park Association.

Toth, C. (1993). Effect of resume format on applicant selection for job interviews. *Applied H.R.M. Research, 4* (2), 115-125.

Zelanski, P., & Fisher, M. (1984). *Design principles and problems.* Fort Worth, TX: Harcourt Brace College Publishers.

Exercise 10.1

Individual Resume Assessment

Six resume examples are used in this exercise and referred to in the text. Look them over and answer the three questions on the right margin for each one. To answer the first question, give each resume a quick once-over. What is your first impression? What catches your eye? How do you feel about the resume? The second question determines the acceptability of the resume. This is a good exercise to do as a group (the question is addressed in greater detail in exercise 10.2). The last question asks you to personalize the resume. Would you use it as your own? Decide for yourself which techniques you like the best and which resume format works the best for you. Which resume did you rate the highest? The lowest? Why?

Sally K. Herr
8310 Oakford Drive
Springfield, Virginia 56001
Home: (507) 555-2223
School: (507) 555-2511
e-mail: skherr@statecollege.edu

OBJECTIVE

Seek an aquatics director position in a community or nonprofit setting

HONORS

All-American—Earned All-American honors in swimming
President—Student Recreation and Parks Club

EDUCATION

State College University
BS degree in Recreation and Parks
Option: Therapeutic Recreation
Expected graduation: May 2008

CAREER EXPERIENCES

Summer 2007 **Rolling Hills AFC**, Rolling Hills, MD
ASSISTANT AQUATICS DIRECTOR and INTERNSHIP
• Administered the pool, including five lifeguards
• Worked with the director and CEO in administering the pool
• Choreographed the women's aquatic exercise program

Summer 2006 **Rolling Hills AFC**, Rolling Hills, MD
HEAD SWIM COACH
• Coached a swim team of over 100 children
• Conducted swimming meets and organized field trips
• Team won first place in regional tournaments

Fall 2005 **American Red Cross**, Harrisburg, PA
ADAPTED AQUATICS INSTRUCTOR
• Taught disabled students to swim as part of an American Red Cross Adapted Aquatics program

Summer 2003 **Browne Summer Camp**, Alexandria, VA
HEAD CAMP COUNSELOR
• Planned special projects and participated in camp productions for children aged three and four

EMPLOYMENT

Spring 2006 **State College University**, University Park, MD
to present RESIDENT ASSISTANT
• Counseled students and worked with seven other resident assistants

Spring 2005 **Springfield High School**, Springfield, VA
SUBSTITUTE TEACHER
• Instructed high school classes in physical education, science, business, mathematics, and art

Do a five-second review of this resume. What are the first five things you remember?

1. _____
2. _____
3. _____
4. _____
5. _____

I find this resume . . .

_____ very acceptable

_____ acceptable

_____ unacceptable

_____ very unacceptable

I would like to use this resume as a model for my resume.

_____ Strongly agree

_____ Agree

_____ Disagree

_____ Strongly disagree

Resume 10.1 Reverse chronological resume.

Do a five-second review of this resume. What are the first five things you remember?

1. _____
2. _____
3. _____
4. _____
5. _____

I find this resume . . .

_____ very acceptable

_____ acceptable

_____ unacceptable

_____ very unacceptable

I would like to use this resume as a model for my resume.

_____ Strongly agree

_____ Agree

_____ Disagree

_____ Strongly disagree

Sally K. Herr

8310 Oakford Drive
Springfield, Virginia 56001
Home: (507) 555-2223
School: (507) 555-2511
e-mail: skherr@statecollege.edu

OBJECTIVE

Seek an aquatics director position in a community or nonprofit setting

EDUCATION

State College University
BS degree in Recreation and Parks
Option: Therapeutic Recreation
Expected graduation: May 2008

HONORS

All-American—Earned All-American honors in swimming
President—Student Recreation and Parks Club

PROFESSIONAL EXPERIENCES

Assistant Aquatics Director—Rolling Hills AFC, Rolling Hills, MD. Summer 2007.
- Managed five lifeguards and worked with the director and CEO
- Choreographed the women's aquatic exercise program

Head Swim Coach—Rolling Hills AFC, Rolling Hills, MD. Summer 2006.
- Coached a swim team of over 100 children
- Supervised assistants, conducted swimming meets, organized field trips
- Team won first place in regional tournaments

Adapted Aquatics Instructor—American Red Cross, Harrisburg, PA.
- May 2006; Wakefield Chapel, Springfield, Virginia, Fall 2005. Taught disabled students to swim as part of an Adapted Aquatics program

Head Camp Counselor—Browne Summer Camp, Alexandria, VA. Summer 2003.
- Coordinated activities, planned special projects, and participated in camp productions for children aged three and four

EMPLOYMENT

Resident Assistant—State College University.
Spring 2006 to present.
- Counseled college students
- Worked with seven other resident assistants

Recreation Assistant—Veterans Administration Center, Martinsburg, WV. Fall 2007.
- Assisted in conducting recreational activities for domiciliary patients as part of a field experience

Substitute Teacher—Springfield High School, Springfield, VA. Spring 2005
- Instructed high school classes in physical education, science, business, mathematics, and art

Resume 10.2 Functional resume.

187

Sally K. Herr
8310 Oakford Drive
Springfield, Virginia 56001
Home: (507) 555-2223
School: (507) 555-2511
e-mail: skherr@statecollege.edu

OBJECTIVE

Seek an aquatics director position in a community or nonprofit setting

EDUCATION

State College University
BS degree in Recreation and Parks
Option: Therapeutic Recreation
Expected graduation: May 2008

HONORS

All-American—Earned All-American honors in swimming
President—Student Recreation and Parks Club

PROFESSIONAL EXPERIENCES

Assistant Aquatics Director—Managed five lifeguards; worked with the director and CEO in administering the pool; choreographed the women's aquatic exercise program. Rolling Hills **AFC**, Rolling Hills, MD. Summer 2007.

Head Swim Coach—Coached a swim team of over 100 children. Responsibilities included supervising assistants, conducting swimming meets, and organizing field trips. Team won first place in regional tournaments. Rolling Hills AFC, Rolling Hills, MD. Summer 2006.

Adapted Aquatics Instructor—Taught disabled students to swim as part of an American Red Cross program in Adapted Aquatics, Harrisburg, PA. May 2006; Wakefield Chapel, Springfield, VA. Fall 2005.

Head Camp Counselor—Responsible for coordinating activities, planning special projects, and participating in camp productions for children aged three and four. Browne Summer Camp, Alexandria, VA. Summer 2003.

EMPLOYMENT

Resident Assistant—Counseled college students and worked with seven other resident assistants in administering policies for a dormitory. State College University. Spring 2006 to present.

Recreation Assistant—Assisted in conducting recreational activities for domiciliary patients as part of a field experience. Veterans Administration Center. Martinsburg, WV. Fall 2007.

Substitute Teacher—Instructed high school classes in physical education, science, business, mathematics, and art. Springfield High School, Springfield, VA. Spring 2005.

Resume 10.3 Functional resume with line dividers.

Do a five-second review of this resume. What are the first five things you remember?

1. _____
2. _____
3. _____
4. _____
5. _____

I find this resume . . .

_____ very acceptable

_____ acceptable

_____ unacceptable

_____ very unacceptable

I would like to use this resume as a model for my resume.

_____ Strongly agree

_____ Agree

_____ Disagree

_____ Strongly disagree

Sally K. Herr
8310 Oakford Drive
Springfield, Virginia 56001
Home: (507) 555-2223
School: (507) 555-2511
e-mail: skherr@statecollege.edu

OBJECTIVE

Seek an aquatics director position in a community or nonprofit setting

EDUCATION

State College University
BS degree in Recreation and Parks
Option: Therapeutic Recreation
Expected graduation: May 2008

HONORS

All-American—Earned All-American honors in swimming
President—Student Recreation and Parks Club

PROFESSIONAL EXPERIENCES

Assistant Aquatics Director—Managed five lifeguards; worked with the director and CEO in administering the pool; choreographed the women's aquatic exercise program. Rolling Hills **AFC**, Rolling Hills, Maryland. Summer 2007.

Head Swim Coach—Coached a swim team of over 100 children. Responsibilities included supervising assistants, conducting swimming meets, and organizing field trips. Team won first place in regional tournaments. Rolling Hills AFC, Rolling Hills, Maryland. Summer 2006.

Adapted Aquatics Instructor—Taught disabled students to swim as part of an American Red Cross program in Adapted Aquatics, Harrisburg, PA. May 2006; Wakefield Chapel, Springfield, Virginia. Fall 2005.

Head Camp Counselor—Responsible for coordinating activities, planning special projects, and participating in camp productions for children aged three and four. Browne Summer Camp, Alexandria, Virginia. Summer 2003.

Resident Assistant—Counseled college students and worked with seven other resident assistants in administering policies for a dormitory. State College University. Spring 2006 to present.

Recreation Assistant—Assisted in conducting recreational activities for domiciliary patients as part of a field experience. Veterans Administration Center. Martinsburg, West Virginia. Fall 2007.

Substitute Teacher—Instructed high school classes in physical education, science, business, mathematics, and art. Springfield High School, Springfield, Virginia. Spring 2005.

Do a five-second review of this resume. What are the first five things you remember?

1. _____
2. _____
3. _____
4. _____
5. _____

I find this resume . . .

_____ very acceptable

_____ acceptable

_____ unacceptable

_____ very unacceptable

I would like to use this resume as a model for my resume.

_____ Strongly agree

_____ Agree

_____ Disagree

_____ Strongly disagree

Resume 10.4   Functional resume with no emphasis on titles.

Sally K. Herr

Residence:

8310 Oakford Drive
Springfield, Virginia 56001
Home: (507) 555-2223

School:

110 Mission Hall
University Park, Maryland 20742
School: (307) 555-2244

OBJECTIVE

Seek an aquatics director position in a community or nonprofit setting

EDUCATION

State College University
BS degree in Recreation and Parks
Option: Therapeutic Recreation
Expected graduation: May 2008

HONORS

All-American—Earned All-American honors in swimming
President—Student Recreation and Parks Club

PROFESSIONAL EXPERIENCES

Assistant Aquatics Director	Rolling Hills **AFC** Rolling Hills, Maryland	Summer 2007
Head Swim Coach	Rolling Hills AFC Rolling Hills, Maryland	Summer 2006
Adapted Aquatics Instructor	American Red Cross Harrisburg, Pennsylvania	May 2006
Adapted Aquatics Instructor	Wakefield Chapel Springfield Virginia	Fall 2005
Head Camp Counselor	Browne Summer Camp Alexandria, Virginia	Summer 2003

EMPLOYMENT

Resident Assistant	State College University	2006 to present
Recreation Assistant	Veterans Administration Center Martinsburg, West Virginia	Fall 2007
Substitute Teacher	Springfield High School Springfield, Virginia	Spring 2005

Name—Does this superlarge font for the name draw too much attention? Think of the potential negative connotations.

Split addresses—Where do they send the correspondence? It leads to confusion. How about an e-mail address. Also, do you like the split address?

Line—Do you find that the line unifies the two addresses, or does the white space between them create too much separation?

White space—Do you find the white space here excessive?

White space—There is a certain order to the column approach, which some people will find pleasing. However, do you find that the white space creates too much separation between the items?

Right justification—Do you like the right justification (aligned with the right margin), or would you prefer a third column?

Do a five-second review of this resume. What are the first five things you remember?

1. _____
2. _____
3. _____
4. _____
5. _____

I find this resume . . .

_____ very acceptable

_____ acceptable

_____ unacceptable

_____ very unacceptable

I would like to use this resume as a model for my resume.

_____ Strongly agree

_____ Agree

_____ Disagree

_____ Strongly disagree

Resume 10.5 Analyze this resume.

Sally K. Herr

8310 Oakford Drive
Springfield, Virginia 56001

School: (307) 555-2244
Home: (507) 555-2223
E-mail: skherr@statecollege.edu

OBJECTIVE

Seek an aquatics director position in a community or nonprofit setting

EDUCATION

State College University
BS degree in Recreation and Parks
Option: Therapeutic Recreation
Expected graduation: May 2008

HONORS

All-American—Earned All-American honors in swimming
President—Student Recreation and Parks Club
First place—Coach of swim team

PROFESSIONAL EXPERIENCES

- **Assistant Aquatics Director**—Managed five lifeguards; worked with the director and CEO in administering the pool; choreographed the women's aquatic exercise program. Rolling Hills AFC, Rolling Hills, Maryland. Summer 2007.
- **Head Swim Coach**—Coached a swim team of over 100 children. Responsibilties included supervising assistants, conducting swimming meets, and organizing field trips. Team won first place in regional tournaments. Rolling Hills AFC, Rolling Hills, Maryland. Summer 2006.
- **Adapted Aquatics Instructor**—Taught disabled students to swim as part of an American Red Cross program in Adapted Aquatics, Harrisburg, Pennsylvania. May 2006.
- **Adapted Aquatics Instructor**—Taught disabled students to swim as part of an American Red Cross program in Adapted Aquatics. Wakefield Chapel, Springfield, Virginia. Fall 2005.
- **Social Chairperson**—Planned program mixers, special event parties, and other social activities, Shaw Hall House Council. State College University. September 2004 to present.
- **Head Camp Counselor**—Responsible for coordinating activities, planning special projects, and participating in camp productions for children aged three and four. Browne Summer Camp, Alexandria, Virginia. Summer 2003.

EMPLOYMENT

- **Resident Assistant**—Counseled college students and worked with seven other resident assistants in administering policies for a dormitory. State College University. Spring 2006 to present.
- **Recreation Assistant**—Assisted in conducting recreational activities for domiciliary patients as part of a field experience. Veterans Administration Center. Martinsburg, West Virginia. Fall 2007.
- **Substitute Teacher**—Instructed high school classes in physical education, science, business, mathematics, and art. Springfield High School, Springfield, Virginia. Spring 2005.
- **Substitute Teacher**—Instructed middle school classes in science and mathematics. Springfield Middle School, Springfield, Virginia. Fall 2004.
- **Substitute Teacher**—Instructed middle school classes in science and mathematics. Springfield Middle School, Springfield, Virginia. Fall 2003.

This resume was purposely created to show what happens when you attempt to put too much information on one page.

Split heading—Do you like this split heading? Does the line help to unify the two elements? Note how this heading was split. The address is on the left; phone numbers are on the right.

Line—Do you find that the line unifies the two addresses, or does the white space between them create too much separation?

Split columns—In an attempt to fill all the space, split columns were used on this resume. Does it work?

Margins—In an effort to fit everything into a limited space, the margins are often encroached upon. Notice the lack of white space when this encroachment occurs.

Font size—This section was purposely written using a smaller font to make the point that once the text approaches 15 words a line, it becomes cumbersome to read. Compare this section with the previous section of text.

Bold, no underlining—This shows the effect of headings that use bold but aren't underlined. On the five-second perusal, does your eye pick up the headings easily? When documents are copied, it often becomes difficult to determine what was bolded because the text bleeds.

Do a five-second review of this resume. What are the first five things you remember?

1. _____
2. _____
3. _____
4. _____
5. _____

I find this resume . . .

_____ very acceptable

_____ acceptable

_____ unacceptable

_____ very unacceptable

I would like to use this resume as a model for my resume.

_____ Strongly agree

_____ Agree

_____ Disagree

_____ Strongly disagree

Resume 10.6   Analyze this resume.

Exercise 10.2

Group Resume Assessment

This is a group, or class, exercise. Have everyone assess the resumes in this chapter in terms of their acceptability (question 2 in exercise 10.1). Use the table below to tabulate the results of the group.

For each resume, have people raise their hands for each category (*Very acceptable, Acceptable*, etc.). Write the number of people who agree with each category in the cell for that category.

To calculate the average score, rate *Very acceptable* as a 4, *Acceptable* as a 3, *Unacceptable* as a 2, and *Very unacceptable* as a 1. Multiply the number of people in each cell by the score. If 10 people rated resume 10.1 as very acceptable, the total score for this cell is 40. Do the same for each of the other three categories. Add the four scores together. To obtain the average score, divide the total score (all four scores added together) by the total number of people in all four categories.

Resume	Very acceptable	Acceptable	Unacceptable	Very unacceptable	Average score
10.1					
10.2					
10.3					
10.4					
10.5					
10.6					

For a more in-depth discussion of the resumes, members of the group could consider the following questions.

1. Circle the most frequently occurring category for each resume. This will give you a quick assessment of the results. Which is the most acceptable? Which is the least acceptable?

2. Are there any resumes with a bimodal evaluation; that is, that were viewed equally by some people as *Acceptable* and by others as *Unacceptable*? What does this suggest, if anything, about using this resume format? Or, would you conclude that you will please some people but not others with this format? Knowing this, should you use the format?

3. Were there any resumes that most people rated as *Acceptable* and very few people, if any, rated as *Very acceptable* or as *Very unacceptable*? These are average resumes. What may account for this?

4. Were there any resumes that most people rated as *Very acceptable* and very few people, if any, rated as *Acceptable* or as *Unacceptable?* What makes this an exceptional resume in the view of those participating?

5. In some cases you will find the average score helpful in your analysis. Which resume had the highest score? The lowest score? Why? Remember that 2.5 is the midpoint. An average score above 2.5 indicates that the resume was viewed favorably, and an average score below 2.5 indicates that it was viewed unfavorably.

Try doing this exercise substituting your own resumes for those used in this chapter.

chapter 11

Portfolios and Business Cards

Do I have the communication tools I need to obtain my job?

This chapter focuses on two tools that students often overlook when developing their promotional tools: portfolios and business cards.

The portfolio is a tool that is gaining popularity outside of the traditional arts disciplines. Unlike a resume, on which you list your experiences, a portfolio allows you to visually display your experiences. Think of it as an expanded resume or as a scrapbook you can use to show others your experiences. However, it is more sophisticated than a scrapbook. You need to present experiences that demonstrate that you have the knowledge, skills, abilities, and experiences (KSAEs) necessary for the job.

Many of the principles used in resume construction also apply to portfolio construction. The following sections present some of the principles that will help you design an effective portfolio.

TYPES OF PORTFOLIOS

The type of portfolio that you develop is determined primarily by its use. If you are going to be presenting your portfolio to an employer in a one-on-one interview or sitting around a table with a group of people in a traditional interview, you may want to develop a traditional flip chart portfolio that you can pull out and use quickly. In this situation, you may find a digital portfolio cumbersome because of the setup time and specialized electronics equipment needed. In contrast, if you want to send your portfolio to someone across the country, a digital portfolio is the better choice. Many people develop both types of portfolios and choose the format based on the situation in which they will be presenting it.

Traditional Flip Chart Portfolio

The traditional flip chart portfolio comes in a variety of sizes. Consider using a three-ring binder format or a small flip chart that folds up into its own container. Both of these formats are portable and lend themselves to individual or small-group presentations.

Although the electronic portfolio is gaining popularity, the traditional flip chart portfolio still excels in many situations. The flip chart portfolio is low tech but functional. If you are in a traditional

A TALE OF TWO MODELS

In the recreation and parks field, portfolios and business cards are relatively new additions for students. Business cards are helpful tools in your networking and they will serve you equally well in both models.

Students should consider developing both a traditional and an electronic portfolio. In the positioning model, the traditional portfolio is a convenient tool you can use during your one-on-one interview. You will find that it helps to stimulate conversation and to display some of your accomplishments. The advantage of the traditional portfolio in this situation is that you can quickly flip to appropriate sections as the conversation develops.

In our electronic age, the electronic portfolio will most likely take on an increasingly important role. In this respect, it will supplement your resume and provide additional information to the potential employer. Be careful of providing the potential employer with too much information too early in the process, though.

The portfolio generally is not as valuable in the traditional model since the interview process is more structured. You may have the opportunity to pull out your portfolio in the middle of a half-hour interview, but often the structure of the interview will not allow this opportunity. Regardless, you should consider developing it as one of your communication tools. If you develop a portfolio, you will most likely use it, and it will most likely enhance your job search.

interview or a small-group situation, you can quickly pull out your flip chart portfolio. The same is true if you are meeting with a potential employer in a one-on-one interview. If you want to show just one program you created, you can quickly page to that section. You don't have problems with specialized electronic equipment, a lack of electrical outlets, or washed-out screens from the sun shining in the window. You simply open the flip chart and proceed with the presentation.

If you are presenting yourself at conferences or at a booth at expositions, you might consider an electronic presentation using a program such as PowerPoint and a rear-view projection system. If you are sending your portfolio by e-mail, you will need to use an electronic portfolio. However, instead of sending it as a PowerPoint file, you might want to send it as a pdf file. The pdf format is a fairly universal format. It has a smaller file size than its corresponding PowerPoint file, which makes it easier to send electronically since many servers have file size limitations. Some people put their electronic portfolios on Internet sites such as Blogspot, Facebook, and

MySpace and then send the address to the site via e-mail. In the future, there may be Internet sites dedicated to portfolios, where people can input their information to create standardized portfolios with little effort.

In the positioning model, most people bring their portfolio to their one-on-one interview. When they meet with the contact person in the organization, they use it as a tool to sell themselves and to convey their experiences. For this reason, the portfolio needs to be portable and convenient to use. You need to be able to access it quickly during the interview if needed. Consider using a three-ring binder format (figure 11.1) or a small flip chart that folds up into its own container. Both of these formats lend themselves to individual or small-group presentations. Regardless, you may still want an electronic portfolio in case the employer asks. As part of the communications between Sally Herr and Mr. Muncheck (see chapter 8), Mr. Muncheck asked Sally for a copy of her resume. She could have just as easily e-mailed him a copy of her electronic portfolio.

Figure 11.1 One example of a flip chart portfolio.

Electronic Portfolios

The electronic, or digital, portfolio is becoming increasingly popular. You may think of it as an expanded resume and use it as you would use your resume. Because the design and technical production of an electronic portfolio can be quite sophisticated, a detailed discussion is beyond the scope of this book. Depending on your production capabilities, you may need to seek technical and professional assistance. In this section, we will touch on the fundamentals of creating an effective electronic portfolio.

As with the traditional flip chart portfolio, how you plan to use your electronic portfolio will determine, in part, the format you use. You may use an electronic portfolio as part of a formal presentation in a traditional interview and leave a copy of it (burned to a CD) with the employer at the end of your presentation. Or, you may attach a copy of your portfolio, in addition to your resume, to an e-mail. An electronic version of your portfolio is also very useful as a repeating presentation at a conference. Be careful, though, that you don't provide too much information to the employer too early in the process. Normally, you want to create a dialogue and avoid providing sufficient information to make an immediate decision.

Although there are many ways to create a digital presentation, the easiest way requires the Microsoft PowerPoint program or similar software program, the ability to print to a pdf file, and the ability to burn a CD. Use PowerPoint to create your portfolio by importing photographs and other electronic documents and moving the text and pictures to compose each page.

The next step in creating a digital portfolio is to print the PowerPoint file to a pdf file. The capability to read pdf files is free; the ability to print pdf files costs a fee. If you don't have the print capability, you may need to find a friend who does. Printing the PowerPoint as a pdf file will reduce the file size so you can attach it to an e-mail. Also, it will give your presentation universality because most systems are capable of reading pdf files. The pdf file is easy to view, and other people can't screw up the presentation by inadvertently manipulating elements. If you are not going to send your portfolio by e-mail, though, you may want keep it as a PowerPoint file because the program offers more presentation options.

If you plan to distribute your portfolio, particularly to the people you have just presented it to in an interview, burn it to a CD either as a PowerPoint or a pdf file.

LAYOUT CONSIDERATIONS

In addition to the general layout principles for resumes covered in chapter 10, consider using the rule of thirds. The rule applies equally well to landscape (horizontal) and portrait (vertical) formats. If you use a three-ring binder flip chart or PowerPoint portfolio, you will be using a landscape format. Figure 11.2 demonstrates the rule of thirds and shows a hypothetical title page for Sally Herr's portfolio. Although she uses a three-ring binder flip chart, she could just as easily have used a PowerPoint presentation.

The rule of thirds is useful in describing how to place objects in the frame that don't occupy a majority of the frame. For example, in figure 11.2 Sally Herr's title page contains three elements: the SCU logo, Sally's mission statement, and the title. The rule of thirds describes how to place these three objects within the frame or on the page. Divide the frame both horizontally and vertically into thirds. This creates four points of intersection and nine quadrants. Begin by placing your objects at the intersections created by the lines. These are your focal points. In figure 11.2, the logo and the title are placed at the intersections. Avoid placing objects in the center quadrant because this has a bull's-eye effect, forcing the eye to focus on the item in the center of the frame and not to rove around the frame. Next, place objects on dividing lines along either the horizontal axis or vertical axis. Sally's personal mission statement is an example of a object placed on the lower horizontal line. In summary, by not placing objects

- Divide the page into thirds horizontally and vertically.
- Place objects at or conceptually near the intersection of the lines. These are the four main focal points.
- Place objects along or conceptually near the horizontal or vertical lines.
- Avoid placing objects in the center quadrant.

Figure 11.2   This title page gives a visual reference for the rule of thirds.

in the center quadrant, you allow the eye to move around the frame.

In addition to the rule of thirds, review the design principles for resumes discussed in chapter 10. Many of them apply to your portfolio page layout also. For example, the objects on the page create shapes, and their absence creates a void, or white space. Objects should be balanced and create a sense of harmony. You can use lines to separate or connect objects. You can emphasize objects by making them larger and de-emphasize them by making them smaller. Also, you can use a contrasting color to create emphasis.

PARTS OF YOUR PORTFOLIO

In planning your portfolio, you must first determine how you will use it. As discussed, this will, in part, determine the format you use, as well as the length of your presentation.

It's useful to consider three situations in which you may be presenting your portfolio to get an idea of how long your presentation should be. The first is a one-on-one interview in which the two of you are having a conversation and discussing the pages of your presentation as you flip through them. The second situation is a traditional job interview in which you are presenting to a group. This is more of a formal presentation and usually has a time limit. In the third situation, you leave a copy of your presentation on a CD, and the employer will review it at her leisure.

A normal rule of thumb for presentations is that you will spend on average a minute per page. A 20-page portfolio will result in a 20-minute conversation. In the first situation, the one-on-one interview, you can easily spend more than a minute on each slide during your conversation. You can skip pages if necessary. In the formal presentation during a traditional interview, you may find yourself talking for less than a minute per slide, particularly if there are few questions from the audience. In the last situation, you are not limited by time constraints because the person will be looking at the presentation at her leisure. Although time is not a constraint, you still want to keep your presentation tight and limit your material.

The following sections discuss the parts of your portfolio. Most likely you will want to limit your material, including only those items that enhance your presentation. Most of the items in the following sections are optional. For example, you may not have letters of reference so you would naturally not include that section. Be sure to check the materials you include for signs of potential safety violations or inappropriate behavior. Some people viewing your portfolio may examine what is going on in the background of a photo. You should do the same. If there is any doubt, don't include it. Remember that sometimes less is more.

Title Page

You can create a title page for your presentation (figure 11.2), or you can use your resume as your title page. Consider including your name, title, and address on your title page or on a separate page. Using the same format that you used on your resume and other documents helps create an aesthetically consistent presentation.

Resume

Include a copy of your resume in your portfolio. Have a copy with you in case the potential employer asks you for one. Review chapter 10 for tips on how to construct your resume.

Cover Letter

Consider writing a cover letter to the person in the organization you are meeting, particularly if it is a one-on-one interview. Even if you are sending the portfolio electronically, this is a nice touch. The cover letter introduces you to the reviewer. Use the format and suggestions described in chapter 12 and used in figures 12.1, 12.2, and 12.3. It's not necessary that you send the cover letter to the individual. Its use as the introduction to your portfolio simply provides a nice touch.

Business Card

A business card is often overlooked as part of your promotional tools. Think of it as a miniature resume. You can include your business card as part of your portfolio, if appropriate. If you do, have a supply of cards to leave with the people with whom you share your portfolio during the

Figure 11.3 Sample business card.

interview process. See the business card section later in the chapter to learn about design considerations. Figure 11.3 provides an example of a student business card.

Significant Samples of Your Work

This section of your portfolio provides samples, or artifacts, that are representative of your work. Artifacts stimulate discussion between you and your potential employer and highlight your experiences. As with resume design, you don't need to present everything you have done; a sampling of your work will suffice. Also, if you use a three-ring binder presentation, you can easily add items or remove them to tailor the presentation to your audience.

Consider the model in figure 11.4 in determining what to include in your portfolio. The model contains three dimensions: amount of experience, magnitude of experience, and relevance of the experiences to the KSAEs required for the position. Many people equate amount of experience with years of experience. The easiest way to portray the amount of your experience is with a log or condensed listing of your activities. For example, an adventure sports student who has taken over 40 outdoor trips could present a log or listing of these trips to quickly indicate the extent of his experience.

Magnitude refers to the quality or importance of the experience. Generally, you want to display your more important experiences. For the same adventure sports student, leading a two-week trip in the backcountry is of greater magnitude than leading a weekend trip. An expedition outside of the country would be considered of greater magnitude than one of the same length locally. He might include a brochure of the expedition in the portfolio or photographs of the trip.

The third dimension is the KSAEs required for the job. This dimension allows you to integrate your findings from chapter 4, Think Evaluation, in which you analyzed job descriptions to determine the KSAEs needed for your next job. Assume that when casing the joint, the adventure sports student determined that the potential employer conducted primarily weekend trips. Based on this analysis, he might also include a section in his portfolio on weekend trips similar to those the potential employer conducts.

When partitioning this section of your portfolio, determine first the KSAEs that are required for the job you are seeking. Then select the experiences in terms of magnitude and amount that best demonstrate these KSAEs. Although it makes logical sense to organize and present your experiences according to the KSAEs, most people find this cumbersome and awkward. A better approach is to present the experiences in reverse chronological order or in order of magnitude. Then, as you discuss each of the experiences, make sure that you highlight the KSAEs they demonstrate. Most people find this approach to the presentation more intuitive and comfortable.

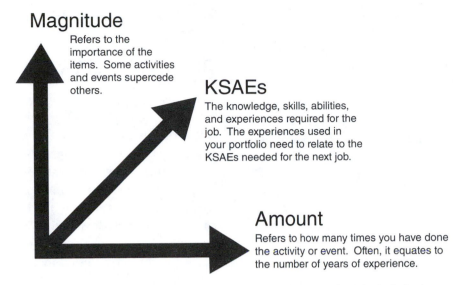

Magnitude
Refers to the importance of the items. Some activities and events supercede others.

KSAEs
The knowledge, skills, abilities, and experiences required for the job. The experiences used in your portfolio need to relate to the KSAEs needed for the next job.

Amount
Refers to how many times you have done the activity or event. Often, it equates to the number of years of experience.

Figure 11.4 There are three factors to consider in deciding which samples to include in your portfolio: amount of experience, magnitude of experience, and relevance to KSAEs.

The artifacts used to describe your experiences should be descriptive of the programs and activities you have done. For example, you might include a brochure of a program in which you were involved. Obviously, if you are listed in the brochure, this helps to showcase you. In addition, it provides the secondary benefit of validating that you actually were involved in the program.

Photographs of the program are good to include in this section. If you do, consider having a title slide or title page. It may be a picture of the building where the program was conducted with the name of the organization on it, or the entrance sign of the park visited. Include a group picture of everyone involved, a picture or two showing the location or site where the activity occurred, and one or two close-up pictures of smiling participants. Try to include at least one picture of you doing something in the activity.

Think of the photographs you use as a tour of your program or activity for someone with little or no understanding of it. Also, don't include too many pictures. Use only the best of the best. In addition, examine the photos for signs of any potential safety hazards or inappropriate behaviors. Examine the action occurring in the background also. When organizing your photos on a page, consider the rule of thirds in determining your page layout.

Self-Statement

A self-statement addresses your philosophy and answers the question, Why do you do what you do? The focus is on *why*. Even if you don't include a self-statement in your portfolio, it is still a good idea to write one to crystallize your thoughts about why you want the job. Your self-statement is not your career goal. It is not about the job. It is about you.

The introduction is the first part of your self-statement. It is normally a short paragraph that contains your philosophy, or why you want to do what you are seeking to do. For example, an adventure sports programmer may write the following statement: *I attempt to create outdoor programs that help adolescents reach their full potential and push them beyond what they believe are their existing limits.* Sally Herr used the following statement of her philosophy on her business card (figure 11.3): *Creating outdoor programs to help adolescents reach their full potential.*

The body is the second part of your self-statement. If you are a programmer or activity leader, think of the programs and activities you have conducted as an artist's canvas on which you have painted an experience. Discuss some of the programs or activities you have conducted in terms of the experience that you created. Describe that experience and how you obtained it through your program or activity.

Your final thoughts are the third part of the self-statement. In this part, draw some conclusions about your work to date. Be honest. In this section, you need to articulate what KSAEs you need to obtain in order to progress along your career path. For example, the adventure sports programmer may need to expand his programming repertoire beyond water and skiing sports to include other sports such as biking or climbing. Or, he may have conducted all weekend (two-day) trips and need to conduct some longer-term expeditions over two weeks in length.

Letters of Recommendation

If you have letters of recommendation, include them in a separate section of your portfolio. Consider pulling out endorsements from the letters to use as part of your presentation and to stimulate discussion (see chapter 10 for a discussion and examples of personal endorsements). Making the text of the quote large makes it is more visible. Include the actual letter also in case the reviewer wants to read further.

Awards

If you have received any awards, you can list them as part of your portfolio. You may even want to include a copy of the artifact or a photo of the award. If the award is a document, consider scanning it and printing a quality color copy. If you are photographing a three-dimensional award, consider using a professional photographer. Taking a quality photograph of a three-dimensional object requires specialized lighting and attention to the background. A photographer who is familiar with shooting small objects for advertising would be ideal.

Professional Memberships

You can list your professional memberships in your portfolio. You can use a format similar to the format used in figure 10.2 to display your memberships. Again, remember that listing your memberships indicates your professional involve-ment and suggests what these connections bring to the workplace.

BUSINESS CARDS

Your business card is often overlooked as part of your promotional tools. In your job search you will probably exchange more business cards than resumes. Think of your business card as a miniature resume. View it as a sales instrument and as a representation of you. The same principles used to design resumes apply to the design of business cards. These include deciding what to include or exclude and treating it as an art form.

It is common practice to exchange business cards anytime you are doing business with someone else. As part of your one-on-one interview, you may be introduced to other key people in the organization. The exchange of business cards leaves other people with reminders of you. This is particularly useful if they desire to contact you in the future.

If you are a student, consider developing a business card. Usually, you can use a format similar to that of the business cards used by faculty. The same design considerations and restrictions apply to the design of your business card as theirs. Figure 11.3 provides an example of a student's business card. In addition, check with school officials to find out whether the school has standardized graphic and design requirements associated with the use of the school logo.

Design and Layout

If you work for an organization, you may already have a company business card. If this is the case, you will probably not have a lot of flexibility in the design of your card because it will need to conform to the design criteria of your organization. Regardless, the same design principles discussed in the resume section apply to the design of your business card: eye movement, shape, white space, line, balance, emphasis, texture, and unity.

Don't overlook using the back of your business card either. Most people leave it empty, but you could use it to include an endorsement or more information about your program.

Front Side

> Organization logo
> Name
> Job title
> Address
> Phone numbers (office, home, cell, fax)
> E-mail address
> Your Web site, if you have one
> Mission statement (the organization's or yours)

Reverse Side

> Endorsements
> Program items
> Photograph or picture
> Items not included on the front side (e.g., mission statement)
> White, or blank, space

Figure 11.5   Items that might be included on a business card.

Parts of Your Business Card

As with resume construction, what you include or exclude on your business card is determined by you or your organization, if its logo is on it. The list of items in figure 11.5 is a starting point for considering what to include on your business card.

PUTTING IT ALL TOGETHER

Portfolios are becoming more popular. Just as you would edit and tailor your resume to fit the situation, consider modifying, editing, and adapting your portfolio to a variety of situations. You may want to have more than one type of portfolio in your repertoire of resource materials. The traditional three-ring binder type of portfolio is a good choice for a one-on-one interview. It also works well with a small-group presentation. It is quick and easy to use. In contrast, the electronic portfolio is portable. You can send it to someone else across the country in a matter of moments. If the equipment is present, you can use it for small presentations also. However, be careful. The dimmed lights and more formal presentation can easily lead to a lecture format rather than a discussion or conversation. It is said that a picture is worth a thousand words. Your portfolio can be those thousand words that make a lasting and positive impression of who you are and what you have done.

Students often overlook business cards as a promotional tool. Usually, people wait until their first job to get business cards. However, they are a valuable tool that students should consider using, even if only for a couple of months until they get a full-time job.

Exercise 11.1

Portfolio Analysis and Review

The purpose of this activity is to provide a review and assessment of your portfolio. You can restrict your review to your own portfolio, or you can make this a group activity. Use the following questions to guide your review of the portfolios.

1. **Is the portfolio appropriate for its presentation format?** Consider whether the portfolio was designed to be sent electronically, to be used in a one-on-one interview, or to be used with a search committee as part of a formal search process.

2. **Are the sections of the portfolio appropriate and informative?** It is not necessary to include all of these, but some elements you might expect to see include a title page, resume, cover letter, business card, significant samples of work, self-statement, letters of recommendation, awards, professional memberships, and business card.

3. **Are the format and layout attractive?** Consider the layout of each individual page. Is the rule of thirds employed effectively? Is color used well? Are pages neat and clean?

4. **Are the samples representative?** Consider each sample of work as a mini-presentation. If photos were used, do they provide a vivid and informative picture of the experience?

Mock Portfolio Presentation

This is a practice presentation of your portfolio. You can record it and review it, if you wish. The exercise can easily be expanded to use a friend who takes on the role of the employer, or a group activity where the group takes on the role of a search committee. In addition, this exercise can be done by itself or as part of the mock interviews (see exercises 9.1 and 9.2).

When performing this activity, consider mimicking the environment or situation in which it will most likely be used (e.g., one-on-one interview, or a search committee presentation as part of the formal interview process). Generally, most people will approach the presentation in a linear manner, starting at the beginning and working their way continuously through their portfolio to the end of their presentation. However, remember that the portfolio is often used as part of an overall presentation where sections are accessed as needed. Develop a format where you access components in the portfolio as part of the overall interview or in response to specific questions. Again, consider using the portfolio as part of the mock interview in exercises 9.1 and 9.2.

Evaluate the use of the portfolio in terms of the following questions.

1. Was the presenter familiar with the portfolio? Could he present without referring to the portfolio, or did he need to rely on it for notes? Did he fumble his way through the portfolio, or did he access elements in the portfolio smoothly? _____

_____

_____

2. Characterize the presentation. Was it animated, bland, monotone? Was it conversational? Did she show enthusiasm? Did she demonstrate command of the subject matter? Were there any good or bad mannerisms in the person's speech or diction? _____

_____

_____

3. Analyze the presentation in terms of time and content. Did he spend too much or too little time on one section? Did the content adequately support the presentation? Was there too little or too much information? Was he able to abbreviate the presentation smoothly if needed? Did he use all of the sections of the portfolio? If not, why? Conversely, were there sections that seemed to be missing from the portfolio? _____

_____

_____

4. What suggestions would you make to improve the presentation, if any? _____

_____

_____

From *Career Development in Recreation, Parks, and Tourism: A Positioning Approach* by Robert B. Kauffman, 2010, Champagn, IL: Human Kinetics.

Business Cards

Collect 20 different business cards (the exercise will also work with only 10). Spread them out on a table and rank them in terms of your preference. Place the one you like the most at the top and the one you like the least at the bottom. Move the cards around until you are happy with the order of the cards.

Analyze your top five preferences. What do you like about the cards? Is it the background or texture? Is it the lettering? Perhaps it is the choice of colors. Are there any similarities in what you like?

Card 1: _____

_____

_____

_____

_____

Card 2: _____

_____

_____

_____

_____

Card 3: _____

_____

_____

_____

_____

Card 4: _____

_____

_____

_____

_____

Card 5: _____

_____

_____

_____

_____

Do the same analysis with the five business cards that you ranked the lowest. Are there any similarities in what you dislike?

Card 1: _____

_____

_____

_____

_____

Card 2: _____

_____

_____

_____

_____

Card 3: _____

_____

_____

_____

_____

Card 4: _____

_____

_____

_____

_____

Card 5: _____

_____

_____

_____

_____

Did you gain insights regarding your business card preferences?

_____

_____

_____

_____

Design your own business card based on your preferences. Use the following guidelines.

1. Describe the background, including its texture.

    _____

    _____

    _____

2. Indicate the type of font you want to use.

    _____

    _____

    _____

3. Check the items you would like to include. Note anything special that you want to do regarding any of the items.

    [   ] Organization logo _____

    [   ] Name _____

    [   ] Job title _____

    [   ] Address _____

    [   ] Phone numbers (office, home, cell, fax) _____

    _____

    _____

    _____

    _____

    [   ] E-mail address _____

    [   ] Your Web site, if you have one _____

    [   ] Mission statement (the organization's or yours) _____

    _____

    _____

    _____

    _____

chapter **12**

Cover Letters and E-Mails

Do I communicate effectively and professionally?

This chapter covers two important forms of written communications that you will use in your job search: cover letters and e-mails. E-mails are becoming the primary mode of communication; traditional letters are used for formal communications or official business. The rules and conventions for corresponding with letters are fairly well established. An examination of the literature reveals that this is not the case for e-mail communications. For this reason, we recommend that you use many of the rules and conventions for writing traditional business letters when writing e-mails as part of your job search process.

COVER LETTERS

Traditionally, cover letters have been used to accompany resumes in job application packages. They still serve this function. In the positioning model, you are more likely to use a letter to thank a potential employer for meeting with you than to introduce your resume. Because cover letters are still used as part of the job search process, the term *cover letter* is still appropriate. Regardless,

the principles used in writing cover letters are useful in writing any communication, including e-mail.

Formats

Generally, both the modified semi-block format (figure 12.1) and the block format (figure 12.2) are acceptable styles for cover letters. The modified semi-block format has traditionally been used by businesses and individuals writing personal letters. It is a little more personal and implies a little more informality than the traditional block format. However, the block format has gained wider use because of its convenience. If you are using the block format and want to tab in five spaces or half an inch at the beginning of your paragraphs, this is acceptable too.

Sections of a Letter

The following sections are normally included in a letter. For your convenience, the topic headings correspond to those listed in the margins on figures 12.1 and 12.2.

A TALE OF TWO MODELS

The cover letter is virtually synonymous with the traditional model. Its name is identified with the process in which you respond to a job announcement by sending the employer a copy of your resume, references, and, of course, a cover letter. In the cover letter you introduce yourself and indicate that you are applying for the advertised position.

The cover letter is not usually required in the positioning model since you are not applying for a formal position. Although it may seem to have little importance, the principles used in writing a good cover letter are fundamental and apply equally to writing e-mails and other written communication. The three-paragraph format and the general discussion of cover letters described in this chapter will serve you well in writing your communications for both models.

Your Address

This section of your cover letter should include your address and the date. It should not include your name because it is at the bottom of your letter. Also, if you are using the modified semi-block or other formats, your address should line up with the complimentary closing at the bottom. It is inappropriate to use your company's letterhead for your application letter because it is personal business and not company business. It can result in the disqualification of your application. Keep in mind that aligning the left margin of your address is not the same as using right justification on your word processing program. Right justification leaves the left margin of your inside address unjustified. Try using tab or indent.

Inside Address

This section of your letter should include the name, title, and address of the person to whom the letter is addressed. Also, note that the envelope should be addressed the same way. You may abbreviate the state or province. Also, note that there are traditionally two spaces between the state and zip code for U.S. addresses.

When possible, address your letter to a person. It may be a small touch, but it is a very important one. It indicates that you have sufficiently researched the firm to know whom to contact. Or, at the very least, it indicates that you know people inside the organization, which can be helpful.

What do you do when you do not know the person to whom you should address your letter?

You can always address the letter *Dear Gentlemen and Ladies* or *Dear Ladies and Gentlemen*. However, there are a few tricks you can use to find the appropriate person. The organization's Web site may have the information. You could also call the administrative assistant and ask. Be sure to obtain the correct spelling of the person's name, the person's precise title, and the correct address. If necessary, be forthright and state that you are seeking a position with the organization and you need to know how to address the letter. The administrative assistant may be very helpful and provide some additional background information. Also, you should be prepared to talk directly with the person you seek. She may answer the phone instead of the assistant, or the assistant may indicate that the person whom you seek is in her office and then ask you if you would you like to speak to her. By all means, your answer should be *yes*.

Salutation

In the salutation you should use the person's last name, even if you know the person: *Dear Mr. Smith* or *Dear Ms. Smith*. A colon should follow the name.

Main Body

Conceptually, you can divide your letter into three parts, or paragraphs. This is a useful approach even in general letter writing. Your first paragraph is the introductory paragraph in which you state your business. The second paragraph is your sales pitch, or what you can do for the organiza-

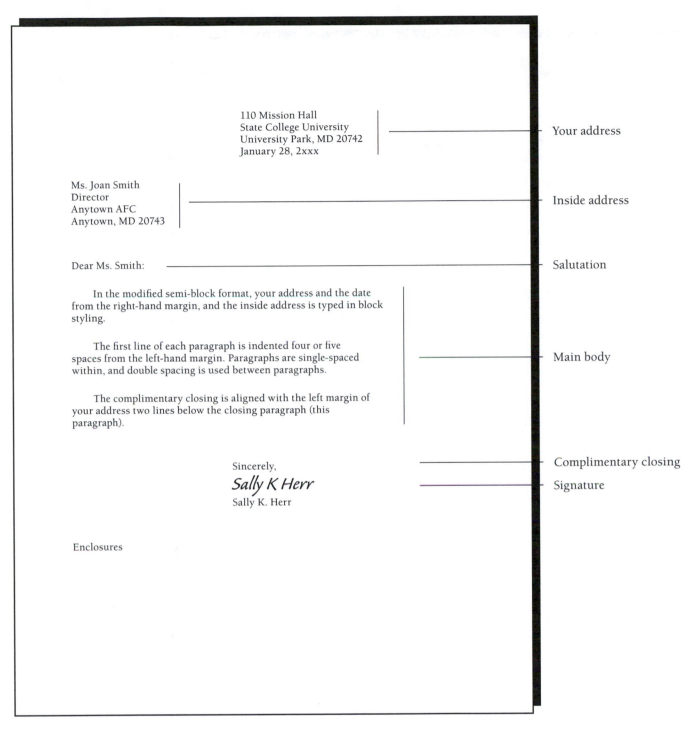

110 Mission Hall
State College University
University Park, MD 20742
January 28, 2xxx
— Your address

Ms. Joan Smith
Director
Anytown AFC
Anytown, MD 20743
— Inside address

Dear Ms. Smith: — Salutation

    In the modified semi-block format, your address and the date from the right-hand margin, and the inside address is typed in block styling.

    The first line of each paragraph is indented four or five spaces from the left-hand margin. Paragraphs are single-spaced within, and double spacing is used between paragraphs.

    The complimentary closing is aligned with the left margin of your address two lines below the closing paragraph (this paragraph).
— Main body

Sincerely, — Complimentary closing

Sally K Herr — Signature
Sally K. Herr

Enclosures

- Use the following margins: left: 1″, right: 1.5″, top: 1″, bottom: 1.5″.
- Although the figure is compressed, the proper proportions, including the use of a smaller font size, were used to maintain correct overall proportionality.
- Some additional spacing notes to consider: First, use two or three spaces between *Sincerely* and *Sally K. Herr*. Second, normally, use one space between your address and the inside address.
- Remember to sign the letter between *Sincerely* and your name.

Figure 12.1 Modified semi-block format cover letter.

110 Mission Hall
State College University
University Park, MD 20742
January 28, 2xxx
————————————————————— Your address

Ms. Joan Smith
Director
Anytown AFC
Anytown, MD 20743
————————————————————— Inside address

Dear Ms. Smith: —————————————————————— Salutation

In the modified semi-block format, your address and the date from
the right-hand margin, and the inside address is typed in block
styling.

The first line of each paragraph is indented four or five spaces
from the left-hand margin. Paragraphs are single-spaced within,
and double spacing is used between paragraphs. ————— Main body

The complimentary closing is aligned with the left margin of
your address two lines below the closing paragraph (this
paragraph).

Sincerely, ————————————————————————— Complimentary closing

Sally K Herr ————————————————————————— Signature
Sally K. Herr

Enclosures

- Use the following margins: left: 1″, right: 1.5″, top: 1″, bottom: 1.5″.
- Although the figure is compressed, the proper proportions, including the use of a smaller font size, were used to maintain correct overall proportionality.
- Some additional spacing notes to consider: First, use two or three spaces between *Sincerely* and *Sally K. Herr*. Second, normally, use one space between your address and the inside address.
- Remember to sign the letter between *Sincerely* and your name.

Figure 12.2   Block format cover letter.

tion. If necessary, divide this paragraph into two paragraphs. The third, and last, paragraph is your closing paragraph. Each of these paragraphs is described in more depth in the following section.

Complimentary Closing and Signature

The complimentary closing and signature should be aligned with the inside address. If you are using the block format, the alignment is the left margin. If you are using the modified semi-block format, the alignment occurs on the left margin of your address. Again, remember that alignment is not the same as using right justification on your word processing program. Right justification leaves the left margin of your inside address unjustified.

Skip a line after the closing paragraph and insert the complimentary closing. Skip two lines and insert your typed signature. Remember to sign the letter between the complimentary closing and the signature. It is surprising how often people forget to sign their letters.

Skip another two lines after the typed signature and note any copies sent to other people. This is a *cc* followed by their names. If you used someone in the introductory paragraph for an entree, it is customary to send that person a copy of the letter to keep him informed and in the loop. If you are not copying anyone, leave this line blank.

If you enclosed a copy of your resume or some other document, indicate that you have done so next. Some people indicate enclosures followed by the number of enclosures; others list the enclosure itself: *Enclosure: resume.* It is a good idea to note your enclosures. If a document is inadvertently misplaced, the fact that you indicated that you included it reduces any doubt that you did submit the item. Also, it provides a check-off item when preparing your materials.

Three-Paragraph Approach

In the three-paragraph approach, you use a slightly different strategy for each paragraph. This strategy applies equally well to cover letters and e-mails.

Introductory Paragraph

In the main body, your first paragraph should come directly to the point and tell the reader exactly why you are writing the letter. In the positioning model, you are generally exploring or seeking a position. If you are applying to an advertised position, state that you are applying and name the specific position. Not doing so suggests indecisiveness (e.g., *I am interested in the position*). Using the word *interested* leaves the person to question whether you are applying for the position. If you are applying for a position, say so: *I am applying for the position.*

If you were applying for a formal position, the following statement would also be considered indecisive. *I am interested in exploring the possibility of developing a position.* However, this statement is very appropriate if you are positioning yourself and this is your initial correspondence with the person in the organization. You are, in fact, exploring the possibility.

Also, you want to establish a rapport with your reader. The introductory paragraph is the place to drop the name of an important person who referred you to the position: *Mr. Jones suggested that I contact you regarding the position.* Last, this paragraph should open the door for the sales pitch or the message in the second paragraph.

Sales Pitch or Message

In the traditional model, this paragraph addresses what you can do for the employer, not what the employer can do for you. By listing your accomplishments, you emphasize what you can do for the employer. Brevity is important in this paragraph. Don't repeat everything on your resume. Rather, present the best of the best.

Figure 12.3 shows the cover letter Sally Herr wrote to Mr. Muncheck in her application for an advertised job. Figure 12.4 is a slightly modified version of the same message as an e-mail; the intent of Sally's e-mail is to position herself for the job.

Examine the strategy of the message in the second paragraph of figures 12.3 and 12.4. The first two sentences indicate that Sally has previous experience in the AFC system. The second sentence indicates that she has an understanding of the organization's culture, that she knows what the job entails, and that she will fit into the organization's culture: *As part of my internship,*

110 Mission Hall
State College University
University Park, MD 20742
January 28, 2xxx

Mr. John R. Muncheck
Executive Director
Anytown AFC
Anytown, MD 20743

Dear Mr. Muncheck:

Per our phone conversation, I would like to apply for the advertised recreation programmer position with Anytown AFC. This May I will be graduating from State College University with a major in Recreation and Parks and would be available for the position shortly thereafter.

Along with my academic preparation, I have considerable programming experience in aquatics. As part of my internship, I was the assistant aquatics director at the Rolling Hills AFC, where I gained an excellent understanding of the philosophy, administration, and programs of the AFC. In addition to these experiences, I have skills in aquatics, slimnastics, aerobics, and youth programs. Based on these experiences, I believe I can make a valuable contribution to your program.

Enclosed is a copy of my resume and references as requested. If you require any further information, please feel free to contact me. I am looking forward to hearing from you.

Sincerely,

Sally K Herr

Sally K. Herr

Enclosures (2)

Introductory paragraph. This paragraph does two things. First, it indicates that Sally is applying for the position. Second, it indicates when she will be available for the position.

Main body. Analyze the main body. The first and second sentences state that Sally has experience. More importantly, she indicates that she is familiar with the AFC system, its culture, and how it works. Then she indicates that she has a diversity of skills and can work most anywhere in the organization. When she states that she can make a "valuable contribution," she is merely summarizing what she has already shown to be true. Why wouldn't Mr. Muncheck want to hire her?

Closing paragraph. This paragraph is functional. There is nothing really special in it. It indicates her enclosures and that she is looking forward to hearing from him.

Figure 12.3 Sample cover letter.

I was the assistant aquatics director at the Rolling Hills AFC, where I gained an excellent understanding of the philosophy, administration, and programs of the AFC. This addresses the employer's worst nightmare, which is that he hired the wrong person and now has to fire that person. The third sentence depicts the diversity of Sally's experiences and suggests the range of potential positions she may be qualified for in the organization. The last sentence summarizes what she already stated, that she can easily fit into the organization and make a valuable contribution.

Subject. The subject line is simple and straightforward. Consider the following alternative subject line: "Follow-up: Recreation programmer position."

Salutation. Note the use of a formal salutation.

Introductory Paragraph. This paragraph indicates that Sally is following up on a phone conversation, that she seeks a position, and when she would be available for the position.

Main Body. The first and second sentences state that Sally has AFC experience. More important, she indicates that she is familiar with the AFC system, its culture, and how it works. Then she indicates that she has a diversity of skills and can work most anywhere in their organization. When she states that she can make a "valuable contribution," she is merely summarizing what she has already shown to be true.

Closing Paragraph. This paragraph is functional. "I am looking forward to hearing from you." It is the same sentence as in the letter. However, it takes on a slightly different meaning.

Signature Block. Sally is using her home address in the signature block. For the e-mail communications, it is not significant since all of the e-mails come back to her e-mail address.

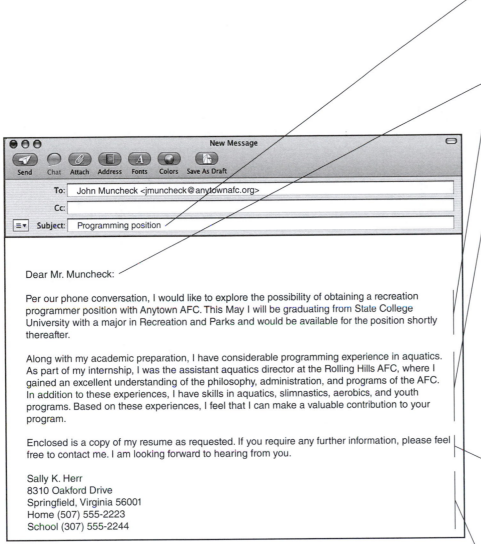

New Message

Send Chat Attach Address Fonts Colors Save As Draft

To: John Muncheck <jmuncheck@anytownafc.org>

Cc:

Subject: Programming position

Dear Mr. Muncheck:

Per our phone conversation, I would like to explore the possibility of obtaining a recreation programmer position with Anytown AFC. This May I will be graduating from State College University with a major in Recreation and Parks and would be available for the position shortly thereafter.

Along with my academic preparation, I have considerable programming experience in aquatics. As part of my internship, I was the assistant aquatics director at the Rolling Hills AFC, where I gained an excellent understanding of the philosophy, administration, and programs of the AFC. In addition to these experiences, I have skills in aquatics, slimnastics, aerobics, and youth programs. Based on these experiences, I feel that I can make a valuable contribution to your program.

Enclosed is a copy of my resume as requested. If you require any further information, please feel free to contact me. I am looking forward to hearing from you.

Sally K. Herr
8310 Oakford Drive
Springfield, Virginia 56001
Home (507) 555-2223
School (307) 555-2244

Figure 12.4 Sample e-mail cover letter.

Closing Paragraph

Generally, the last paragraph is the shortest paragraph. However, it is still extremely important. In this paragraph, you want to close your letter, indicate any enclosures, and indicate your desired follow-up. It is always good to note which enclosures you are sending. Although the closing sentence in both figure 12.3 and 12.4 is the same, it has a slightly different meaning in the positioning example (figure 12.4): *I am looking forward to hearing from you.*

In the positioning example, you might want to consider a more assertive sentence. You have talked with the potential employer on the phone. You are now following up with an e-mail. You are creating a dialogue. You may want to consider suggesting a one-on-one interview. Either way, the dialogue is moving forward and it is only a matter of time before you move to the next step.

Diction

Your choice of words in a cover letter or e-mail is of utmost importance. Choose your words carefully. Diction is not what you say, but how you say it. Try to avoid emotionally charged words. Think of the implications of what you write. What picture are you drawing about yourself with the words you are using? Are you full of yourself? Are you too aggressive? Conversely, are you not assertive enough and perhaps a wimp? Do you seem sincere? These are all things that your writing conveys between the lines.

Consider the following closing sentence of a cover letter: *If you feel that it would be helpful, I would like to set up an interview with you.* Do you sense the writer's hesitance and lack of assertiveness? This example is more neutral and acceptable: *I would like to set up an interview with you at your convenience.* In this example, you are merely expressing what you would like to have happen. Consider the statement this example makes about the writer, particularly if this is an introductory letter and the first contact with the employer: *I will be contacting your secretary to set up an interview with you.* Do you think, Who is this person to set up an interview without asking me first? Isn't this being presumptuous? However, this may be a perfectly acceptable statement later in the process after the employer suggests that you set up an interview. In that case, you may write: *As we discussed, I will call your administrative assistant and set up a meeting with you at your earliest convenience.*

The following example demonstrates the importance of choosing your words wisely. The student is explaining how she became involved in therapeutic recreation. Examine her choice of words used and what they imply about her: *My sister has a physical disability that was received in her earlier years. Ever since that tragic accident, I have dedicated myself to working with the disabled. It is particularly important to do so because they have*

been cheated out of a meaningful life. My sister has really opened my eyes about the disabled. Words such as *tragic, cheated,* and even *meaningful life* may suggest a particular attitude by the person writing the passage. The phrases *in her earlier years* and *really opened my eyes about the disabled* are awkward and suggest poor diction. Would you want to hire the person who wrote this passage? Do you wonder if she is going to be a zealot rather than just an advocate for the disabled? Is this person going to create more problems for you than she will solve?

Consider the following alternative passage and what it says about the writer (although some may suggest that the best option is not to say anything about her sister at all): *My involvement in therapeutic recreation stems from an accident involving my sister. Several years ago she was in an automobile accident that left her partially paralyzed. My involvement in her rehabilitation program resulted in my seeking a professional career in therapeutic recreation.* Note the more neutral words such as *professional career* and even *rehabilitation program.*

E-MAIL AND OTHER ELECTRONIC COMMUNICATIONS

Within the last 20 years there has been an information revolution. This revolution has profoundly affected the traditional job search process. The Internet, cell phones, e-mail, instant messaging, text messaging, and constantly changing communication technologies comprise the communications landscape today. In his 1982 book *Megatrends*, Naisbitt noted that one of the significant communications trends occurring even then was networking. He noted a profound change in the organizational structure from hierarchical structures to networking or more horizontal structures. For the most part, electronic communications were still relatively unknown to the general public in the mid-1980s. The change Naisbitt noted led to a corresponding change in communication structures also. Actually, his book understated the transformation that would occur.

Your electronic communications should retain the formality of professional correspondence.

The changing communications environment is demonstrated in the simple act of sending someone an e-mail. As Naisbitt suggested, you can create networks with numerous other people across the country and communicate with them almost instantly through e-mail and instant messaging.

In addition, you can avoid the chain of command and go directly to the person with whom you want to communicate. For example, you can send an e-mail directly to the person in the organization with whom you would like to work and bypass human resources, at least initially. Unlike 30 years ago, today, we have direct access to virtually anyone we want.

As much as things change, they don't change. E-mail has pretty much replaced regular mail. It is quick. It is easy to use. It is readily available. Most people have computers on their desks and hookups to the Internet. Originally, e-mails replaced memos and were used primarily within the organization. Today, they are used so universally that most people don't differentiate between the two environments. They simply send the communication to whomever they need to. The medium is informal, and people are used to writing cryptic messages because it is simply quicker.

Correspondingly, e-mail has become a valuable tool when casing the joint and when setting up a one-on-one interview with someone in the organization. You may be tempted to be informal in your e-mail communications with your contact in the organization. Don't. Use the formality associated with letters. If you look at figure 12.4, the e-mail contains many of the same elements found in a letter (figure 12.3), including the salutation, main body or message, and signature block. *Dear Mr. Smith* is more appropriate than *Dear John*. In this sense, as much as communications have changed, they haven't really changed all that much.

E-mail is a valuable tool in positioning yourself in the job search process. You will probably use it to make your initial contact with the organization and to set up your one-on-one interview. This section provides some tips on how to use e-mail to position yourself.

Parts of an E-Mail

The focus of this section is on the parts of an e-mail that affect your message. Consider applying the basic principles of letter writing to e-mails that involve your job search. Err on the side of formality rather than informality.

Subject

The subject is the title of your e-mail. Use a brief summative statement that describes your message. Consider writing the message of your e-mail first. The writing process can help you organize your thoughts. Then write your subject line. It will most likely be more summative and more succinct if you write it after you have composed the message.

Copies

In the days of typewriters and carbon paper, *cc* stood for *carbon copy*. Today, the acronym *cc* refers to the people to whom you are sending copies of the e-mail. As a general rule, if you refer to someone in your e-mail, or if you refer to a topic that directly relates to something that is this person's responsibility, you may want to consider copying her in your e-mail.

The acronym *bcc* indicates that you are sending a blind copy to this person. It is blind in the sense that the person to whom you are sending the e-mail is unaware that you are copying this other person. Use *bcc* very sparingly, if at all. First, ask yourself why you want to send this other person a copy of the e-mail without the principal person knowing. Usually, there is no really good reason. Second, in the electronic age in which everything is easily forwarded, consider that your blind copy may be forwarded to someone you didn't want to see it in the first place. As a general rule, if you copy someone else, assume that everyone else will see it also.

Attachments

People have an inherent reluctance to open e-mail attachments. First, it is inconvenient to do so. Next, they fear that the attachment may contain a virus or something else that will infect their computer. Third, they may not have the software with which to open the file. If they do, it may be a different version from the one used by the person who sent the attachment, which may result in a document that isn't the same as the original.

If you are sending your resume as an attachment, make sure the person to whom you send it can open it and view it as you viewed your original. Be sure to state in the body of the e-mail that you have included an attachment. Consider attaching the resume as a pdf file, which usually avoids this problem because the file prints fairly accurately on most computer systems. Another option is to paste the document directly into the e-mail. You can also do both: paste it into the e-mail and attach it as a pdf file.

Salutation

Differentiate casual communications from those used in your job search. When writing as part of your job search or when writing in other more formal situations, consider using a salutation as you would in a typical cover letter: *Dear Mr. Jones*. If the person is a friend or someone you know on a first-name basis, you may use her first name: *Dear Sally*.

In contrast, if you are positioning yourself or applying for a formal job position, use the person's last name, even if you would normally send an e-mail using her first name. Because you are applying for a position as the in-house candidate, err on the side of conservatism and formality and address this person in the salutation using her last name.

Message

Use the three-paragraph approach when composing an e-mail. The first paragraph states your business and why you are writing. The second paragraph is your message, or your sales pitch. It is what you want to happen because of your e-mail. The closing paragraph suggests what needs to be done next. Do you want to meet with the person, or will you wait to hear from him? See figure 12.4 for an example of the three-paragraph approach used in an e-mail communication.

Signature Block

Don't overlook the value of the signature block in providing useful information to the potential employer. In a cover letter, it is inappropriate to use the letterhead of the organization for which you work. Your application or your inquiry is not company business. Generally, this is not the case with e-mail regarding the signature block. In most programs, the signature block is automatically inserted into the e-mail document. For this reason, and because people use e-mail for business and semipersonal communications, it is generally not considered inappropriate to send an e-mail using your organizational e-mail account. If there is any doubt, check your organization's policy regarding the use of e-mail. You may need to create your own e-mail account outside the organization to handle your nonbusiness correspondence.

Your signature block tells the person you are writing to that you are employed, and if you include your title, it tells them your current rank and position. In addition, it gives the person the necessary contact information so he can contact you.

If you include your Web site as part of your signature block, don't be surprised if the person checks it out. Make sure that everything on your Web site is appropriate. In addition, remember that the signature is inserted automatically; if you don't want this information sent as part of your e-mail, change the signature block. In general, you don't want to provide so much information that your signature block becomes cluttered.

E-Mail Tips and Etiquette

The following e-mail tips include both general tips and tips to help you position yourself.

Don't Write Anything You Don't Want Someone Else to Read

Click once on Forward, click again on a server list, click once again on Send, and in this electronic age, the world is now reading your e-mail. The rule is, *If you don't want someone else to read your e-mail, don't write it.* Conversely, *assume that anything that you write in an e-mail will be read by the world.* These rules cannot be overemphasized. Obviously, never write an e-mail in anger. Also, your e-mails can become very informal and you can become very intimate in your back-and-forth correspondences with others. Always consider whether there is anyone you would not like to see your writing when you are corresponding back and forth by e-mail. Avoid using slang, obscenities, and vulgarities for the obvious reasons. Remember, you can always use the phone to say what you really want to say without leaving a record of it. Again, it is a sound practice never to write anything that you don't want everyone else to read.

AVOID USING ALL CAPS; IT SHOUTS!

The use of all capital letters shouts at the reader. Yes, it stands out and brings attention to what you have written. It is one thing to use it in personal correspondence, but avoid it in more formal e-mail communications.

Avoid Using Only Lowercase Letters

One way to increase text messaging and typing efficiency is to jettison words or simply use only lowercase letters: *i would like to discuss the topic... what do you think.* This may be okay between

friends, but not in the more formal situation of a job search. When in doubt, err on the side of more formality, not less.

Body Language and Inflection

Although electronic communications are a tool, they also have the effect of eliminating face-to-face communication. In fact, it is now commonplace to communicate with someone by e-mail or over the phone without meeting her in person. In doing so, we develop a mental picture of the person. When we eventually meet the person, we are surprised to find that our mental picture is often quite different from reality. He may be taller or shorter than expected, weigh more or less than predicted, be more or less attractive than expected, or be younger or older than the tone of his voice suggests. Regardless, it is amazing how well people can pick up on voice inflection and nonverbal language while on the phone. It is amazing how well people do the same with e-mail also. Regardless, don't assume that the reader understands the inflection in your writing. If you are joking, try placing *just joking* in parenthesis. It leaves little or no doubt of your intentions, particularly if the e-mail is copied or forwarded to someone who may not be in on the joke.

Your E-Mail Is Probably Public Property

You may mistakenly think that your e-mails are private property. If you work for someone else and use their server, they aren't. Particularly at work, e-mails are backed up and archived, to be resurrected at a later date if needed by administrators.

Proofread Your E-Mail

E-mail is quick, and in an effort to get things done quickly, people don't always use spell-check or check the grammar in their messages. It is the message itself that is considered important. Usually, the communications occur between fellow employees or friends. When you are communicating with someone as part of your job search, proofread your e-mails for punctuation, spelling, and flow, and always use a pleasant tone. Just as in a letter or any other formal communication, your errors will reflect negatively on you.

Form Over Function

E-mail is designed to be a quick and dirty form of communications. People don't expect it to look good. Think for a moment about how you may impress someone if you focus on how your e-mail looks. When discussing resumes and cover letters, we emphasized the importance of the presentation. Look at the formatting of your e-mails from an aesthetic perspective as much as you can, particularly when you are using them as part of your job search.

Emphasize Formality Over Informality

When in doubt, write your e-mail with the same cordiality and formality that you would use in a letter. Just as you can never overdress, include *Dear Susan* in your salutation—or better yet, *Dear Ms. Smith*—in a job search–related e-mail. Avoid the use of all lowercase letters. Although it is quicker to type, it is inappropriate. Write coherent paragraphs and not in little snippets as you might with friends.

Don't confuse being personable with informality. You wouldn't make small talk in a formal letter. However, you might in an e-mail even if it's part of your job search. Because it is a more informal medium, there is no problem with being personable even in job search–related e-mails.

Develop a Dialogue or Story

A basic technique of sales is to have the buyer buy into the product. The more she has invested in the product, the more likely she will be to purchase it. In a sense, she has made too much of an investment in the product not to buy it. This technique applies to your job search communications. By creating a dialogue with a person within the organization, you create an investment on his part in you. If he spends time communicating with you, he gets to know you. It is harder to say *no* to someone you know. At some point, he will want to make it work because he has spent time and energy on you. He has an investment in you and in making it work.

Consider developing the following story line with the person in the organization with whom you are communicating. This will stretch across several e-mails. In the first e-mail you introduce

yourself. It is the teaser, in which you provide enough information that she wants to come back for more but not so much that she can make her decision whether to hire you. Depending on the situation, you may choose to not include your resume with your first inquiry. You may choose instead to provide a brief summary of your experience. This is your teaser.

The person in the organization replies. She may outline some possibilities and ask for some additional information, including your resume. If you haven't provided the resume with your first e-mail, you might include it with this e-mail even if the person doesn't request it. The conversation continues and includes setting up a one-on-one interview and moving toward your eventual employment. Don't string out the dialogue too long, however, because at some point the employer may conclude that you aren't worth the investment she is putting into you. She too wants to move toward a conclusion.

PUTTING IT ALL TOGETHER

In the positioning model, the employer's first contact with you, before the one-on-one interview, may well be an e-mail. This is in contrast with the traditional model, in which the employer first sees your resume and cover letter. In a world turned upside down, today, you will deliver the cover letter at the end of the process, when the employer formally offers you the job. Regardless, the formality and the approach used in writing your cover letter are directly applicable to writing your introductory e-mail. Although the format has changed, the approach hasn't.

REFERENCES

Enelow, W., & Kursmark, L. (2007). *Cover letter magic: Trade secrets of professional resume writers*. Indianapolis, IN: JIST Works.

Kauffman, R.B. (1989). Writing your cover letter. *Employ, XV* (1, 2).

Naisbitt, J. (1982). *Megatrends*. New York: Warner Books.

Zelanski, P., & Fisher, M. (1984). *Design principles and problems*. Fort Worth, TX: Harcourt Brace College Publishers.

Writing a Cover Letter

Identify someone in an organization where you would like to work and write a cover letter addressed to that person. Use the three-paragraph approach to write the body of your letter. Give your letter to a friend to review in terms of its message and content.

chapter 13

Putting It All Together

It was summer and I had just visited a student who was completing his senior internship during the summer at a Boys and Girls Club in northern Virginia. This is a good a place to end this book because Marty's story is typical of the many stories of students who have positioned themselves. I met Marty and chatted with him briefly, and then we both met with his supervisor, Connie. It didn't take long to find out that they had hired Marty on as program director at the end of summer. The job had opened suddenly toward the end of the summer when their program director left for another position. I smiled and felt happy for him, but I wasn't really surprised, either. As noted throughout this book, variations of his story happen all the time.

The three of us chatted about Marty's new position and how he had positioned himself for it. I noted that Marty had gotten a position that wasn't advertised. It had just appeared. I noted in our conversation that the majority of positions are never advertised. The previous program director had taken another position, and they needed someone to fill his position. Marty was there, and he was already doing a similar job. They liked what he was doing. For them, it was an obvious choice. They simply moved him into the program director's position.

As part of the discussion, I noted that the biggest fear of employers is that they will hire someone they don't really know off the street and then have to fire this person because he couldn't do the job. Connie nodded her head in agreement. Connie was happy. She was reasonably certain that she wouldn't face this unpleasant situation.

She had hired someone she knew could do the job, because he was already doing it. Marty was happy because he had employment after his internship. Also, he was flattered that they thought enough of him to hire him. And it was a position for which he had prepared himself. I was happy because they had both satisfied their needs, and we had placed a student, in a manner of speaking. Actually, Marty had positioned himself for his new job.

After our meeting with Connie, I chatted further with Marty. I asked him why he had originally taken a position with the Boys and Girls Club. His answer was typical. He said that he had needed a summer job the previous year. Because the club was related to his major and because it was something he thought he would like to do, he applied for a summer job there. They hired him and it was both convenient and a logical choice for him to do his internship there the following summer.

In chapter 1, positioning was defined as *the technique of placing yourself in close proximity to the person for whom you want to work, the organization in which you want to work, and/or the position that fulfills your career goal.* The model has several steps that we can examine to see how well Marty fared in positioning himself.

The first step in the positioning model is deciding on your career goal, or what you want to do. Marty identified that he wanted to work in his major and at the Boys and Girls Club. He wasn't sure what he wanted to do in terms of his long-term career goal, but this is understandable. Most people don't know their long-term goals. When I asked him where this position would lead him in a year or two, he said he wasn't sure. He said that he might get a promotion. Like many other young people his age, he knew something about his next career step but not much about his long-term career goal. For Marty, this will come in time and, perhaps, with additional focus on his part. However, what was clear to him was that the choice he had made to seek a summer job at the Boys and Girls Club and in his major had helped to position him for the position of program director that he had just earned.

In the next step of the positioning model, you identify positions in firms that will potentially advance your career goal and research them in terms of their viability in advancing your career. You ask yourself several basic questions: *Is this a firm where I would like to work? Will this firm advance my career? If I take a position with this firm, how quickly will it advance my career?* Actually, Marty did this when he researched the organization the previous summer and when he identified the Boys and Girls Club as a place he would like to work. Marty researched the organization the previous summer and made decisions regarding its suitability in terms of his major and career. Marty does not yet have a clear picture of advancement and his future.

The next step in the positioning model is to identify and approach a person in the firm to

explore how you can become involved with the firm, the one-on-one interview. Depending on the situation, your involvement could be volunteer, part-time, or even full-time employment. Again, Marty did this with his summer position the previous year and this year, again, with his internship. In addition, Connie was showing signs of taking on a mentoring role for Marty. She had already shown signs of protecting him by not advertising the program director position. Because she had a vested interest in his success, she was already sponsoring him within the organization.

Involvement with the firm can lead to full-time employment or to a promotion depending on whether you were previously employed full- or part-time. Often, a new position simply appears, and you are the only one interviewed. This was the situation for Marty. If the position is opened up to the public, the job search process may become more of a formality to satisfy human resources because it has already been decided internally who will be hired. This was true for Katie at park and planning, who took a lesser position while she waited for a position at the new recreation center to become available (see chapter 2). She positioned herself for the newly created position and will be a candidate in the traditional job search to fill the position. There is always the chance that she won't get the job, but she is the odds-on favorite. Both Marty and Katie had successfully positioned themselves.

Finally, the positioning model suggests that you develop an individualized job announcement and then accept the position. In this case, they didn't really need to define a new position since Marty was filling an existing position. They both knew what the job would entail, and that is what is important. Marty accepted the position. Why shouldn't he? He had positioned himself for the job.

As part of his internship, Marty was required to complete a comparative analysis of a similar organization to the Boys and Girls Club in terms of size, program, and clientele. Marty, Connie, and I discussed what he might do in this regard. We selected a nearby Boys

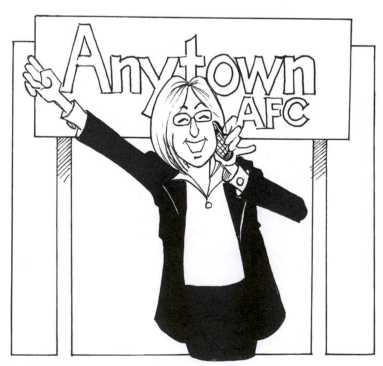

I got the job!

and Girls Club that would give him additional programming skills that Marty could specifically adapt to his facility. Again, Connie demonstrated an interest in mentoring Marty. In addition, the contacts that Marty would make through his comparative analysis would help him develop his professional network, which would help him in his current job and in the future.

On my drive home, I reflected on Marty's experience. It was a classic case of positioning, even though he had not consciously applied all of the positioning principles. He had placed himself in close proximity to the position that he wanted, or rather, a job that became available to him when it opened up. Its geographical location was good for him. And, he was already doing the job. It reinforced the adage: if you want to work there, work there. In time, he will use the techniques

described in this book to position himself for his next job or promotion.

I smiled to myself. For Marty, most of the elements of positioning were in play. Positioning is a natural process. This book formalizes what many people have done naturally at an elemental level in the workplace. Also, it provides specific techniques that you can use to help position yourself for your next job.

If you want a job, you should position yourself in close proximity to the person you want to work for or the firm in which you want to work. Marty's new position was a testament to the concept of positioning. Marty's experience is a variation of Sally Herr's experience, which was chronicled throughout the book. As the examples used in this book demonstrate, positioning is a new way to approach career development.

Exercise 13.1

Applying the Positioning Model

Normally, this is a group activity. Positioning is a general concept that you can apply to other aspects of your life. Reflect on movies or books you have viewed or read. Do any of the story lines reflect the positioning model? If so, share your example with others. Can you apply the positioning model to other aspects of your life? If so, make a list of these applications. In these situations, which aspects of the model change and which remain essentially the same?

INDEX

Please note the following abbreviations that follow page numbers in the index:

Italicized *f* or *ff* refers to a figure or figures.

Italicized *t* refers to a table.

Page numbers in **bold** refer to worksheets.

Internet. *See also* e-mail
  demographic information 103
  for identifying an organization's purpose 103
  for identifying the administrative structure of an organization 103-104, 104*f*
  job announcement exercise 20*f*, **27-28**
  job hunting using search engines 48, 49*f*
internship
  as employment opportunity 16-17
  as a transition phase 4-5
  using academic experiences in bridging 62-65
interviews, formal 155*f*
  being yourself 148-149
  gotcha questions 158-160
  inappropriate or illegal questions 161-162
  individualized job announcement **144-145**
  mock interview **165-167**
  mock phone interview **168-170**
  overview 7
  phone interviews 162-164
  post interview 167, 170
  putting it all together 164
  questions for recent graduates 156-157
  reversal 149-150
  strategies overview 147-148
  talking to your talking points 149, **171**
  three-doors questions 160-161
  transition questions 157-158
  typical questions 150-154
  your questions 154-160
interviews, one-on-one
  close the deal 130
  design step 129-130
  dressing for success 137-138
  engage the decision maker 129
  follow up 130, 131*ff*-134*ff*
  identifying your prospect 128-129
  individualized job announcement 135-137, 136*f*
  overview 7, 127-128
  perfecting your greeting and introduction **143**
  propose 130
  putting it all together 139-140
  seating arrangements 138, 138*f*, **141**
  seven-step sales model overview 128
  starting the conversation 139
  survey the organization 129
  using the seven-step model 134-135
introducing yourself at an event 85-86, 86*f*
investigating a community 99*f*

J

job announcements
  example of 21*f*
  individualized 136*f*, **144-145**
  on the Internet **27-28**
  one-on-one interview and 135-137
job descriptions
  creating a working table 48, 50*f*
  example of one used for evaluation 46*f*
  individualized 129-130
  writing 111-112
job search. *See also* casing the field; casing the joint
  determining the career track 107
  hidden positions 2-3, **10**, **11-12**
  identifying major players 102
  proactive **40**
  proactive skills **41-42**
  proximity 14-18
  researching an organization 98-99
  researching the position 106-107
  statistics on 1-2
  through internships 16-17

K

Kopiske, W. 1-2
KSAEs (knowledge, skills, abilities and experiences) 76-77
  acquiring 67-75, 68*f*-74*f*
  determining the ones you need for the job 51, **56**
  identifying skills needed for a job 47-51, 49*f*-50*f*
  matching to the position you are applying for 107-108
  proximity by 18
  synthesizing of 51
  tailoring the categories to your needs 50
  what to include in your portfolio 200, 201*f*
  worksheets 68*f*-74*f*

L

layout considerations for portfolios 198-199, 198*f*
learning experiences 61-62
legal liability 100
length of service 153
letters of recommendation 202
living legends library 95-96

M

magnitude of experience 200
main body of a cover letter 210-211
mainlining 107